FADE TO BLACK

Hard Rock Cover Art of the Vinyl Age

FADE TO BLACK

Martin Popoff

with contributions from celebrated cover artist

Ioannis

STERLING
New York

STERLING
New York

An Imprint of Sterling Publishing
387 Park Avenue South
New York, NY 10016

ISBN 978-1-4027-7817-9

Distributed in Canada by Sterling Publishing
c/o Canadian Manda Group, 165 Dufferin Street
Toronto, Ontario, Canada M6K 3H6
Distributed in the United Kingdom by GMC Distribution Services
Castle Place, 166 High Street, Lewes, East Sussex, England BN7 1XU
Distributed in Australia by Capricorn Link (Australia) Pty. Ltd.
P.O. Box 704, Windsor, NSW 2756, Australia

Book design by Ellen Nygaard

Photographs of album sleeves by Mark Weiss, Lisa McKeever,
and Martin Popoff

Please see picture credits on page 276 for image copyright information

For information about custom editions, special sales, and premium and
corporate purchases, please contact Sterling Special Sales at 800-805-5489
or specialsales@sterlingpublishing.com.

Manufactured in China

2 4 6 8 10 9 7 5 3 1

www.sterlingpublishing.com

DEDICATION

For Beth and Trevor
—M.P.

For my mom, Maria, and my dad, Niko;
also for my wife, Lisa,
and my daughter, Maria; my brother, George,
and my sister, Liz;
and for Caylene and Sophia.
I love you all.
—I.V.

ALSO BY MARTIN POPOFF

FOR ORDERING INFORMATION, PLEASE SEE WWW.MARTINPOPOFF.COM OR E-MAIL MARTIN AT MARTINP@INFORAMP.NET

TO SEE MORE OF IOANNIS'S ARTWORK AND PURCHASE FINE ART LIMITED EDITION PRINTS, GO TO HIS WEBSITE AND STORE AT WWW.DANGEROUSAGE.COM

CONTENTS

INTRODUCTION BY MARTIN POPOFF

Being a card-carrying metalhead since 1973, when I was ten years old, as well as a frustratingly occasional but lifelong artist, I have always been crazy about album covers. As a kid, I had a huge, perfect Eddie that I drew in pastels on a nice linen, then put up on my bedroom wall; Motörhead skulls done in ballpoint pen on the front of my social studies book; a full-on Whitesnake's *Lovehunter* on the back of my math book. My meticulous pencil repro of Roger Dean's cover for Yes's *Relayer*—still got that somewhere— and then there's an oil repro of ZZ Top's *Tejas* (eh, not great) and a few pencil sketches of budgies on horses (see Budgie: *Bandolier*).

Logos, we got logos. I'm still knocking off UFO and Kiss logos while I work (if I'm not drawing flaming Flying Vs, like the ones on the UK cover of Accept's *Restless and Wild*), and I do recall theming a schoolbook or two with New Wave of British Heavy Metal (NWOBHM) logos, inventing them if a band didn't get it together to have one themselves. Then there's the standard of those actually way better than me, enough to become actual rockers: the sketched-out stage show, stacked with pyro, amps, wicked backdrop, the massive drum set (okay, I was actually a bar-band-level drummer).

The memory floodgates are opening . . . I designed my own *Sad Wings of Destiny*–based silkscreen T-shirt in high school, 'cause I wanted the Halford holding the mic looking like Jesus, but had to have the new *Stained Class* logo with it. Hell, I hooked a rug (remember that craze?) with a big blue BÖC Kronos cross on it. And that Scorpions logo in the old-school computer font? Well, my bedroom had individually cut letters (white gloss affixed to cardboard) hung on fishing line from the ceiling and draped in Christmas lights (how come no one ever took pictures of this stuff?).

Fact is, I love what goes into these kooky album covers—the type as much as the picture—and would chuck all the book writing to paint album covers full time and to be a gallery artist and just paint, paint, paint, and draw. Alas, however, I just haven't gotten around to throwing those hours at it. I keep saying yes to books. I don't like the setup and mess that painting puts on my office. Excuses, excuses, excuses.

The great heroes of mine all through this book didn't make excuses. They just got on with it. I know because I've fawningly gotten their stories from them, or their stories secondhand from the bands for which they doodled and scribbled. And as it does when I talk to producers, the hit rate on these artists and their cover stories being interesting actually eclipses what you usually get from the rock stars themselves about the music enclosed. A bunch of those stories are here, but let it be known that I couldn't concentrate and spend words on getting them all because as I write this intro, I know I'm way over my allotted word count and have no idea what's gonna be (or has been) done about it.

In any event, enough about me and my unfulfilled work life. It's time for a few comments on the following plush pages about why things were done a certain way. The picking of the sleeves that we've deemed fun and fundamental to shower with praise was a collaboration between myself and this book's contributor Ioannis—a force of nature basking in and through a great career I wish to emulate one day. It's been a blast picking these with him, because we're roughly the same age with pretty close (superlative) tastes in music, not to mention the fact we both grew up placing outsize importance on album cover art.

Having said that, you'll notice a few things we've done to rein it in, so to speak, and that is the following: (1) we went with a pretty loose definition of *hard rock* to widen the tent, most pertinently so we could slide a few things in there from the '60s; (2) we've tried not to be too, too obscure, meaning we've stayed somewhat mainstream, especially making sure (most) everything in here was issued in the U.S. and has at least a minimum level of recognition. Sure, many readers may think, "Who the heck is Legs Diamond?" but those head-scratchers are actually, one would hope, pretty few and far between; (3) we've tried to restrain ourselves in picking what we truly believe are the great covers in our hearts of hearts, in the name of variety. Heck, I could have put every last Blue Öyster Cult cover in here, for truly, I'd say they are all in my Top 200. As to other bands, easily, I could have put three, four covers for a few dozen of them. So instead, we curtailed our choices, ignored the math and the rankings, and wrote about some other perfectly good sleeve so you weren't reading about the same twenty-five bands over and over, dig?

Enough with the formalities. Hope my manic panic words of praise go a little way toward either teaching you some new trivia tidbit or enhancing your appreciation of a sleeve you know well. Or maybe these little reviews will have you pondering a sleeve you never gave a first or second look. At base, of course, is the artwork itself, these hard rock wrappers for the ages. I mean, additionally, may you be sufficiently inspired upon gazing at them to seek out other works by the artists at hand, draw similarities between one work and another album cover you know, hit the net for the full story of its birthing, or indeed be inspired to take up the profession of pictures yourself as this writer hopes to before it's too damn late.

INTRODUCTION BY JOANNIS

Okay, so I am a self-confessed album cover fan. You know, one of those insane guys who buys records for their covers, spends countless hours in old antique shops, record stores, record conventions, yard sales, and flea markets looking at the art and design credits.

I think I own every book that ever came out on this subject. I never got as swept away by famous classic artists and painters as I was by my personal childhood album-art heroes—folks like Roger Dean, Rodney Mathews, Hipgnosis (Storm Thorgerson and Aubrey Powell), Russell Mills, Derek Riggs, Hugh Syme, Peter Saville, Mick Rock, Kelley Mouse Studios, John Pasche, Mick Haggerty, Peter Lloyd, the Hildebrandts, Brian Griffin, George Hardie, and Bob Carlos Clarke. Man, I can go on forever and bore you to tears. Led Zeppelin, Queen, Yes, Pink Floyd, Black Sabbath, Rush, Genesis, Deep Purple, Judas Priest, ELP, Iron Maiden, U2—their music and their album cover images worked a perfect experience. When I spoke to Martin about this, we found we shared a common passion for the subject in addition to our fanatic love of Black Sabbath, Deep Purple, and hard rock in general. So the idea for this book emerged, since, to our amazement, it had not been tackled solely within and about the hard rock genre. Ergo, the book you are holding in your hands today.

My love affair goes way back in time. Art and music were a main part of my life as far back as I can remember, way back in my home city of Athens, Greece. In the cinema, the cartoons that I saw before the main movie—you know, the ones that had an orchestra soundtrack—had me amazed. Later on when my family moved to America, I, like every ten-year-old, was transfixed watching Batman and animated Saturday morning fare like Jonny Quest and Spiderman. You see, to me, the music and art were meant to be enjoyed together. I mean, Batman would not be as good without that great 1966 theme. So when I got into rock and roll later, well, the music would continue to create images in my head and those were the album covers, right?

My first attempt at an album cover career was in 1972, when I absentmindedly started to draw Roger Dean's cover for Uriah Heep's *Demons and Wizards* in pencil on my school desk during a very boring math class. The teacher was lecturing as he walked through the aisles, and I was so absorbed in my creation that I did not notice him stopping over me. "Well," he said. "Looks like we have an artist in our midst, one who likes defacing desks." I had to stay after school and scrub every desk.

Moving on, I had dreams of becoming a comic book artist and had developed my own scripts and characters. And then one summer day in 1975, I walked into my favorite record store, Cutler's in downtown New Haven, Connecticut, in the heart of Yale University. Bob Briar, my friend who worked there, showed me a book they had just received. There was one copy, as record stores did not sell books back then, just posters. This was a very special event. The book was *Views* by Roger Dean, a collection of his work, mostly his record cover art. I immediately recognized *Demons and Wizards* and a lot of other treasured art I had in my vinyl collection. I bought the book, ran home, and did not put it down for the next eight months. After that, I knew all I wanted to do was to work in rock and roll and create record cover art.

I received my first commission from a local band as I was finishing high school, and later I designed my first international release and art-directed an MTV video in 1983, while in college. It's been a long roller-coaster ride since then. My craft has allowed me to travel far and wide, see amazing places, go to incredible shows, parties, and events. Most important, it allowed me to work with some of my music heroes—Mick Box, Roger Glover, Butch Trucks, Bob Weir, and others—and in some cases become friends with them.

It's also allowed me the opportunity to work with some of my art heroes, such as Neal Adams, Ed "Big Daddy" Roth, Mick Rock, and Bob Carlos Clarke. My work has had its ups and downs, as the creative world is a very opinionated place, but never has it been dull, and it's what gets me up in the morning, always wondering what's coming next.

So it's really a thrill and an honor that with this book, Martin and I can give credit to the people who have created these amazing images that continue to inspire and give visual punctuation and identity to the music that they represent.

STEREO PS 420   LONDON

THE ROLLING STONES, NOW!

THE ROLLING STONES THE ROLLING STONES, NOW!

LONDON, FEBRUARY 1965
COVER PHOTO: DAVID P. BAILEY

I wanted to kick off this tome with two established and anchored heavies from an era perhaps two years earlier than when rock really begins to supercharge into hard rock. By that I mean the Who and in this case, the Stones, who draw upon the aptly dark and weighty image from this classy cover that's stepped a couple of paces outside the box. A pleasing collage of shadowy photographs perpetuates the vibe established with all the earlier covers, namely, that this is perhaps not a cheery lot of popsters, but rather a serious bunch of miscreants willing to dig deep under the blues and come back with tales of derring-do.

THE WHO THE WHO SINGS MY GENERATION

BRUNSWICK, DECEMBER 1965
COVER PHOTO: DAVID WEDGBURY

The history of hard rock arguably kicks off with the Who (or the Yardbirds) in '65, quickly gaining volume through Cream and Hendrix as we lurch toward Blue Cheer, the Stooges, MC5, and, finally, trouncingly, the first Sabbath album. Cover art intensifies through that lineage as well, with our ground zero jacket (changed for the U.S. Decca release in April 1966) being none too heavy, the guys at least looking laddish, punkish, lightly sneering at the camera above their mop-topped heads.

THE JIMI HENDRIX EXPERIENCE ARE YOU EXPERIENCED

REPRISE, AUGUST 1967
DESIGN AND PHOTOGRAPHY: KARL FERRIS

Jimi's debut, *Are You Experienced*, was issued in a number of different slapdash sleeves, but the U.S. and Canadian versions came closest to a winner with a psychedelic blowout evocative of Blue Cheer, Cream, the Stooges, and MC5. *Electric Ladyland* gets the razzie for its incendiary (and blotchy) naked-women cover in the UK and then a pointless blurry photo in the States. *Smash Hits* and *Axis: Bold as Love* got Jimi's American Indian heritage crossed with East Indian. But yes, the debut is a triumph, given the playful psychedelic text,

purple on funky '60s yellow, both colors picked up from the band photo in the middle. And the guys? Well, Noel Redding (left) and Mitch Mitchell flank a bulging-out Jimi, hands on belt buckle, all looking ridiculously psychedelic and foppish. Jimi had thought the UK cover lacked energy, so he set upon photographer Karl Ferris to improve upon it. The final shot, cooked up at Kew Gardens, makes use of a fish-eye lens to capture a spacey vibe, the emphasis on Jimi's talented hands completely intentional.

STEREO

reprise 6261

PRINTED IN U.S.A.

CREAM DISRAELI GEARS

REACTION/ATCO/POLYDOR, NOVEMBER 1967
ART AND ILLUSTRATIONS: MARTIN SHARP
COVER PHOTOGRAPHY: BOB WHITAKER

Cream covers were as psychedelic as the band's smothered music, but *Disraeli Gears* is the most explosive,
lunging at the looker like an acid-dosing. The chaos of
this sleeve becomes a metaphor for the heaviness of
the times and the heightening of all senses as Cream
turns up the volume sonically, lyrically, and visually.
Rules are to be broken, and the psychedelics of *Disraeli Gears* is a direct provocation of the squares, the
underlying message being that Ginger, Jack, and Eric
are tripping.

PHILIPS

PHS 600-264 STEREO

BLUE CHEER VINCEBUS ERUPTUM

PHILIPS, JANUARY 1968
PHOTOGRAPHY: JOHN VAN HAMERSVELD

This is a savage, scary record, like something made by a garage band gone possessed. That's as far I'll go to calling this the very first heavy metal album (actually, its follow-up equally qualifies!). But I do love the way the cover art screams acid rock hoodlums, bad trip guaranteed, time in the hoosegow, very likely. Dickie, Paul, and Leigh look like a cross between the Alice Cooper group and the Manson gang, and that text couldn't be more luridly antiestablishment. "The first album, originally, was an embossed album," notes Dickie. "You could feel the bubbles and the grooves on that cover. We did this because, when you're high on acid and you're tripping . . . well, years and years later I was playing with a band called the Longhorns, one night up in Chico. This guy comes up to me and says, 'Hey, I have a friend who wants to meet you, but he can't come back here because he's in a wheelchair.' And I said, 'Well, take me to him.' So he takes me to this guy who's in a wheelchair and he's also blind. And

he says, 'Man, I want to thank you so much. Because you've made the only album cover I've ever been able to read.' But yes, we were very, very, very into drugs, particularly LSD. The name partially comes from that, and another part of it is that we were all into the blues, but we weren't into being sad. And actually, in the blues medium, they have a name for this, and it's called jump blues. And the album title, *Vincebus Eruptum*, that came out of a friend of ours by the name of Richard Peddicord ["architect, artist, musician, freak, eccentric, acidhead," according to drummer Paul Whaley], who showed up one day at the commune with a big piece of butcher paper with the name on it and put it on the kitchen wall. And we all looked at it for quite a while, didn't say anything, and finally said, 'Richard, what is this?' And he said, 'This is the name of your new album. This is what you should call it. *Vincebus Eruptum* means *We Control Chaos*.'"

IRON BUTTERFLY HEAVY

ATCO, JANUARY 1968
ARTWORK AND COVER DESIGN: ARMANDO BUSICH
ART DIRECTION: GEOFF GANS

Much psychedelic artwork came off as chaotic and ill-composed, but *Heavy* makes synchronized use of type, keeps the vibe calm with a conservative blue and yellow color scheme, and then presents an amusing scenario depicting the band jamming away to a big, concrete ear god, with vocalist Darryl DeLoach irreverently perched atop the monolith. Type and illustration fuse acid-trippingly to form a complex yet squarish sculpture that sits diagonally on a white background. The totality emerges as a butterfly viewing the cosmic jam.

IRON BUTTERFLY IN-A-GADDA-DA-VIDA

ATCO, JUNE 1968
DESIGN: LORING EUTEMEY
PHOTOGRAPHY: MICHAEL OCHS AND STEPHEN PALEY

This darkly psychedelic classic made a disturbingly big impression on the American rock landscape, selling four-times platinum on the strength of its endless and apocalyptic title track. And its cover art was the perfect visual, the band looking like servants to something larger and more evil above them (Satanic cell division?), in a live performance juxtaposition that evokes similar portrayals of the Butterfly's dark psychedelic doppelgänger from o'er the amniotic ocean, Pink Floyd. Wild green and pink type, oddly placed, completes the bad acid trip.

LED ZEPPELIN LED ZEPPELIN

ATLANTIC , JANUARY 1969
COVER DESIGN: GEORGE HARDIE

Striking in its simplicity, the cover for the first and hugely important Zeppelin album was essentially a visual play on the band's odd name—i.e., a zeppelin made of lead was one sure to crash. Of course, the name itself came from the Who, with Keith Moon remarking that the new band would go over like a lead balloon, the laconic Entwistle supposedly chiming in with "a lead zeppelin!" The grainy monochrome treatment applied to the original photo of the Hindenburg exploding adds frenzy, energy, and a hint of psychedelia. The solid bold type applied to the band name corrects the chaos, quietly emitting its own kind of power. Of note: original UK copies featured this type in turquoise, with a quick switch to the common brownish orange, causing prices on first copies out to blow up like the blimp.

MC5 KICK OUT THE JAMS

ELEKTRA, FEBRUARY 1969
ART DIRECTION: WILLIAM S. HARVEY
PAINTINGS: GARY GRIMSHAW
DESIGN: ROBERT L. HEIMALL

The word that comes to mind is *frenzy*. The vibe is emphatically not of Detroit's famed Grande Ballroom, where this album was recorded, but more the atmosphere of protest surrounding the 1968 Democratic National Convention in Chicago, at which MC5 staked its claim. There's a weird juxtaposition of old, moldy hippie images with glam, and as always, the American flag incites drama. But of course none of this was the plan, and this was not supposed to be the cover. "That cover was by Bill Harvey," explains band manager John Sinclair. "What it said to me was they rejected the cover we submitted, and then they made that one. We were never happy about it. When they made that CD reissue in the '90s, they also printed Gary Grimshaw's

original cover design, the burning flag and marijuana leaf, psychedelic lettering. It wasn't what they were looking for. What they came up with wasn't what we wanted, but on the other hand, we wanted to have a record out on Elektra. So we were happy." Yet the official sleeve certainly communicates a sense of power and chaos. "Yeah, and it also spotlighted the audience," agrees Sinclair. "That was the one thing I liked about it. Because really, everything that MC5 was about was thrilling these kids, and I imagine that's a component that carries forth now down through your heavy metal chronicles. That was the one thing about them—they thrilled their audience."

FREE TONS OF SOBS
ISLAND/A&M, MARCH 1969
PHOTOGRAPHY: RICHARD BENNETT ZEFF

Tons of Sobs featured a more conceptual and psychedelic wrapper in the UK—one theory about why it wasn't used Stateside was that the U.S. label was legally spooked by the use of Mickey Mouse. Nonetheless, I've always dug the U.S. issue for its squalid, decadent quality, much more druggy than the meat-and-potatoes blues-rock enclosed. The four-square photo idea anticipates the sleeve for Van Halen's debut, but the vibe is far from California sunny, more akin to Alice Cooper's *Love It to Death*, with Paul Kossoff—soon to be dead from drug and drink—looking particularly vampiric, cosmic, and Syd Barrett-ish, underscored by the solar system painting used as a backdrop for all four shots. And yeah, notice how you never see Paul Rodgers and (Robert) Plant in the same room together? Hmm. Trivia note: "tons of sobs" is slang for lots of money (specifically UK pounds), a phrase cooked up by producer and "mad genius" Guy Stevens.

KING CRIMSON IN THE COURT OF THE CRIMSON KING

ISLAND/ATLANTIC, OCTOBER 1969
COVER: BARRY GODBER

Call this one Edvard Munch's *The Scream* updated and intensified for a rock-and-roll generation struggling through a particularly bad time, namely the death of the '60s and the attendant rise of downer rock, plus, more gravely, a bloody Vietnam conflict only half over at this point. Okay, only Sabbath got stamped as downer rock, but there were other forms of hard and heavy music boiling and bubbling alchemically, Robert Fripp and Michael Giles representing the Crimson King at the progressive-rock tea party, mercury-poisoning the idyll that Yes was busy planting. The painting disturbs us not only because it claustrophobically crowds the frame but also because it is a nightmarish adjunct to the horrific words (and music) to "21st Century Schizoid Man," and because this would be the only piece of cover art to come from Barry Godber, who would be dead from a heart attack at the age of twenty-four only four months after the album's issue.

FREE FREE

ISLAND, OCTOBER 1969
DESIGN: RON RAFFAELLI, VISUAL THING, INC.

Quite the creative artifact for record covers this early in the rise of rock, Raffaelli's cover for Free's second album features a silhouette of a leggy model, shot in bounding stride from below—Raffaelli had her catapult off a four-foot-high pile of wooden crates into a bunch of pillows a good twenty times to get the effect. Her presence is then converted into a sky of stars (actually strobe lights). The real sky above her is benign, and in smart Vertigo-like fashion, her hand reaches out to a tiny Free logo, perfectly top-centered on the cover. Crazy idea if you think about all the pieces, with the bonus being its instant recognizability from afar.

ROLLING STONES LET IT BLEED

LONDON
STEREO NPS-4

THE ROLLING STONES LET IT BLEED

DECCA/LONDON, DECEMBER 1969
DESIGN: ROBERT BROWNJOHN
PHOTOGRAPHY: DON MCALLESTER

Fitting our devious plan of including hard rockers that were heavy for their era (and the Stones were definitely considered loud ruffians, especially versus the Beatles), *Let It Bleed* makes the grade both on riffs and cover art absurdity. *Let It Bleed* had been provisionally titled *Automatic Changer*, and hence the nonsensical Robert Brownjohn sculpture of a record playing but threatened by the likes of a cake, a bike tire, a reel of itself, and then the band itself. One might consider this the third of the Stones' creatively outstepped covers and arguably the best of the early ones, given that *Their Satanic Majesties Request* was cynical and opportunist. And for *Let It Bleed*, it's almost as if the band is letting the music speak for itself, and sod what's on the gritty, dirty, haphazard garbage pile of an album cover. Plus the sleeve turned out to be striking enough for the Royal Mail to turn it into a commemorative postage stamp.

STEREO SKAO-406

GRAND FUNK GRAND FUNK

CAPITOL, DECEMBER 1969
NO IMAGE OR DESIGN CREDIT

Flint, Michigan's, Grand Funk got somewhat heavy with their second record, nicknamed *The Red Album*, given its lurid red-and-white color scheme and the confusing fact that it didn't have a title. The band members are depicted in close proximity to one another, energetically adding to the power-trio vibe the guys embodied. Drummer Don Brewer laughed at the suggestion that the album was known as red because the guitars were turned up (i.e., sent into the red on the meters) to correct for a thin mix on the first album (the "vibrating" lettering supports this reading as well). "No," says

Brewer with a laugh. "I just think just the fans took it on themselves to call it *The Red Album* as opposed to *Grand Funk*, which is what it was—it was self-titled *Grand Funk*. Also, the fans really came up with the short name for Grand Funk Railroad: Grand Funk. A lot of people thought that we actually changed the name or there was some sort of legality that we ended up going to Grand Funk instead of Grand Funk Railroad, but it was just the fans calling us Grand Funk instead of Grand Funk Railroad."

MC5 BACK IN THE USA

ATLANTIC, JANUARY 1970
DESIGN: JOAN MARKER
COVER PHOTOGRAPHY AND ART DIRECTION: STEPHEN PALEY

Sure, the album is a rarity, a collectible, but it looks like one as well, like a garage-rock grail, like a dangerous and druggy Velvet Underground joint. The heavy, black, in-your-face text that uses the same font for the band name as for the title is placed simply above a photo of the band, depicting them as the worst type of wasted, long-haired hippies, so sweaty that they confound the picture-taking process. The black-and-white palette and the ill-fitting text and photo within the square provide a definite retro vibe, matched by the music—which was, on the whole, more garage rock and '50s retro than the sum total of the band's *Kick Out the Jams* debut.

MC5 / BACK IN THE USA

BLACK SABBATH BLACK SABBATH

VERTIGO/WARNER BROS., FEBRUARY 1970
ALBUM DESIGNED AND PHOTOGRAPHED: KEEF

Sabbath's debut album is the record most agreed upon as ground zero for heavy metal proper, and its doomy, protoprogressive rock strains are reinforced by the crushingly depressive sleeve: a pink sky that appears overcast and a green-faced woman who all too frighteningly resembles a witch. Set amid the scrub in front of an old mill, she is unknown to this day even to Tony, Geezer, Bill, and Oz. "We didn't pick the album sleeves; they were given to us," says their manager at the time, Jim Simpson. "Olav Wyper, who ran the record label, got a designer named Keef, and he had done stuff for him, I think, in the earlier days, with CBS, and he was doing the whole Vertigo series, as I recall. And then he came up with the *Black Sabbath* photograph. Frankly, Vertigo and Olav Wyper didn't really think much of the album at all. They didn't really want it. They only took it because another title had fallen out, and the catalog number of VO 6 was empty, and they needed

[a] product to fill that gap. They already turned it down once. But without ever talking to Keef, the designer, I think he got it straightaway. Olav didn't, Tony Hall didn't, even Essex Music didn't get it. But I think the designer did. I only say that because he created the perfect album sleeve, and I think the second album is certainly not so good, and neither is the third." Adds Geezer: "We had a gig in, I believe, Lincolnshire in England, and this girl came up to us, dressed just like the cover. And she was allegedly that person. Whether it's true or not, there's no way of proving it. And I just found out, again, from the Internet . . . someone had gone there and got a photograph taken there, and I was actually going to use that as the album cover for my new solo album. I was going to go to that exact place and have the band stand in front of it, that mill; it's a place in Oxfordshire, not far from where I live in England."

URIAH HEEP URIAH HEEP

MERCURY, JUNE 1970
ART DIRECTOR: DES STROBEL
COVER DESIGN: JOHN CRAIG

You know, the predictable tack would be to go with the original, and thus more intentional, cobweb-strewn howler fronting the UK issue of this record, complicatedly called . . . *Very 'Eavy . . . Very 'Umble* for the home territory. To be sure, that's a barrier-shattering spot of scariness for album sleeves circa '70, but so is the U.S. sleeve, which features a ghoulish, crazy-eyed reptile of the lake, basically Eddie before Iron Maiden, if Riggs's night prowler were an inky-sea swimmer instead.

LED ZEPPELIN LED ZEPPELIN III

ATLANTIC, OCTOBER 1970
VISUAL CREATIONS: ZACRON

The psychedelic pinwheel design of *Zep III* has been discussed and celebrated many times over, but what it signifies is almost as important as the mechanical operation of the thing: that Zeppelin breathes rarefied air and deserves plush outside-the-box graphics in accordance with the band's creative audacity and subsequent mythical rise as a rock phenomenon more intense and moody than any band before. Be that as it may, one nevertheless could play with this thing for hours, pontificating on the interdependent significance of what shows up through the holes on the underlying

rotating disk, known as a vovelle. As the story goes, the idea was created by an art school student named Zacron, whom Jimmy Page had met in '63. Zacron had subsequently set up his own design house, and Page reintroduced himself and asked him to put something together. The two artists were both aware of vovelle construction, Zacron having fiddled with them as far back as '65. The imagery is a bewildering mix of graphical patterns without meaning, although a sense of intention is achieved through recurring band shots and a theme of images relating to flight.

GRAND FUNK LIVE ALBUM

CAPITOL, NOVEMBER 1970
COVER DESIGN: MARK AMERLING
COVER PHOTOS: MARK AMERLING AND JOE SIA

I swear, there's some crazy conspiracy, and I'm the only one not in on the joke, but the whole world except me thinks Grand Funk is squarely a hard rock band. Yet I still play the records. . . . Seriously, though, I would bet that impression is based half on the strength of the blunt-yet-somewhat-raving music on this live album and half on the depiction of Mark Farner on the cover looking as violently heavy metal as possible. In the blurry, black-and-white, almost protogrunge live shot, Farner is seen whacking out some godforsaken chord sequence as if he's chopping wood, flanked closely by Mel Schacher and Don Brewer, who are going all-out as well. The type screams out a similar high-volume message: band name in lurid fire-engine red, album title stamped with army letters 'cause we're all in such a hurry. "It's that image of three guys in a very rock-and-roll style, with

the black and red, and the shirtless Mark Farner—and the Afros," says drummer Brewer, still the engine room of the band after forty years. "I had an Afro and Mel had the beard, very much descriptive of the time period, and it was just a very rock-and-roll image—that was really what was coming across. And I think that record is really special in that it was done in a couple of days; it was truly live. There were no overdubs at the time; it is what it is, and the energy level that was apparent from listening to that record . . . there was no metronome; nobody was playing with a click track. It was just, play with random abandon and get the energy from the audience; you had this thing going back and forth between the audience and the band, and it was like, harder! faster! bigger! harder! faster!"

MOUNTAIN NANTUCKET SLEIGHRIDE

WINDFALL, JANUARY 1971
COVER DESIGN, PAINTING, AND PHOTOGRAPHY: GAIL COLLINS
CALLIGRAPHY: MICK BRIGDEN AND GAIL COLLINS
DRAWING OF A NANTUCKET SLEIGHRIDE: ROY BAILEY
LITTLE DRAWINGS: MICK BRIGDEN AND GAIL COLLINS
WINDFALL VISUAL DIRECTOR: GAIL COLLINS

Mountain was a hit and miss with its album sleeves, but the best ones were outlandishly illustrated by Mountain bassist Felix Pappalardi's wife, Gail Collins, who was found guilty of criminally negligent homicide in his shooting death, maintaining to this day that the events of April 17, 1983, were accidental. In any event, the historical whaling concept for *Nantucket Sleighride* was amplified in this record's gatefold as well as booklet, with Collins's cover painting being more of a fanciful psychedelic trip, accentuated by groovy custom type that was also used for the credits on the back. The art has helped anchor Mountain, in a pique of revisionist history, to the '60s acid rock movement—a case of product positioning that has aided the band through the decades of plodding along, recording occasionally, but mostly performing as a raucous live act not for fainthearted audiences, a style that never was psychedelic rock, despite the present-day positioning.

ALICE COOPER LOVE IT TO DEATH

STRAIGHT/WARNER BROS., JANUARY 1971
ALBUM COVER AN ALIVE CONCEPT
COVER PHOTOGRAPHS: PRIGENT
INSIDE PHOTOGRAPH: DAVE GRIFFITH

Uh, frankly, the front cover is no great shakes, the controversy about Alice's thumb notwithstanding. But the grainy sleeve takes on extra resonance when coupled with the fantastic decadence of the back cover shot, not to mention the eyes of the gatefold. Still, even considering just the front cover, I feel there's a link between *Love It to Death* and both *Back in the USA* and *New York Dolls*. It's this idea of garage music, filtered through psychedelic, arriving at the laconic thuggishness of glam as it existed in a crumbling New York. Recalls drummer Neal Smith, "There was the thumb thing, which was just a fluke, about the way Alice was holding that shawl that he had around himself, and you know, and then he said—I've always said, everybody said—his thumb looked like a penis. I said, 'Well if that was my penis, I'd be totally embarrassed.' But I just couldn't believe that; that was one of those fluky things. We had some things that accidentally happened in our career, and that was one of them. All of a sudden, they had banned the album; they had to change it and airbrush it out. Give me a break. That's the most ridiculous thing in the world. With Alice Cooper, people were trying to find things that were outrageous. And so from that standpoint, if they really thought Alice is sitting there holding his dick in the picture, first of all, I wouldn't be in the picture with Alice if he was holding his dick, but at any rate, it was one of those great things, and I love it from that standpoint. Also, when I'm standing there in the back, if you look on the back cover . . . I'm holding a cane. See, in 1968, we had a hunting accident, when Alice shot me in the foot, and I still have the bullet in my foot; I used to use a cane for quite a while to help me walk, and so on that cover I still had one of my canes. So I just wanted a prop to use, and if you look on the back cover, holding my hands out with the cane going straight down, and sitting on that seat, and then on the front cover, there on the left, I had the same cane, but I had it over my shoulders, and I'm draping my arms over it. So that was the first time the cane was used on the stage, and to this day Alice still uses a cane." Open the gatefold, and you will find the germination of another milestone rock tale. "We were very anti-hippie all the time," continues Neal, "and the thing is, as things progressed, we were always decadent, but we were decadent even when we were poor. And so, you know, it was Dennis's idea, when you open up the album cover on *Love It to Death*, the most unusual thing was Alice's eyes, and it was the whole inside of the album cover, and when you look inside the pupils, you see a picture of the band. But that idea for the eye makeup came from Dennis. He found a handbill in New York at Carnegie Hall with the eyes on it, and he suggested that Alice try it onstage and we did, and of course we've used it ever since."

JETHRO TULL AQUALUNG

ISLAND/REPRISE, MARCH 1971
LAYOUT: CCS
PAINTINGS: BURTON SILVERMAN

Quite odd, but Jethro Tull made its own bed, folks subconsciously positioning the band as a grizzled collection of old men long before the guys got that way. The main origin of that identity is the cover of the band's debut, *This Was*. But *Aqualung*, featuring a painting of the vagrant that brings to life the very literary, disturbing, though poignantly sympathetic lyric, fuels the fire as well: it's essentially a likeness of mad flautist Ian Anderson himself! Says Ian, evoking for us the menace of the piece as contained in the lyric: "I think more than anything else, it's a song that has a grim reality. It's about something that's very real. Hardly a day goes by when I don't confront that sort of a person and feel the same mixture of guilt and embarrassment and a degree of confusion. But at the same time you

have to think, well, hey, it's not going away; it's part of every day. Having to sing that song is a means of continuing to look at something. It's not exactly cathartic, but it's something you have to do. You have to keep confronting it and not pretend that it's something that doesn't exist. I don't necessarily find it very comfortable to sing, but they are things that I have to keep saying to remind myself of the degree to which they are important subjects. I guess I don't enjoy singing the song because I do focus very much on the words when I'm singing, visualizing what I'm singing. It's very important for me to do that, and so it's not always an easy or comfortable song to do, not in the way that some other songs are upbeat or fun or humorous and lighthearted. But that's part of balancing up a show."

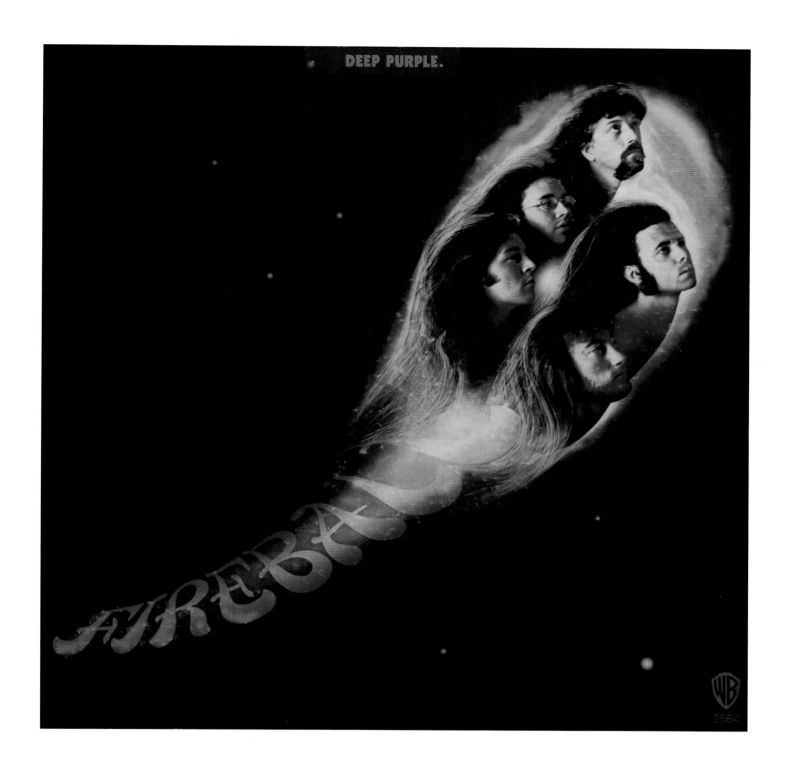

DEEP PURPLE FIREBALL

HARVEST/WARNER BROS., JULY 1971
COVER DESIGN: CASTLE, CHAPPELL AND PARTNERS LIMITED
PHOTOGRAPHY: TONY BURRETT, CHAGFORD STUDIOS

Is this a "good" sleeve or merely an eye-grabber? What-ever your aesthetic acceptance toward the unwieldy idea of sticking five disembodied Purple heads onto the front of a comet, one can't escape the fact that this cover's top-heaviness, its stark juxtaposition of pink on black, the odd small type for band name (with a period!)—it all adds up to a lovable mess, a refreshing willingness to take risks and not worry about the consequences.

ALICE COOPER KILLER

WARNER BROS., NOVEMBER 1971
DESIGN: ALICE COOPER
PHOTOGRAPHY: PETE TURNER

Three records in, Alice Cooper had not really made full use of cover art to summarily shock to the degree his garish horror show did. That all changed with *Killer*, which—well, if you have a fear of snakes, makes you want to quietly step away. Drummer Neal Smith's snake, Kachina, leers, frowns, and promises death as only snakes can, emerging from the side of the sleeve on a lurid red backdrop, framed by the shock of that childlike text. The *Killer* cover instantly shakes something inside the viewer. Flip the album over, and you have the gang-band equivalent of Kachina's threat, and you just have to hear what was inside. Art school students that they were, the guys in the band had layers of meaning in mind. "On the *Killer* album, we had this concept," recalls bassist Dennis Dunaway, who only took up rock and roll full-time because he had found a way not to forsake his huge amount of talent in things visual. "We were going to make every song about a different kind of killer. 'Desperado' was the gunslinger, and 'Halo of Flies' had the James Bond *License to Kill* guy and whatnot, and even though Michael came up with this incredible song, 'Be My Lover,' which we were thinking, 'Well, I don't see a killer in there,' and you're really stretching to say it's a lady-killer, but that song is so good we couldn't say it can't go on the album. So

the snake, we thought, 'Okay, the ultimate killers are a shark or a snake.' Well, Neal had a snake: okay, the snake is going to be on the album cover. The handwriting on the album cover is me writing with my left hand because I wanted it to look like a demented ransom note kind of thing. So when we did the photo session with Pete Turner in New York City, who took the band photo on that album as well, we had them do the picture of the hanging at the same time, and then we had them do the picture of the snake for the cover. Now, Neal was holding the snake, and that was not a little snake. So holding his arm out and trying to hold still for as long as it took, Neal started losing his patience with them. Because they would wait until the snake's tongue came out and then they would snap the picture, and it would be too late. And Neal kept telling them, 'No, you missed it!' And he'd say, 'Well, you're making the mistake of waiting until you see the tongue, and it's too late. Just snap when you don't see the tongue.' And anyway, they took a ton of pictures of the snake, and when we looked through all of them, all of the contact sheets, there was one picture where the snake had his tongue out, and that's the one that's on the cover."

DUST DUST

KAMA SUTRA, 1971
COVER DESIGN: DOMINIC SICILIA
FRONT COVER PHOTO: FROM THE ARCHIVES OF THE CATACOMBS

I'm not sure anybody could challenge this obscure two-record power trio from New York for ghoulish when it comes to early scary cover art, save for maybe Coven or Black Widow. In any event, the album's music didn't quite live up to this archival shot of three former humans slowly yet inexorably returning to dust. "Well, yes," says Marc Bell, a.k.a. Marky Ramone, "we were the first band in America to have skulls on their cover like that, obviously. That was from the catacombs in Mexico." The red text outlined in white picks up and amplifies the subtle glow of what is in the deathly photo. Perhaps it's a shot of a band's forward motion summarily stopped dead in its tracks through the picking of album art too scary for mainstream consumption.

DEEP PURPLE MACHINE HEAD

PURPLE/WARNER BROS., MARCH 1972
COVER DESIGN: R. GLOVER AND J. COLETTA
PHOTOGRAPHY: SHEPARD SHERBELL

Like a fuzzed depiction of Purple's career arc over the previous four years, the *Machine Head* cover painted a picture of a band leaving psychedelic metal behind for tantalizing new alchemical alloys. Talk about downer rock—this could have been a Sabbath cover, given the sense of brain damage evoked by no less than type, title, band shot, and even the actual "machine head" on the back. "An American photographer called Shep Sherbell was put in charge of doing the cover," recalls bassist Roger Glover, "presumably by our management. He came out to Montreux to shoot the piece while we were recording the album. Since our previous two albums had images of us cast in various substances—rock and fire—we were wondering what we could do next. I can't remember who came up with the idea of it being metal. It was either me or John Coletta, one of our managers at the time, but it had nothing whatso-ever to do with the phrase 'heavy metal,' a term that was not yet in mainstream circulation; we were hard

rock and that was that! Shep Sherbell procured a sheet of metal from somewhere, roughly five feet square, and managed to find some wooden letters, like those used in early printing presses, which he then hammered into it. It was a bit tricky because the harder the letters were hammered in, the more the metal tended to warp, and since the result was going to be a shot of our reflected images, we wanted to keep the smooth quality of the sheet as intact as possible. The embossed metal sheet was then suspended vertically in front of a blue cloth backdrop, and the five of us in the band, suit-ably lit, sat in front of it with the backdrop behind us. Shep—disguised by some sort of dark material so that his face and camera were as unobtrusive as possible—positioned himself just in front of the backdrop, seven or eight feet behind us, and shot the pictures over us, capturing our reflections in the metal underneath the roughly stamped letters of the name and title."

STEREO
DL 7-5347

WISHBONE ASH ARGUS

DECCA/MCA, APRIL 1972
DESIGN AND PHOTOGRAPHY: HIPGNOSIS

Not quite hard rock, Wishbone Ash is nonetheless perennially part of the heavy metal conversation due to its pioneering of twin lead-guitar solos. But we may not have even taken notice of that were it not for the quietly menacing warrior standing vigilant guard on the front of this, the band's third and signature album.

It's an early piece for Hipgnosis and not much to it, perhaps betraying the resources of those fledgling days. Still, it did the trick of making the band seem "heavy," as per the pre-heavy-metal definition of the term, namely, "heavy of vibe."

URIAH HEEP DEMONS AND WIZARDS

BRONZE/MERCURY, MAY 1972
DESIGNED AND DRAWN: ROGER DEAN

This early Roger Dean work, twinned with his follow-up cover, *The Magician's Birthday*, went a long way toward positioning Heep as conceptual, mystical, and, somewhat in error, a card-carrying member of England's progressive-rock phalanx. Additionally, the wizardry embodied unwittingly represented the ground-level communion between fantasy themes and heavy metal, a literary and visual marriage that would develop through Rainbow into the NWOBHM and Dio, exploding thereafter into an entire thriving genre known as power metal. Explains Roger, "This is a painting of a wizard holding a small island of reality in the vastness of the universe. His cloak is made of real butterfly wings, partly because I thought it would work. It would be from a different reality, a sudden flash of color in the darkness of space. It was also a way to finish the painting, as I had a fall and broke my right wrist and sprained my left!" Adds Heep lead guitarist Mick Box: "They were very, very strong covers and were picked up everywhere in the world. *The Magician's Birthday* was just a reflection of—and an obvious move on from—*Demons and Wizards*. Unfortunately, I don't have any of the originals." Box continues, with a laugh: "He was a canny artist—kept them all."

DUST HARD ATTACK

KAMA SUTRA, 1972
ART DIRECTION: GLEN CHRISTENSEN
COVER PAINTING: FRANK FRAZETTA

Sure, Dust members were somewhat of an early "power metal" trio, featuring a couple of future second-tier musicniks in Marc Bell (Marky Ramone) and bassist-about-town Kenny Aaronson, not to mention the Kenny Kerner–Richie Wise–Kiss production connection. Anyway, Dust is, weirdly, best remembered for its two album covers—the first, previously discussed, and this second and last, a true protometal/proto–power metal cover along the lines of signature fantasy cover art, featuring three Vikings battling it out on a wind-swept mountaintop. It's more than that, though: this is a painting by Frank Frazetta, the notable, collectible fantasy artist (deceased in 2010), also part of the rock-and-roll world through his Molly Hatchet covers. "It was free," says Bell. "He loved the band, and he was a big fan, and he loved helping out on it. And he was just happy to do it. He gave us the rights, but he owned the painting. And you see, at that point in time, a lot

of people in the industry would borrow and lend. Not necessarily steal, but it would be like a professional courtesy, you know what I'm saying? It wasn't till later on that a lot of the lawyers got involved, stealing and taking samples from other bands. It's not like today—everybody just steals. If you go hear a band that sounds like the Ramones, they won't admit where they got their influence from." I can't stress enough how this cover establishes an aesthetic that moves through the imagery of *Lord of the Rings*, *Heavy Metal* magazine, *Conan the Barbarian*, and Manowar, slouching toward the vast and mostly European power metal genre—essentially a speedy, classical-based, melodic, tradi-tional heavy metal often wrapped up in fantasy themes both lyrically and graphically. This is where that whole thing starts, coupled with Uriah Heep's *Demons and Wizards* wrapper, also from 1972.

T. REX THE SLIDER

EMI/REPRISE, JULY 1972
PHOTOGRAPHY: RINGO STARR

The Slider presents Marc Bolan as the original top-hatted dandy of hard rock, a mantle rattled by Slash, and, to some extent, Alice Cooper before him. Not that T. Rex was incredibly heavy, but covers like this, as well as *Electric Warrior*, helped push the quasi-band in that direction, in the firmament of minds superficially stimulated by the visual. *The Slider* is arch-glam, but the cover suggests a drug-corrupted—if not smarter, more art-minded—version of glam, along with a time-less (or Gothic, or Victorian) quality. Ultimately, this striking image helped position Bolan as the Lord Byron pixie wizard of a strange, roughed-up-yet-fey rock not unlike that which fellow glam noisemaker Mick Ronson provided for Bowie.

STATUS QUO PILEDRIVER

VERTIGO/A&M, DECEMBER 1972
NO IMAGE OR DESIGN CREDIT

Piledriver found Status Quo gradually transitioning out of the British blues boom into something a little tougher and riffier. Little did the players know that their habit of "headbanging" in blue-jeaned unison, long hair flying, would become an iconic image for the metal minions. So yeah, due equally to the music on this album (e.g., "Big Fat Mama," "Paper Plane," and "O Baby") and to the all-business live shot emblazoned between that bright and shouty text, Status Quo would be perceived as helping fly the flag for hard rock, albeit that of a boogie sort, roughly akin to Foghat and ZZ Top.

ALICE COOPER BILLION DOLLAR BABIES

WARNER BROS., FEBRUARY 1973
ALBUM CONCEPT AND DESIGN: PACIFIC EYE & EAR
PHOTOGRAPHY: DAVID BAILEY, LYNN GOLDSMITH, AND NEAL PRESTON

Gorgeous and expensive, the *Billion Dollar Babies* sleeve, brightly burnished, combines the evil of snakes and the innocence of babies for a chilling effect—chilling because the baby becomes corrupted, comparisons to *Rosemary's Baby* notwithstanding. Rounded corners and embossing work on the ingenious snakeskin wallet design, continued inside with money and punch-out wallet-style photos, plus more incendiary shots of the filthy rich band—it's the third Coop cover to include fancy-print doodads, but it's also the most artistic and disturbing, helping fuel the fire that the band (Alice Cooper being still denoted a band) started with its lyrics, clothes, stage show, and, well, its lanky, smarmy countenance. "I don't see anything shocking about it, myself," notes band bassist and resident conceptual artist Dennis Dunaway. "It was just a snakeskin wallet, and I guess people got shocked because it had the crying baby. Alice is holding the crying baby, which was baby Lola, whose mother, Carolyn Pfeiffer, still works for Live Enterprises after all these years. She worked in publicity with the Beatles, with Derek Taylor. That's where we got her from, and that was her daughter. That's the only thing I can see that was shocking. I guess it was just because it was so blatantly, 'Hey, we're rich, and we're rock-and-roll,' and we had a picture with a big, gigantic pile of money and a crying baby with Alice Cooper makeup on. That's all I can see that was shocking about it. It seemed pretty mild to me." Yes, but then there're those rabbits: "Well, that actually came from an idea I had when the band lived [on a farm], all the way back before *Love It to Death*,

going back to that concept of the white and the black on that album. Cindy, my wife, who was Neal's sister, at the time had rabbits on this farm that the band was at in Pontiac, Michigan. And I got this idea for the white part of the album, which I thought would be the back of the cover, all of us sitting in a white bed wearing white, and we would have these bunny rabbits in bed with us. So it would be the opposite of the dark. See, I wanted to contrast happy and innocent and dark and evil. So we brought in a photographer, and we did this shoot. I have seen some of these pictures crop up, all these years later, but at the time, the guy wanted to be paid a few hundred dollars, and we're like, 'You've got to be kidding, man. Look in our refrigerator. We don't have any food! Take pity on us and do a spec deal.' And the guy wouldn't do it. And I was so pissed off, after we went through all this trouble. I told him, 'Well, we're going to redo this picture someday, and then we're going to use it and you're going to be sorry.' And so eventually we got around to it. We even got rabbits in London. That was David Bailey, who photographed the Beatles and all kinds of people. And that shot was taken in London. But the night before, I was up all night, because Cindy was in my room sewing, making those outfits, because she made all the clothes for the band. But she was up all night, and I'm trying to do a photo thing at nine o'clock in the morning with no sleep. None of us had any sleep, really—we were partying in London. But the hard part about that photograph was trying to get that much American money in England."

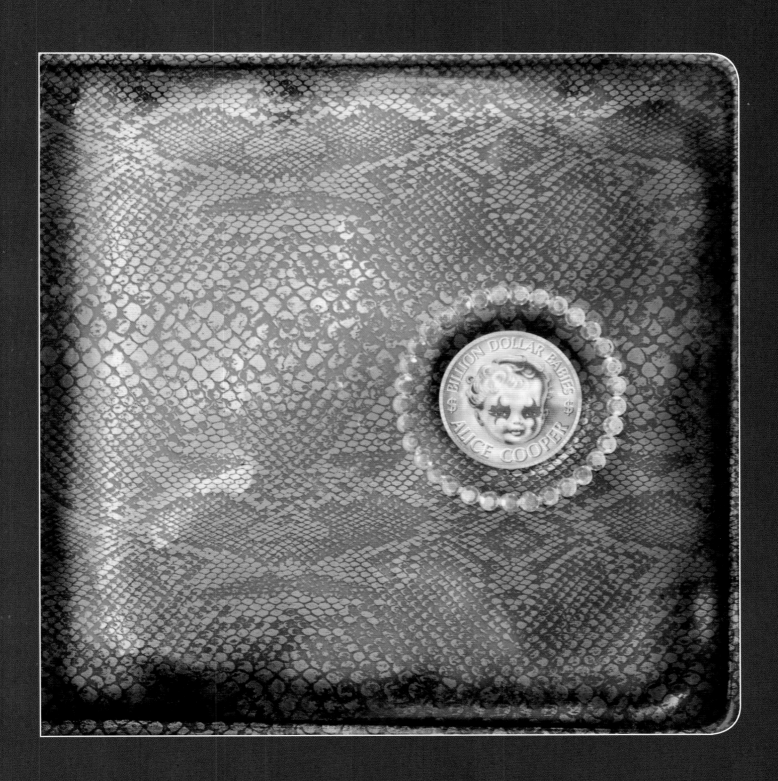

BLUE ÖYSTER CULT TYRANNY AND MUTATION

COLUMBIA, FEBRUARY 1973
COVER BY: GAWLIK

No one had infused mystery into metal so quickly and efficiently as Blue Öyster Cult—through its band name, its record and song titles, and the first three record covers, all black-and-white, none with a band photo. *Tyranny and Mutation* (complete with archaic *V* instead of *U*) is the work of the equally mysterious Gawlik, who manipulates this idea of black and white into a disorienting vortex. Explains BÖC manager and colyricist Sandy Pearlman: "Gawlik had gone to the Rhode Island School of Design, and he had left there and transferred to [the State University of New York at] Stony Brook. He was living in the dorms, and I had run into him, quite literally, on the day when he was unfurling the huge scroll on which he had all of his architectural designs. He was sort of like the Albert Speer of H Quad at Stony Brook. You know, Speer was commissioned by Hitler to design all of future Europe. And Bill Gawlik was designing all of future America, although he was not being commissioned by Hitler or anyone else. And so a lot of the cover art really is on those original scrolls, which were so long that they would go the entire length of the building. It was like four o'clock in the morning when we were unfurling these things, and anybody who was up and moving around at four o'clock in the morning didn't seem to mind. Anyways, that's where I first ran into the stuff."

LED ZEPPELIN HOUSES OF THE HOLY

ATLANTIC, MARCH 1973
SLEEVE: HIPGNOSIS

Like *Zep IV*, part of the mystique of the *Houses of the Holy* sleeve is the lack of text anywhere on the front or back of the thing. However, this allowed for an extra doodad, applied to the U.S. and UK issues of the album, a Japanese-style obi strip, which also served the purpose of covering up a bum. This amazing shoot was conducted at the Giant's Causeway in Northern Ireland,

Aubrey Powell enlisting for the role of the ritualistic children a brother and a sister, who were shot and replicated a bunch of times, for a photo that is an homage to the conclusion of Arthur C. Clarke's book *Childhood's End*. No question that there's mystical menace to the thing, fueled by Jimmy Page's oft-reported ties to the occult.

BACHMAN-TURNER OVERDRIVE BACHMAN-TURNER OVERDRIVE

MERCURY, MAY 1973
ART DIRECTOR: JIM LADWIG
ALBUM DESIGN: ROB BACHMAN
COVER SCULPTURE: PARVIZ SADIGHIAN
COVER PHOTOGRAPHY: TOM ZAMIAR

BTO guitarist and vocalist Randy Bachman, having recently decided that his post–Guess Who country rock act, Brave Belt, was dullsville, came up with the idea of trying his hand at the new brutish hard rock storming ashore from the UK and rumbling across America through the likes of Cactus and Mountain. Thus BTO was born heavy, the manly mood of metal evoked on the band's debut wrapper through the weighty presence of a sculpture of cogs within gears and more cogs forged in fire by the stoners at the end of the hall in machine shop, up to no good come lunchtime with their muscle cars and Black Sabbath eight-tracks.

IGGY AND THE STOOGES RAW POWER

COLUMBIA, MAY 1973
PHOTOGRAPHY: MICK ROCK

The cover of the third Stooges album broke the creepy door open between garage rock and punk, then grunge, sending off signals that glam had gone very wrong, that celebrity is a sham, and that rock could be dangerous again. Iggy, in this impossibly iconic Mick Rock shot, ever the confrontational contortionist, is caught in coiled wait, praying for provocation from the crowd, jet-fueled wider up top than he is in the engine room. He floats above an oblivion of black, and then that Munsters text (not on all versions) stupidly offers up a tossed-off band name and a warning of an album title. "I think the band was always shock," notes Stooges guitarist James Williamson. "But not in the sense of an Alice Cooper or somebody like that, who actually had a kind of artificial show that he did, that had shock value. I think that we were a band that was, for lack of a better word, an experiential band. Because you couldn't tell . . . I mean, it was spontaneous. There were no two shows alike, and in fact, in later years, there were no two shows that contained the same music. But *shock* isn't a good term, I don't think, for us, but then neither is *glam* at first. I mean, we went to London, and we're a bunch of Midwest guys, and so we're over there just trying to make sense of everything, and it's right at the beginning of the glam rock thing—Marc Bolan and David Bowie and all those guys—and we weren't going to be left behind, and so I remember our first gig, our only gig in London, we went out and wanted to get some makeup and stuff, but we didn't have any skills or know what to do, so we bought a bunch of kind of clown makeup, and so you see us in that *Raw Power* album picture in whiteface and all that stuff. It's just because, you know, we didn't know what to do. At first we were laughing our asses off, basically. But later on, we started to integrate some of that; you want to look contemporary, if you're in a rock and roll band. And I think kind of everybody fell into that. Anyway, that morphed itself into something completely different, because the experience of going to watch the Stooges, no matter what we wore, was entirely different from the songs that were coming out of the glam guys' bands." Admissions or not from Williamson, the beauty of the *Raw Power* cover is in the idea that no amount of half-assed glamming up can cage the power of deconstructed rock wattage, of miscreants messing up rock and roll. Thus the music inside this record serves as the Friday night meet-thy-doom slaughterhouse of the half dozen or so records that coalesce as the pillars of punk.

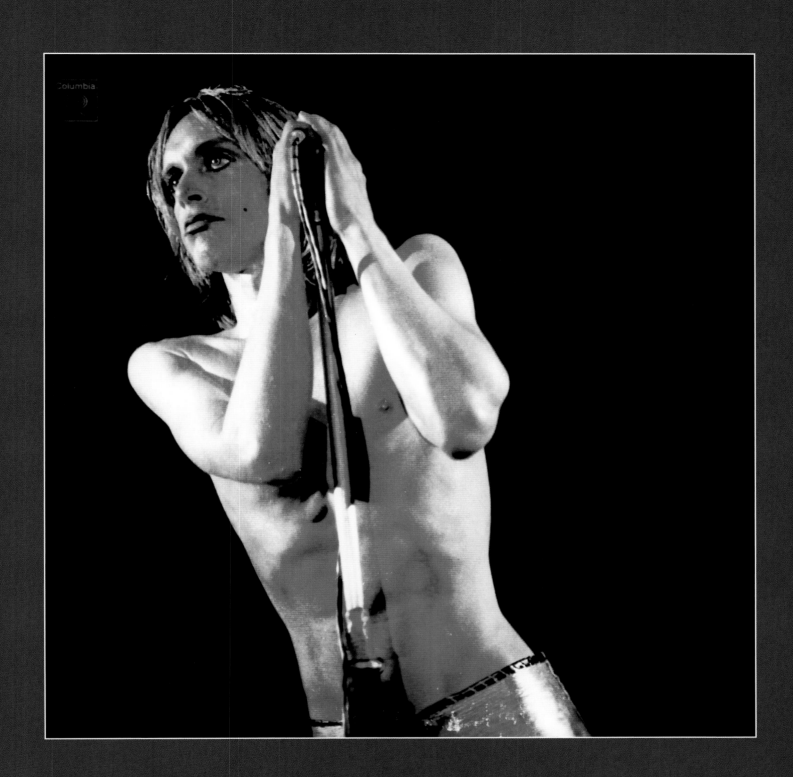

NAZARETH RAZAMANAZ

MOONCREST/A&M, MAY 1973
DESIGN: DAVE FIELD

Precursor to Metallica's *Ride the Lightning*, the *Razamanaz* sleeve captured the magic power of hard rock, especially given that snazzy title, rendered so big and bold it had to be broken up like a bad mob and segregated into groups of three. It's a brilliant text treatment to be sure, utilizing what is now the time-honored tradition of Nazareth putting to punned use part of their name and, more so, their jagged slash of an *N*.

HAWKWIND SPACE RITUAL

UNITED ARTISTS, MAY 1973
ART DIRECTION: PIERRE
PACKAGING: BARNEY BUBBLES
PHOTOGRAPHY: LAURIE LEWIS AND GABI NASEMAN

Hawkwind's incendiary double live album turned up the jets on the band's reputation by adding an extra level of brutality to the band's psychedelic drone rock. But its sleeve, well, it opened like a drug flower to fully six panels of chaotic spiritual mumbo jumbo. The inside was forest-green ink on a white background and, textually, was the height of nonsense. The six sides of color offered, of course, the epic frontal image, which looks like the Starbucks logo after you gulped a dosed caramel macchiato, plus jerky live shots that played up the band's pioneering light show. These also offered a disparate, disconnected bunch of pop-art images, topped or titled with the sentiments "Flying is dying is trying," "Brainstorm here we go," "Master of the Universe," "We were born to go as far as we can fly; Turn electric dreams into reality," and the infinitely more utilitarian "Recorded live at Liverpool Stadium & Brixton Sundown." It all must have been very expensive, especially for a band of anti-money bandits like the Hawks. "Actually, funny you should mention that," notes founding member Dave Brock, "because we didn't realize that artwork used to come out of the band's wages. We always thought the record company paid for it. As you well know, it was always paid for by the bands, so you didn't see very much royalties. I mean, I went up to RCA in the '80s, actually, and they had a skip around

the back of their office, which is just off of Tottenham Court Road. I walked past it, and if you can believe it, the actual artwork for Elton John's *Yellow Brick Road*, it was in a glass frame, and all the glass had been smashed, and it cut the picture. I'm thinking, fuckin' hell, these people are just chucking all this stuff out. This is what used to go on. You think you could give it to the band, sort of, 'Here you are, chaps,' and there it is dumped. But *Space Ritual* cost probably about fifteen hundred quid. All our stuff at the time, we had Barney Bubbles, who was a wonderful artist who worked with us. Barney designed a lot of our stage sets as well. We were doing this thing with colors going round these spheres, certain colors with certain sound frequencies. You would get the red and orange mixing, and red and orange had a certain sound and so on—the sound of the spheres. You can check out all this; all colors are supposed to have a sound that works wonderfully well with the color. And he had it worked out where we'd stand, and certain sounds would help us feel better. Healing sounds, they are, and it's quite interesting. So this was all Barney's idea and his artwork. Barney probably only got paid a few hundred quid for it, and somebody else in the art department did all the writing over it, and no doubt they charged a lot of money."

NEW YORK DOLLS NEW YORK DOLLS

MERCURY, JULY 1973
DESIGN: ALBUM GRAPHICS, INC.
PHOTOGRAPHY: TOSHI ASAKA

A masterful, provocative slice of shock is this *New York Dolls* sleeve, so bold that in one stroke it upstaged—and in fact embarrassed—anything coming out of the paltry glitter rock movement in the UK, where all this was supposedly invented. But talk about stopping your career dead. These boys were beyond pretty, their thuggishness shining through, their inscrutable New Yorkness alienating most of the country and, yes, scaring them away in droves. Homosexuality, if you thought about it for more than a knee-jerk second, didn't even enter the picture: this was no less than anarchy in the making, welling out of a bankrupt city of grime and crime. As Syl Sylvain explains, this incendiary sleeve was a bit of an accident. "Yes, well, Mercury took us into this antique shop on Third Avenue in New York. And basically, when we made ourselves up, we kind of looked like whatever, what Aerosmith looked like back then. And they did this scene . . . it costs a lot of money for them to shoot it and all this. We were basically like dolls in this antique shop, supposedly. And it looked like crap—I hated that cover. It just didn't do anything, and as a matter of fact, we never even showed those pictures, that session, to anybody else. But anyway, I got on my horn and got back to all the people that I knew in the rag business, and I had these two friends, Pinky and Diane, who had a clothing line, like a Paradise kind of look, and I told them my situation and everything else, and they said, 'Oh man, the Dolls can't go out like that. That's going to be so damn boring.' And they actually may have been

right. Had it happened, I predict you wouldn't be talking to me right now. So anyway, got all my friends together, I got the hairdresser, a photographer, Toshi, who is like a Vogue photographer, and he was doing covers and everything else, and this makeup artist who is like an Andy Warhol sort of, one of the guys that was hanging out at Max's Kansas City. Now, the couch that we're on? Okay, we found that; me and Pinky and Diane found that couch downstairs on the street in New York not far from the studio. And we brought it up to the studio and we tacked it with some of the materials that we had left over from making pants and stuff like that, which was a white stretch satin, and that's the couch that we used. And, of course, the makeup artist, he went nuts on us. He wanted to make us look like we were in some Andy Warhol movie or something, and Toshi just snapped those pictures, and hence the whole thing that happened to be shock and androgynous and all this other shit. And yeah, we used to have fun with sex. We were still, I would say, very adventurous in trying to find out what we liked and what we didn't like, and so you tried everything, in a way. And you know, hence, that's the reason why they say that. But it was a natural thing for us, being the outgoing lads that we were. And we were doing it to get even more girlfriends because we all turned out to be kind of straight, if I can use that word, as boring as that might sound."

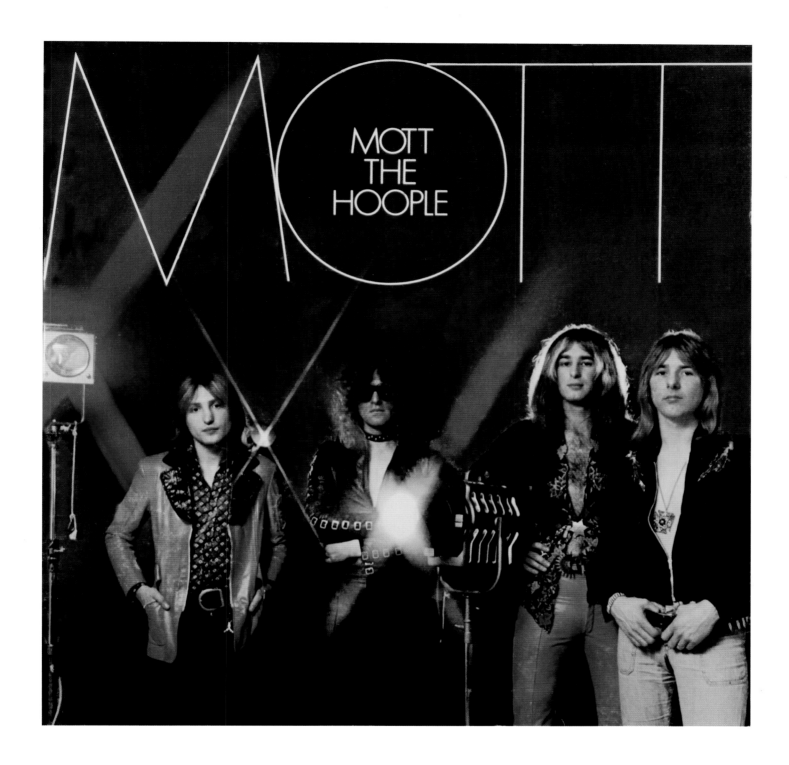

MOTT THE HOOPLE MOTT

COLUMBIA, JULY 1973
NO IMAGE OR DESIGN CREDIT

The UK cover is crap, wrecked by anemic color, stodgy type, and a dumb Roman bust, but the U.S. sleeve hums like bad grounding, presenting the band in a simple posed photograph, two lights projecting rays straight out, the effect subconsciously adding rock-star glamour to the scene. Upscale type dominates, but not really, over the shot of the band members, who are each dressed to the nines in the post-hippie rock garb of the day, save for Ian Hunter, who goes for a considerably hard rock look, black leather from head to toe to dog collar, made even meaner by his trademark scowl and dark glasses.

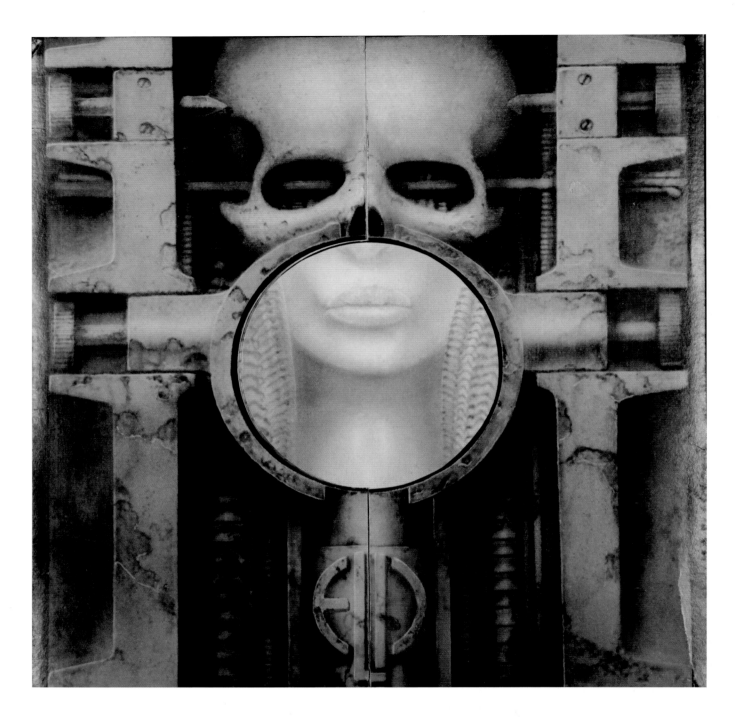

EMERSON, LAKE & PALMER BRAIN SALAD SURGERY

MANTICORE, NOVEMBER 1973
ARTWORK, COVER PAINTING, AND PAINTINGS: H. R. GIGER
ART DIRECTION AND DESIGN: FABIO NICOLI

Not exactly a hard rock band, ELP could nevertheless be classed as heavy progressive or protoprogressive metal, due to the aggression with which they attacked their complex numbers and to the grinding nature of Keith Emerson's keyboard work, insinuating in tandem with Purple's Jon Lord that keyboards could be menacing. And talk about menacing—*Brain Salad Surgery* makes use of specially commissioned artwork by H. R. Giger, namely, *Work #217 ELP I* and *Work #218 ELP II*, the two "biomechanical" paintings layered through the use of a novel center gatefold design.

Giger is also responsible for the "keyhole" ELP logo (massaged into the art, usually a no-no), that would from here on in be regularly used by the band. Some trivia on this: the paintings were either stolen or lost in 2005, after a Giger exhibition in Prague; in addition, Giger has stated that he was never paid for the paintings. In any event, this is a case of artwork boosting the mystique of a band, with ELP hereafter viewed as dark and wizardly, nudged toward King Crimson and away from the lightness and being of Genesis, Yes, and Jethro Tull.

NAZARETH LOUD 'N' PROUD

MOONCREST/A&M, NOVEMBER 1973
SLEEVE: DAVE FIELD

A refreshing burst of uninhibited color and maybe somewhat of a last gasp, for after a few more years, hard rock clichés would build into stacks of ossified rules, and something like a blue peacock surrounded by verdant green feathers would be considered uncool for a metal album. "We didn't have a lot to do with the *Loud 'n' Proud* sleeve as such," explains guitarist Manny Charlton. "We took that title from a headline from one of the musical papers. That was a quote from Ritchie Blackmore, actually; he came up with that phrase, and the title came from that. And of course, don't forget that the album was produced by Roger Glover, so there's an association there. We thought, 'Well, we'll call the album

Loud 'n' Proud,' and we said to our manager, 'That's the album title,' and they went off and commissioned different people to put forward ideas for the sleeve. And the one with the peacock, our management liked it and we liked it; we thought, 'That's cool.'" What's also cool is the use of type, with the album title strutting like a peacock many times the size of the band name, further accentuated with a black drop shadow, whereas the band name is rendered in simple black. In addition, the album title makes use of the iconic band name font that had, four albums in, been used every time, a further tie-in being the massive, long-legged *'n'* anchoring boldly the *Loud* to the *Proud*.

BLACK SABBATH SABBATH BLOODY SABBATH

VERTIGO/WARNER BROS., DECEMBER 1973
ALBUM CONCEPT AND DESIGN: PACIFIC EYE & EAR
ILLUSTRATIONS: DREW STRUZAN
PHOTOGRAPHY: SHEPARD SHERBELL

No cover spoke to the Satanic panic of the early '70s—fueled by *Rosemary's Baby*, *The Exorcist*, *The Omen*, and this writer's fave, *Race with the Devil*—as much as this aggressively society-baiting sleeve from the mighty Sabs. From the nasty fascist type through to the exotic ways and means of evil all over this deathbed, Pacific Eye & Ear (essentially Ernie Cefalu conceptually and Drew Struzan, through daunting and imaginative illustration) resolutely stoked with a direct gaze the fires of Sabbatherian mystique. This gave the band its first sleeve since the debut that said much of anything, and then did so as loudly as one could envisage on a one-foot square of scare. "I thought *Sabbath Bloody Sabbath* was incredible," agrees drummer Bill Ward. "That's one of my favorite all-time album covers. On just a personal note, I love the back of that album cover, really nice. I guess if I ever wanted to die, in a certain way, that's how it would be, with all the animals and everything, everybody just around me, or whatever. It was interesting actually to see what it did do to people. But we really did try in the press, when we did interviews, to really say where we were at, and I don't think we did any interviews where we said we were demonic and really go into a black area. As far as

I'm concerned, Black Sabbath went into enough black areas anyway that weren't anything to do with being demonic, and it was still hell as far as I was concerned. We'd certainly been through all of that. To be honest with you, the people that I feared the most personally, back then, and I don't think this is a very admiring name, you know, back then they were called Jesus freaks, and it's something that's not a particularly nice way of calling people. They're still human beings, you know? But unfortunately they were just caught up in this obsession, and I feared them a lot because they could be very violent at the same time. Or individuals could be very violent. And if anybody was going to try to pull a gun and shoot one of us, I'm sure it would have come from there. But there were attempts on our lives over the years, through different sources and things like that. It's not something that happened all the time, but there were some incidents, and we were well protected at the time, well policed, and the FBI were involved. But it was the people who believed in Jesus Christ who really bothered me; they really got to me. Only because I feared that they were mental enough to really go over the top."

BUDGIE NEVER TURN YOUR BACK ON A FRIEND

MCA, 1973
SLEEVE DRAWN AND DESIGNED BY ROGER DEAN

Budgie cranked all sorts of wacky sleeves featuring their bird warrior, and Roger Dean was involved more than once. But *Never Turn Your Back on a Friend* (oddly, the only early Budgie album not issued in the U.S.) sports the spiffiest, classiest, most vibrantly colored sleeve of any cooked up by Dean, this plush gatefold rivaling the best of his work for Yes. I recall, as a young teen, seeing within the scene some sort of malevolent capture-and-convert-into-humanoid narrative, but with a clearer mind now, it looks to me like the parakeet dude

is essentially taming a wild bronco. Notes Roger, "Back then, in the days before I had designed full fonts, *Never Turn Your Back on a Friend* was really too long a title to make into a satisfactory logo. But the budgie in a flying suit became an unofficial logo for the band. My favorite of the Budgie covers was *Squawk*. Decades after I had painted it, I met an engineer from the research works where they built the Blackbird, and he told me that a copy of the *Squawk* plane was painted huge on the side of an aircraft hangar. I wish I had seen it."

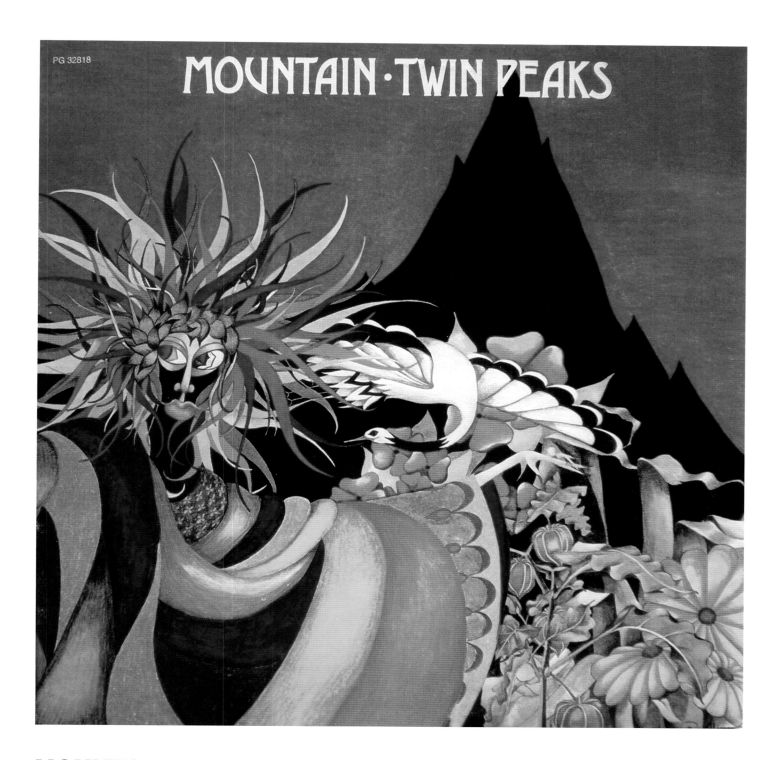

PG 32818

MOUNTAIN · TWIN PEAKS

MOUNTAIN TWIN PEAKS

WINDFALL/COLUMBIA, FEBRUARY 1974
COVER ILLUSTRATION: GAIL COLLINS

Turn back to the *Nantucket Sleighride* (page 27) write-up for a quick reminder of the bad vibes surrounding our Gail Collins. But putting that aside, this is the cover on which her exotic and oddly Oriental floralscapes of the mind bloom most forcefully. Elsewhere throughout the band's ragtag catalog is a frustrating combination of partials and rushed text choices, but come *Twin Peaks*, yes, there's finally a sense of balance and belonging (and even two peaks, once you include the wraparound).

DEEP PURPLE BURN

PURPLE/WARNER BROS., FEBRUARY 1974
ART STUDIO: NESBIT PHIPPS AND FROOME LTD.
PHOTOGRAPHY: FIN COSTELLO
CANDLES: © CANDLE MAKERS SUPPLIES

The Purps hadn't been known to be rockin' the album covers up until this point, but *Burn* knocked it out of the park, its explosion of color announcing the Mk III version of the band with stunning lushness. Of course, the predominant color is purple, but beyond that, Ritchie's occult leanings are highlighted with the burning candles idea—these candles being, in essence, voodoo candles, two sets having apparently been made for the occasion. Decadent, druggy, and dramatic, the sleeve art is enhanced by the album title's psychedelic text, resembling a flickering tip of flame, with white-tip coloring used in the quiet, polite text for the band's name, nudging off the top of the conflagrated scene.

QUEEN QUEEN II

EMI/ELEKTRA, MARCH 1974
PHOTOGRAPHY AND ART DIRECTION BY MICK ROCK
SLEEVE CONCEPT BY MICK ROCK AND QUEEN
TYPOGRAPHY BY RIDGEWAY WATT

The audacity of Queen matches that of Led Zeppelin, as well it should, because Queen has the greater talent—is it a dig at the Zeps to call their vastly superior second album *II*, too? Anyway, it's no conceit that the band, gracing the sleeve of what is only their second grasp at greatness, pose in contempt of lesser rock bands and perhaps even those so base as to attend rock-and-roll concerts of any sort, including Queen's. Explains photographer Mick Rock, "The brief the band gave me for *Queen II* was that it should have a black-and-white theme, it should feature the band, and that it was to

be a gatefold cover. Around that time, I came across a book of photos of Marlene Dietrich, which included a shot of her on the set of *Shanghai Express.* It's hard to explain in words but I made an immediate connection with Queen. It had something to do with Freddie's personality and the general aura of the group, which was somehow outrageous and also magnificent. And, of course, no one was ever more glam than the divine Ms. Dietrich. So I showed the photo to Freddie, and he immediately got it and corralled the others into going along with it."

UFO PHENOMENON

CHRYSALIS, MAY 1974
COVER DESIGN AND PHOTOS: HIPGNOSIS
TINTING: MAURICE TATE
GRAPHICS: RICHARD EVANS

Concocted during that fecund period when Hipgnosis could do no wrong, this is one of the gang's more pastoral presentations, a tinted scene that amusingly captures a young couple perpetrating a UFO hoax rather than a mighty heavy metal UFO itself. A small white line by the tire betrays the removal of a hubcap, as does the visible enough contrast of no hubcap up front versus hubcap at the back. Mr. Muttonchops has flung the hubcap inelegantly into the air, and his wife was just about to snap a shot of it while the all-seeing eye of Hipgnosis catches her in the act. She stares

daggers and is clearly perturbed. The *Phenomenon* sleeve improbably inaugurated quite the run between these barroom rock-and-rollers and the world's most esteemed design team. Frankly, as much as UFO is vastly underappreciated for Phil Mogg's Springsteen-esque storytelling, the austere cover art did more than its part to help people take UFO seriously as a first-rate organization, *organization* being the last word to get close to anything Pete, Michael, and Phil could ever accomplish.

NEW YORK DOLLS TOO MUCH TOO SOON

MERCURY, MAY 1974
GRAPHIC SUPERVISION: ALBUM GRAPHICS
PHOTOGRAPHY: BOB GRUEN, HANS G. LEHMANN, AND PIETER MAZEL

The Dolls' second and last incendiary sleeve presented a rough-and-tumble glam band in potent, live, action-hero mode. Usurping similar vibes ascribed to Slade and Mott the Hoople, the cover easily outrocked the Stones as well, but definitely evoked images of Jagger and Richards (and Wood), given all the bedhead-edness on protopunk display. "To me what it says is, here's a couple of great-looking guys having a lot of fun," muses legendary photographer Bob Gruen, who took the iconic cover shot. "You can kind of tell that it's loud, fast music from just looking at the picture. That was taken at the Don Steele show in Los Angeles. The band picked that shot. There's a doll pinned on Jerry's drums. They didn't really use dolls in their act or in their persona or their visuals at all, actually. Somebody had given Jerry a doll that day or that week, and he stuck it on his drums, so it happened to be there. Actually, the thing with the Dolls, they didn't want to play with dolls, they wanted girls to play with them, you know, and

they dressed themselves up to look like dolls so the girls would play with them. They weren't attempting in any way to look like girls. People tend to look back and think they were drag queens or they were gay or they were trying to look like women. Quite the contrary; they were very much men who were trying to be as beautiful as they could in order to attract women, which they did." Asked if the band members were ever physically threatened for their fashion sense, Bob confirms, "On occasion, yeah. People who are afraid of any kind of change, of anything different, tend to get scared. There's a great line by Dennis Hopper in *Easy Rider* where he says people talk a lot about individual freedom, but if you show them a free individual, they get scared. And they don't get running scared; they get dangerous. And that really applies in this case because people would see the Dolls and they'd be so frightened for their own values, they'd want to strike out and destroy what they're looking at."

BACHMAN-TURNER OVERDRIVE NOT FRAGILE

MERCURY, AUGUST 1974
ART DIRECTION BY JIM LADWIG/AGI
DESIGN BY JOE KOTLEBA
COVER CONSTRUCTION BY PARVIS SADIGHIAN
PHOTOGRAPHED BY TOM ZAMIAR
PHOTOGRAPHY BY JOHN BROTT AND BRUCE LARSON

Sticking stubbornly with the metal-shop theme, Bachman-Turner Overweight added a li'l inside joke, responding to the lily-livered Yes, who, in the opinion of the nudie-suited trucker wannabes in BTO, had meekly pronounced their music *Fragile*. A couple of sweet details: first, the bolts and crate and gears all get a light embossing, an appointment no doubt earned through the band's solid-hit status; and second, a crude tag is attached at the bottom of the box, upon which the album's catalog number is scrawled in red.

ALICE COOPER GREATEST HITS

WARNER BROS., AUGUST 1974
ALBUM CONCEPT AND DESIGN: PACIFIC EYE & EAR
ILLUSTRATION: DREW STRUZAN AND BILL GARLAND

Rock royalty and illustration royalty combine for a spot of class on this Pacific Eye & Ear design. Alice had always worked a Hollywood complexity of inspiration into his game. I stand short of calling it a shtick, because there's a serious artful shock to what Alice does, and even quite directly on the glitz front, there's a bit of the old junk-culture-leads-to-disaster thing going on, with Alice and his lanky band of antihippies being the result of too much eye candy—or worse, Charlie Manson. So there's an unease with such miscreants infiltrating the sacrosanct, inclusive celluloid world that is supposed to be easy listening and watching. True, Alice and his band are portrayed as villains, but the underpinning is that they are more villainous than this playacting would suggest. The sleeve is the work of hugely famed artist Drew Struzan, under the direction of Ernie Cefalu, who further clarifies, "That was Drew on the outside and Bill Garland on the inside. Two different illustrators, which makes that piece even more desirable, because Drew never really . . . he's only worked on the same piece with another illustrator three times. The first one was the first *Star Wars* poster, when he worked with Charlie White, who could draw figures. So Charlie did the background, and Drew did the figures. Bill was very much a very versatile illustrator, like Drew, and Drew was a mentor to him, and we all worked at Pacific Eye & Ear together, and they did it like an animation cell. Drew did the background, and then Bill did the cartoon characters on an overlay. What happened was, we did that album cover, we submitted it to the record label, and the record label said, 'Well, you know, you're going to have to change . . . anybody that is still alive, you have to take out.' So we had to change twenty-three faces. And it wasn't just as easy as going in and changing the face. You had to find somebody who was the right physical height and weight. For example, on the inner sleeve, I think we have Judy Garland dancing with Alan Ladd. Well, originally it was Mickey Rooney. What's her name, Judy Garland, and Mickey Rooney were teenagers together in movies, all the Andy Hardy movies and stuff, and they were sort of a known couple, so it was a no-brainer to have Judy Garland dancing with Mickey Rooney. Well, when they said Mickey Rooney is still alive; you can't have them in there, you have to change it, we had to find somebody who is his same height and weight and physical makeup. So it wasn't just as easy as changing heads. And those two drawings are graphite pencil. So it's not that easy to work with graphite, once you start erasing. So it was a real tedious kind of . . . you can't just go in and take the face out and just redraw it over. You had to lift the graphite that was on the board off, and then redraw on top of it. So it's an interesting cover. It was really neat watching." Of note, a brilliant touch is the firing squad motif around the classic retro lettering of the band name and album title. All told, it's an ambitious and conceptually ripe cover, especially for a hits pack.

HAWKWIND HALL OF THE MOUNTAIN GRILL

UNITED ARTISTS, SEPTEMBER 1974
FRONT COVER: BARNEY BUBBLES
BACK COVER: DAVID HARDY

Despite their hopeless hippie underpinnings, Hawkwind albums were always nudged into the hard rock realm through their quite manly and epic cover art. *Hall of the Mountain Grill* is one of the band's most forceful, featuring dramatic Gothic type set above what looks like a prototype for the *Starship Enterprise* crashed in a marsh. As with many Hawkwind images, this one is also due to the genius of one Barney Bubbles (although the idyllic and disconnecting back cover painting is by David Hardy). Asked to shed some light on Bubbles, Dave Brock explains, "Barney went on to work with Stiff Records, but we knew him, first off, because we lived in the Notting Hill Gate area of London, which was a bit like Haight-Ashbury. It was a cheap area to live. There were always lots of things going on there—arts center, arts labs, interesting places—and Barney lived there as well, and so did [science fiction writer] Mike Moorcock. We all lived in that same area, so we all knew

each other, and we used to go down to the workmen's cafe, which was where *Hall of the Mountain Grill* comes from: the Mountain Grill was a café, believe it or not. And it ended up being a crashed spaceship; that was *Hall of the Mountain Grill*; the Hawkwind spaceship had crashed. And now with the new [2010] album, *Blood of the Earth*, if you look at the album sleeve, we've got the same spaceship now rusting. We've got a wonderful new guy who is quite ingenious with our work—and who is very similar to Barney, actually—does fantastic stuff. Barney was a delicate character, I'd say. He was . . . well, about five foot six, had a beard, used to draw a lot. Used to work for a free magazine called *Friends* in their office doing artwork for them as well. Yeah, but in the end, poor old Barney committed suicide. He was, as I say, one of those delicate characters, and eventually he killed himself."

QUEEN SHEER HEART ATTACK

EMI/ELEKTRA, NOVEMBER 1974
ART DIRECTION AND PHOTOGRAPHY: MICK ROCK
SLEEVE CONCEPT: QUEEN

After two standoffish and aristocratic sleeves, Queen portrays itself as the rock-and-roll machine it is, the guys looking either coked-up or collapsed post-gig, likely having just ripped and roared their way through this album's egregiously heavy "Stone Cold Crazy." The image captures as well the band's frantic stuffing, genius-like, of a bewildering number of ideas into one song, their overactive imaginations manic at the possibilities before them. Recalls photographer Mick Rock: "*Sheer Heart Attack* was the group's idea. The

brief was, 'We want to look wasted and abandoned, like we've just been thrown up on the shore of a desert island.' They also wanted really bold lettering on the front. So they got what they wanted and then some! As Freddie is quoted in our collaboration, *Killer Queen*, 'God, the agony we went through to have the pictures taken, dear. Can you imagine trying to convince others to cover themselves in Vaseline and then have a hose turned on them! We suffered for art that day!'"

VEL-2002

THIN LIZZY NIGHTLIFE

VERTIGO/MERCURY, NOVEMBER 1974
SLEEVE DESIGN FRONT: JIM FITZPATRICK

Fitzpatrick's Roger Dean–esque *Nightlife* illustration marks a dramatic upgrade for Lizzy; Jim depicts a Gotham-like cityscape ripe for the picking by a black panther, yet another in a growing queue of vagabonds and villains that roam the Thin Lizzy storybook. Yet the album's music is not exactly the apt soundtrack to the aggressive scene, its composite effect evoking more of a smooth R&B nightlife, a languid limo cruise quite devoid of dogfights for survival. This has always been the conundrum of the *Nightlife* record: upon each revisit comes a sense of disappointment at the lack of power once past the wrapper. Coupled with that feeling comes the realization that the record before it, *Vagabonds of the Western World*, rocked harder, as did, by a long shot, every album to be cut and beloved afterward. "That's a composite from a number of different photographs," explains Jim, addressing first the skyline of the piece. "I was very influenced by an artist called Jim Steranko, who was a friend of mine at the time, and it's kind of based on one of his images. I was also influenced by Jack Kirby, who did these montages in Marvel Comics, so there's an element of that to it as well. And the black panther . . . I can talk about it now, but I couldn't talk about it then, but I was a great admirer of the Black Panthers. A lot of people will disagree with me on that, but I lived in New Haven and met some of them; I lived outside New Haven in a place called Madison, Connecticut, and these, to me, weren't terrorists; they were people who had a political agenda that I agreed with. So before I ever got near Madison, Connecticut, or New Haven, where their headquarters were, I knew the writings of Huey Newton and Bobby Seale, and I talked to Philip [Lynott] a great deal about them. But we sort of put the panther in without saying it was a Black Panther, or any reference to the movement. So it was kind of political, to be honest. Philip was a very patriotic Irish man. He never saw himself as a black black man. And I suppose I was trying to point him in that direction. But that was a very political album. Martin Luther King, I did work for his widow, actually, and Malcolm X—those were two of my heroes. The whole civil rights movement was forced on America by Kennedy, and I remember reading a story about Jack Kennedy, when he was standing for election; it was a very fine-run thing, and he only won by a hundred thousand votes or something. For a vast country like America, that was very close. When Martin Luther King was arrested by the FBI, before the election, Jack Kennedy picked up the phone, to Coretta King, to say how outraged he was. That could have cost him the election. When Bobby Kennedy marched in the funeral for Martin Luther King, that was a seminal moment. And our civil rights struggle, which actually became a war over here, and in Northern Ireland, was actually based on the black civil rights movement."

MOTT THE HOOPLE LIVE

COLUMBIA, NOVEMBER 1974
DESIGN: ROSLAV SZAYBO
PHOTOGRAPHY: DAGMAR

Half the reason folks tumble Mott into the heavy metal travel trunk derives from the band's visual presentation, most notably the U.S. cover for the *Mott* album and the decadent glam-rockin' sleeve shot out of a cannon for *Live*. And hey, that's how you panned for heavy ore in the old days, by squinting hard and trying to divine through live shots and wardrobe whether a band looked like they were stacking up enough power chords. This image promised that (forgetting the fact that it only somewhat delivered), the guys projecting to a loud place somewhere between Kiss, Alice, Sweet, Be Bop Deluxe, and, with Ronson's crazy getup in particular, the Tubes.

ROBIN TROWER BRIDGE OF SIGHS

CHRYSALIS, 1974
COVER DESIGN: FUNKY PAUL

Add up the golden-period Robin Trower wrappers and you wind up with cogent reinforcement of the hazy, druggy, thick, and hot psychedelic–hard rock gumbo one attributes to the Trower catalog. They all work together and they all emit Zen heat, simplicity in soul-searched motion. *Bridge of Sighs* is no exception; artist Funky Paul explains that he wanted to come up with a three-dimensional representation of a Mobius strip, a mathematical concept describing time and space seeming to fold in on themselves. As he did for the debut album, Paul used oil paints, coming up with a three-foot-square masterpiece, constructed in forty-two hours without sleep—a flagrant defiance of time in itself. He was painting from a clay model he had first worked up, and then from a sketch of his sculpture. The original painting was accidentally turned on its side for the actual album cover shot. The piece is now hanging in the Chrysalis offices, having been bought by Chris Wright, owner of the company.

DEEP PURPLE STORMBRINGER

PURPLE/WARNER BROS., DECEMBER 1974
ART DIRECTION: ED THRASHER
ILLUSTRATION: JOE GARNETT DESIGN, JOHN CABALKA

First off, *Stormbringer* ushers in what would become the closest thing to a Deep Purple logo we'd get to this day, this iconic and dramatic text rendition being periodically used on merch now and forever as long as Purple's freak flag flies. Beyond that, *Stormbringer* offers a gorgeous, motion-filled illustration: a winged horse (prophetically rainbow-charged) riding the hurricane that was Purple at this juncture, a loud and hard funk machine not averse to hard drugs. The painting is based on a 1927 photo, taken by Lucille Handberg, of a hurricane in Jasper, Minnesota. (The shot is also featured on the cover of *Tinderbox* by postpunkers Siouxsie and the Banshees.) "I can definitely remember that Linda Gray from *Dallas*, her husband did the artwork for *Stormbringer*," recalls bassist Glenn Hughes. "I

remember that very well. There was no other alternative art. You may know different, but looking back to 1974, I can't remember if there was. And I don't think anybody had any say in the art. I think it was left to the Warner Bros. art department. If someone came up with something now, I have total control over it, but then someone just came up with an idea, and we liked it—very simple, I thought." Ironically, this arguably quite heavy metal cover art, certainly epic, would enclose the band's lightest record to date, one so rhythm 'n' bluesy that guitarist Ritchie Blackmore would soon uproot himself to try his hand at a heavier, more medieval, and timeless form of metal, a music that Glenn Hughes and David Coverdale found essentially juvenile.

ALICE COOPER WELCOME TO MY NIGHTMARE

ATLANTIC, FEBRUARY 1975
CONCEPT AND DESIGN: PACIFIC EYE & EAR
ILLUSTRATION: DREW STRUZAN
PHOTOGRAPHY: BRET LOPEZ

The striking showbiz images Alice had been building, formerly as a band called Alice Cooper, reach an acme here with Alice presented in top hat and tails. Type reinforces the old-time show-tune tradition of Alice's new presentation (most prevalent musically on the album's swingin' Las Vegas–style title track). The only clue that something might not be right is the presence of all those bugs. Very cool that what we are looking at here is the work of legendary movie poster illustrator Drew Struzan, then a Pacific Eye & Ear guy and later the iconic-image magician for *Star Wars*, *Back to the Future*, and *Indiana Jones*. "Extremely famous cover, but I don't know, I've actually never been asked that question before," muses the now-retired Struzan. "I do remember where the idea came from. We wanted to make something classy, so we put him in a top hat and tuxedo and made it very clean and welcoming— you know, 'Welcome to my nightmare.' I do remember, because Alice was so very kind; he hung around when I penned it, and we got to be pretty good friends, really nice, kind, quiet man. We got along really well, and he would come over and visit, but when we shot the picture of him, we actually went up in the Hollywood Hills, where his house was, and I just brought the camera, and I said, 'Take the pose, so we can get an idea.' We needed a dark background. We weren't prepared much at all, so I said, 'Stand in the closet,' so he stood in the closet, so the background was dark, and I took his picture. And then I just painted it, oils on canvas." Boss of Pacific Eye & Ear, Ernie Cefalu, attests to the modesty in that telling: "We had talked about this nightmare of being like a three-ring circus, Barnum and Bailey and stuff, and that's where I came up with this idea of him being like a ringmaster. And Drew did this beautiful illustration with graphite pencil on canvas. The piece is probably fifteen inches by twenty inches. So yes, Drew always stretched his own canvas, and he did this beautiful drawing of Alice tipping his hat. We'd taken some photography, and he did this tipping his hat, and he did this magnificent drawing. It took him, I don't know, a whole day, so at the end of the day, I remember everyone had left. Because Drew only worked nine to five. He had a family. But he did more work from nine to five than most people did in two days. He was very fast and very confident. And I swear to God, I don't remember him ever making a mistake. You know, I really don't. This drawing of Alice on canvas . . . if it was flesh-colored, you'd think it was real. And I remember being with my partner smoking a doob and looking at it at the end of the day, and thinking, 'Man, they're just going to love this.' We thought he was going to go back on top of that and add a little color. So Drew got in before we did the next day, and by the time I got in, he'd taken a sienna wash and put it over the entire canvas—you could hardly see the drawing underneath. And I was like, 'Drew, what did you do?! What happened? You can't even see it!' And he said, 'Don't worry about it.' And I said, 'You can't see the drawing.' 'Don't worry about it. That's my middle tone. That's my middle tone.' And what he did over the next couple of days is took all the color and used that sienna as a middle tone and worked the dark tones in—it was amazing. When he was finished, well, you see the painting, that's it. And if you look in the textured background, there's an actual pattern of insects and stuff he did as a separate illustration, and we put that photo together mechanically. But the actual painting, if you look at the background, it has that deckled kind of style, that chiseled style, and if you look in the background there are still pieces of sienna floating around."

HUMBLE PIE STREET RATS

A&M, FEBRUARY 1975
ART DIRECTION: FABIO NICOLI
DESIGN: MICHAEL ROSS
PIE PHOTOGRAPHY: ROGER STOWELL

Crap album and not heavy to boot (long story—confiscated tracks, unauthorized by the band, etc.), *Street Rats* nonetheless got many a listen and a good old college try from rockers, 'cause the cover was, well, it's beyond metal into punk—certainly a perfect image for the Stranglers. Flip over to the back and one can't help but think there's a dig in that, an equating of the four broke and indentured Humble bums with the four rodents crowding the grimy street scene on the preferred real estate of the front cover.

BLUE ÖYSTER CULT ON YOUR FEET OR ON YOUR KNEES

COLUMBIA, FEBRUARY 1975
DESIGN: JOHN BERG AND GERARD HUERTA
COVER PHOTO: JOHN BERG
SKY: BELINDA RAIN
BACK COVER PHOTO: DON HUNSTEIN

Much as the *Alive!* cover brought it all home for fellow New York anglers Kiss after three wobbly studio records, Blue Öyster Cult worked the same pattern, coming up with a double-live wallop called (nay, emblazoned) *On Your Feet or on Your Knees.* The record offered the band's first photography and indeed first color after three illustrated black-and-white sleeves. "One of my favorite covers," notes bassist Joe Bouchard. "It certainly has this sort of church-of-the-occult reference to it. I think it's a pretty outrageous-looking cover, to have

our limousine in front of this church. Even the promotion for that album was going to be more radical. There was a very controversial ad with a preacher at a pulpit, in bondage gear—it was pretty radical." Indeed it was, picking up on the imagery of the back cover's Bible full of song titles. But back to the front: here we had BÖC massaging in all one's uneasy queasiness about the stratified conspiracy among us at all levels, with the fascist flag bearers in the rock-and-roll cabal paying a visit to the vicar for God knows what reason.

KISS DRESSED TO KILL

CASABLANCA, MARCH 1975
PHOTO MANIPULATION AND DESIGN: PETER CORRISTON
PHOTOGRAPHY: BOB GRUEN

In contrast to the two solid sleeves preceding it, here Kiss provokes subtly, with the idea that it can infiltrate positions of power by suiting up and mingling among us. Throwing a few dollars at embossing got across the suggestion that Kiss was indeed destined to be a viable business (like Alice Cooper and Aerosmith, both audacious embossers). But so did the combination of humor and understatement, especially after the bacchanal that was the *Hotter Than Hell* cover. "Fire and brimstone, blood and gore, to get out there and get in your face," is the way band photographer Bob Gruen sums up the Kiss philosophy. "I mean, they're superheroes; they look like monsters. I remember doing the photo session where the pictures from *Dressed to Kill* came from. And it starts off with Kiss wearing business suits and going to work in the morning, mild-mannered, secret identity, and then they change into Kiss. They run into a phone booth and they pull off their suits and they emerge as superheroes. When in fact, when we were doing the session, they came back to my house. We went out and they got dressed, put the makeup on, and then they put the suits on. We went out and did the first part of the photo shoot. Then we came back to my house, and I was changing the film and dealing with my cameras, and they were changing their clothes. And at one point I felt this presence behind me, and I turned around, and Gene was a foot taller and he looked like a monster. It really was like superheroes who changed from the secret identity into the superhero monster identity. It was as if they were different people, different beings. They really went through a transformation. I was scared. I felt this presence, and

I turned around and you kind of jump, 'Oh my God, what's that?'" There's more to this shoot than what we see on the *Dressed to Kill* cover. "Oh, that was all used," confirms Gruen. "It was a comic book in *Creem* magazine, a two-page comic book about basically how Kiss is going to work and they read the newspapers and discover how there's going to be a concert by John Cleveland, I think—or John Pittsburgh is how they referred to it, but they were talking about John Denver—and Kiss is horrified that the world is falling into such mediocrity. So they put up posters for a fake John Pittsburgh concert, and when everybody shows up, Kiss comes out on the stage and they save the world with rock and roll. It's a funny little story, and it ran in *Creem*. And actually that's how Kiss saw it. And you know, I didn't pull that picture out. We weren't shooting that picture for an album. They were in the studio recording when the comic book came out, and they saw the picture and they called me up and said, 'Can we use that for an album cover? We want to call our album *Dressed to Kill*. We love the picture.' And then I had to go to the recording studio—the Electric Lady studio—and they put the suits on again, and we did a whole series of pictures of them as if they were recording wearing the suits, to make it look as if that was their normal, everyday clothes. The one in the street's from the original shoot; the one on the cover is the original shoot. There's a couple others—I don't know if they're in the album or not; certainly they were in the publicity kit—that show them in the studio wearing the suits . . . again."

NAZARETH HAIR OF THE DOG

MOONCREST/A&M, APRIL 1975
SLEEVE ILLUSTRATION: DAVE ROE

Man, how many kids with bad hair like me reproduced this cover art on our schoolbooks back in the copacetic mid-'70s? I'd venture to say as many as those who scribbled Eddie and Motörhead skulls a few years hence. In any event, *Hair of the Dog* sports a stunner of a sleeve: quite strange upon close inspection, combining an odd number of dogs, miniature skulls, and a sort of coral formation in which we searched in vain for secret messages. Equally arcane, exotic typeface completes the geometrically pleasing tableau. "*Hair of the Dog* was great," recalls Pete Agnew. "We did the album, and as you know, there's a song on it, and we were going to call the album *Son of a Bitch* because where we come from, *son of a bitch* is not even a saying. That's just a thing John Wayne said in movies. It's not a British thing . . . We took it to A&M in California, and they went, 'Oh, no, you can't call it that.' You've got to remember, this is back in 1975—'Oh, you can't call it that. Sears

won't sell it.' So you can't say that. And everybody in America used to say 'son of a bitch,' so we thought was fair enough. Anyway, we couldn't use it, and so we thought we'd be really smart and we'd call it *Heir of the Dog*—h-e-i-r. And basically the guys said, 'Oh, we're all Scottish; let's call it *Hair of the Dog*.' So once the dog was mentioned, we went to this guy, and we actually never met him. We never did. I mean, we saw the thing, we saw the finished album sleeve and we thought it was . . . well, for the time it was very, very . . . you've got to realize, I'm not really a monster guy. I'm a little more laid-back. They're not my favorite thing. But I was outvoted, and the band loved it. And it is a fantastic painting, I've got to admit. But it came from that. I mean, we never had anything to do . . . we never suggested anything. Management just showed it to us after the guy did it, and the guys thought, 'Yeah, that's punchy,' and that was about it, really."

AEROSMITH TOYS IN THE ATTIC

COLUMBIA, APRIL 1975
DESIGN: PACIFIC EYE & EAR
ILLUSTRATION: INGRID HAENKE

Aerosmith finally gets a classy sleeve in accordance with the quality of hard rock the band was able to muster despite the drugs and infighting (no superlative adjectives need to be added at this early stage). Still, there's a hint of that through the sly turn of the phrase *toys in the attic*. Top illustrator Ingrid Haenke also injects a bit of menace, in that the scene depicts a baby, having absconded with the keys to the attic, being dragged into the surreal scene by animated toys, each and all malicious of gaze. A nutty bit of trivia for you: Ingrid is one of the ladies whom the designers at Pacific Eye & Ear had used as a model for one of the most notorious album covers of all time, *Sabbath Bloody Sabbath* (page 54–55). Explains Ernie Cefalu: "Yes, the girl on the left is Ingrid Haenke, who did the

final art on the *Toys in the Attic* illustration. She was a girl who worked with us; she lived with us because she was a friend, and she worked downstairs. She had her own little business going [on] downstairs in the office because we bought a fourplex, and we had put Pacific Eye & Ear in the bottom unit, and we lived in the top unit, and rented the other ones out. So she sort of moved in with us. She was married one time to a guy named Ed Silvers, who was the president of Warner Bros. Music, so we became really good friends. So when they split up, she came and lived with us for a couple years, and we helped her get going as an illustrator. So she is one of the models that Drew Struzan used, and my wife, Bonnie, is the other one."

ZZ TOP FANDANGO!

LONDON, APRIL 1975
ALBUM DESIGN: BILL NARUM
ALBUM CONCEPT: BILL HAM
COVER PHOTO: JOHN DEKALB

The sense of subversion here is that guys who look like country-and-western snoozers—nudie-suited like BTO, who were Canadians, oddly enough—could rock so hard, especially on this album's studio side, possibly the best half record ZZ Top ever sent upriver. Delving further into the scene, it's a live shot that celebrates the chemistry of the power trio: the telepathy, the interaction, the eye contact, and the subsequent cues. And when has an album title ever splashed such pizzazz?

HAWKWIND WARRIOR ON THE EDGE OF TIME

UNITED ARTISTS, MAY 1975
CONCEPT AND ART DIRECTION: COMTE PIERRE D'AUVERGNE, EDDIE BRASH

Hawkwind's mysterious cover art arguably outstripped the quality of the monochrome noise rock packaged within, but from another angle, the visuals made whatever space warrior was strapped under them 'phones study the sound track more seriously, parsing the lyrics, searching for links with the 'scapes draped on the jacket. The *Warrior on the Edge of Time* sleeve dutifully complies, but with an uncharacteristic washed-out comic-book feel, placing in the mind of the owner the thought that he has stumbled upon an old collectible book of wisdom. Both type choices at the top are congruent with this feeling of discovery, the Gothic band name, rendered in pink with a black outline, adding a jolt at the end of the sensual trip of sight, sound, and imagination.

URIAH HEEP RETURN TO FANTASY

BRONZE/WARNER BROS., MAY 1975
DESIGN: LOGO LTD.
ILLUSTRATION: DAVE FIELD

Even though Heep's music power was on the wane, they propped it up nicely with spiffy cover art. *Return to Fantasy* is filled with motion, firepower, and even a title that promises much. However, there's also a disturbing, druggy quality and even a sort of religious-cult vibe—similar to the effect one gets from various Santana sleeves.

THE TUBES THE TUBES

A&M, JUNE 1975
ART DIRECTION: ROLAND YOUNG
DESIGN: M. COTTEN AND P. PRINCE (AIRAMID DESIGNS)
FRONT COVER AND POSTER PHOTOS: HARRY MITTMAN
HANDS AND BODY: RE STYLES

A delightful and upscale Roxy Music decadence wafts sensuously from this clever sleeve, announcing the lascivious world created by San Francisco's favorite art provocateurs—part pop, part Zappa, part tongue-in-cheek rhinoceros rock. All the elements of the sleeve feel alive, right there, from the bracelets through to the cellophane, the vinyl, those fingernails, and, above all, the yummy (flavored lube?) of the stuff from the tube. "We did them all ourselves," notes Fee Waybill. "Prairie and Mike did the album covers, and the first

album cover was just . . . you know, it was just called *The Tubes*, and they just liked that image [on the back] of the inner tube around the girl—inner tube as a bra around the girl's chest. They loved that image. And that toothpaste is actual toothpaste, that new red toothpaste they had out, which was squirted out and made into that logo, which is called the 'toothpaste logo.' Then we had the fake shrink-wrap over it, to look like it's being ripped open. All of that was Prairie's and Mike's idea: to be arty."

UFO FORCE IT

CHRYSALIS, JULY 1975
COVER DESIGN AND PHOTOS: HIPGNOSIS

Hipgnosis turns in a second strong sleeve for UFO, the heavy rock band most associated with that venerable design house through the golden '70s. The shiny, aseptic, weirdly futuristic bathroom scene is classic Hipgnosis. Wrapped up in that is a certain krautrock vibe, which accentuates the band's Anglo-German merger (UFO consisted of four fast London buddies and Michael Schenker, shy, misunderstood, misunderstanding, and very much German). "I don't know if you've seen the difference in the European and the American cover," notes drummer Andy Parker, concerning the controversy around the naked couple getting it on in the shower. "You know, that's all down to Kmart, that American cover, because Chrysalis came up to us and said, 'Kmart won't stock this album with

that cover on it. If you want to sell them, they need to be . . .' That was before Walmart got huge. So we had to go with a steamed-out, watered-down version in order for Kmart to stock it. It was the right decision because obviously that was about the only place kids could buy records—like Walmart today. Small record shops are gone. But that was just something that Hipgnosis came up with. They were just amazing, those guys, Powell and Storm. They always came up with something spectacular. They just chucked us ideas and you go, 'Yeah, I like it.' I don't remember them giving us an idea that we didn't like, to be honest. They seemed to be in tune with us and the direction we were going; the covers just spoke volumes."

RITCHIE BLACKMORE'S RAINBOW
RITCHIE BLACKMORE'S RAINBOW

OYSTER/POLYDOR, AUGUST 1975
COVER DESIGN: DAVID WILLARDSON AND FIN COSTELLO

You can call Rainbow's *Rising* cover the bold actualization of fantasy-based metal cover art, much the way the music inside improves upon the sea-legs wobble of this, the band's debut. Still, the *Ritchie Blackmore's Rainbow* cover art reinvigorates elements seen shortly before on Deep Purple's *Stormbringer* and then back to the Roger Dean sleeves for Uriah Heep. Notes the bassist for the band, Craig Gruber: "The medieval motif, if you will, it was Deep Purple—castles, that medieval feel—and the rainbow is obviously a reference to Ritchie Blackmore's Rainbow. The colors . . . if you look at the band Deep Purple, that's obviously a kind of a color scheme, and it was a natural transition that felt right. But directly speaking, there was no castle involved. We didn't really have that in our mind, and then we contacted this graphic artist, Dave Willardson, when we were recording the album in West Germany. We were in Munich for about six months, seven months, but he was a graphic artist and photographer, and he got involved with Deep Purple and us there and actually came into Musicland Studios with us and listened to what we were doing. I saw Ritchie and him having a chat at the hotel. I didn't even get to see any of the artwork, but when it came out, it was iconic; that's the word I like to use. It's iconic: something that creates a very powerful image in your mind. In fact, I have a ten-inch tattoo of that on my right shoulder from the top of my shoulder to my elbow. The original's got a Fender Stratocaster coming out of the middle of the castle, as that's what Ritchie played. But I had the guitar taken out of the center of the castle, and I had my bass put in there, to commemorate the multimillion-selling album. That album changed everybody's lives in the band." Of note: Willardson worked for Disney, and the tone and vibe of this illustration is strikingly Disneyesque, back to the early days of television, and decisively non–heavy metal, almost the good witch to *Rising*'s wicked witch.

MONTROSE WARNER BROS. PRESENTS MONTROSE!

WARNER BROS., SEPTEMBER 1975
COVER ILLUSTRATION: HARRY ROSSIT

Two previous wishy-washy covers for Montrose made
it high time for a good one, and *Warner Bros. Presents
Montrose!* delivers, suggesting the band as movie and
movie poster, brightly illustrated and then punched up
by a solid hard rock band logo, rendered in a grada-
tional fiery-red-to-yellow that would look killer on the
side of a tricked-out '70s van.

SCORPIONS IN TRANCE

RCA, SEPTEMBER 1975
COVER DESIGN BY CODESIGN/DIRICHS
COVER PHOTO BY MICHAEL VON GIMBUT

The Scorpions inaugurate a string of arguably sexist sleeves here, but mildly so, pretty much merely presenting a good-looking gal (granted, flashing a bit of breast, even if this was censored in the U.S.) in cool metal pose with a guitar. In fact, the whole thing looks quite hip, like Nico and the Velvet Underground or like a punk cover, the cool factor enforced by the strict black-and-white palette from the photography through to the type.

RUSH CARESS OF STEEL

MERCURY, SEPTEMBER 1975
ART DIRECTION: AGI
GRAPHICS: HUGH SYME

After a pair of fey wrappers, Rush proves its mettle:
Caress of Steel suggests hot days in the forge of heavy
metal, like a cross between Purple's *Machine Head* and
the first three covers from BTO. As well, there's a near-
oppressive sense of both the mystical and the medieval, to match the album's similar sense of history, both
real and imagined.

KISS ALIVE!

CASABLANCA, SEPTEMBER 1975
DESIGN: DENNIS WOLOCH
CONCEPT AND PHOTOS: FIN COSTELLO

The beauty of the *Alive!* cover was that the band was finally presented neck-deep, practicing their profession—smoke, lights, and leather aiding and abetting the massive sound that guys who look like that would produce. Tantalizingly, the iconic Fin Costello shot looked live but weirdly composed at the same time; those stances and that configuration of the guys come off as poetic and loud and rock-and-rollish beyond a young teen male's wildest protometal fantasies. And if occasionally the guys could be captured looking a little goofy or fey or tired, this was emphatically not the case here—oddly, Peter manages to look more evil than Gene, Paul exudes the good looks that guys and gals alike could admit were there, and Ace looks like he's about to whip up a space spitball and stun-guitar the crowd.

BUDGIE BANDOLIER

MCA/A&M, SEPTEMBER 1975
ART DIRECTION: JOHN PASCHE
COVER ILLUSTRATION: PATRICK WOODROFFE

This was the first Budgie album for me, at all of twelve years old, and like any metal miner, I couldn't help but be shocked by this surreal image, at least to the point of picking it up and scrutinizing the back—which means it did its job. I recall that I still felt doubtful that the music itself would rock, but I took the risk anyway, the scales of my judgment shifting ever so slightly due to the riveted metal heft of the band name and title treatment. In any event, it all turned out well, and Budgie had a new fan for life. Explains Burke Shelley about this silly yet striking sleeve: "*Planet of the Apes* was on at the time, and we just said to the artist, 'What we want is *Planet of the Apes*, but could you make it *Planet of the Budgies*?' So essentially, if you look at the beginning of *Planet of the Apes*, there they are, riding up on their horses. They are apes, and they've got their guns, and they've got their bandoliers about them, so we said we want something like that, but we want budgie men. But he put some beaks on there, didn't he? Which I can do without. And they had bandoliers on. But it's

a pointless bloody name, if you want my opinion. But there you go; that was my choice. I get a bit cheesed off of people who just dream up words for no reason, just for the word. I tend to want to know why they want that word. And it's a play on the word *band*, isn't it? That's all. I have something against people trying to change Budgie into hawks. Budgie is, you know, it's ironic; it wasn't meant to be sort of like tough. Everybody was using occult names like Black Sabbath or Led Zeppelin, which had connotations of heaviness; people went for those sorts of titles. We were originally called Six Ton Budgie, which you could say had that sort of inflection, but by the time we became Budgie, we lost that weight, and we were just called Budgie, which appealed to me much more. And so, like I said, every time somebody would do a design for us, whether it was a T-shirt or a cover or a poster, it would inevitably have some bird with a huge beak, as if they screwed on an eagle's head. It was just huge and nasty, so there's no irony in it, and it looks a bit stupid in the end."

ANGEL ANGEL

CASABLANCA, OCTOBER 1975
LOGO DESIGN AND ART DIRECTION: JEREMY RAILTON

Here's a hard rock band lacking at this point a logo, but
wielding a sort of icon or talisman—the next best thing.
And it's quite the piece of jewelry: all gold and blue, a
mystical metal woman protecting the realm, her winged
shape suggestive of Aerosmith's graphic identifier. As a
cover, it's a simple one, but imagine the stoner at your
local record emporium and head shop circa '75 building
a window display of these shaped like an *A*. Yeah, now
you're on board, aren't you?

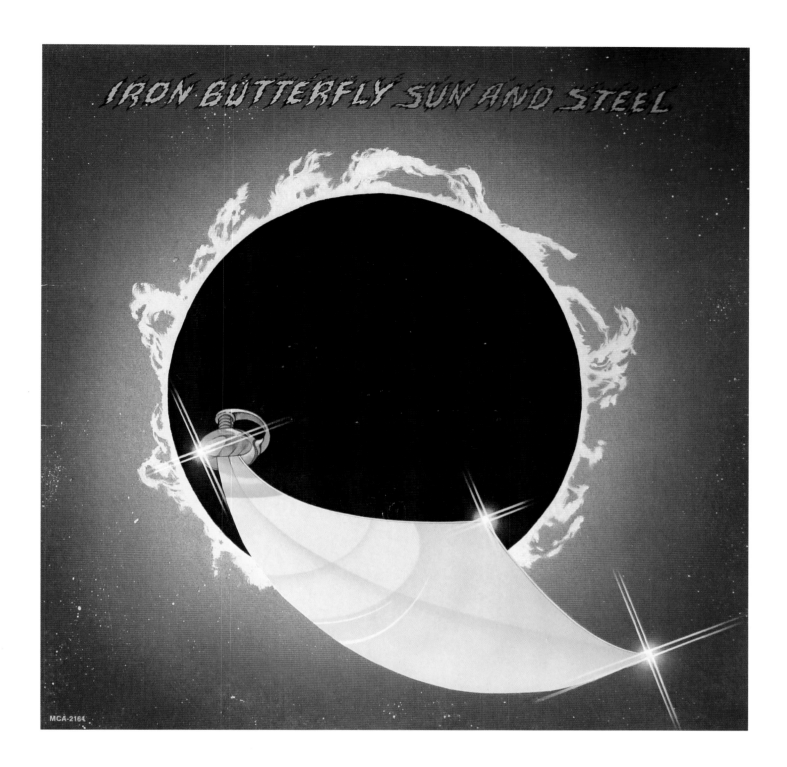

IRON BUTTERFLY SUN AND STEEL

MCA, OCTOBER 1975
ILLUSTRATIONS: CRAIG NELSON

No one was paying much attention to Iron Butterfly up around this sixth and last for the band, but the final two records were weirdly heavy and interesting, and both had intense and psychedelic sleeves, wrappers that tilted the band Hawkwind-ward, much like the loopy music inside. *Scorching Beauty* displayed exactly that, and *Sun and Steel* was as self-evident, combining a black sun and scimitar, an image druggy, like Morocco, an effect heightened by the text ablaze.

1980

GOLDEN EARRING TO THE HILT

POLYDOR, JANUARY 1976
COVER: HIPGNOSIS
CONCEPT: GEORGE HARDIE
PHOTOGRAPHIC RETOUCHING: RICHARD MANNING

Golden Earring is a Dutch hard rock outfit best known for the 1982 hit "Twilight Zone." But the band's morbid and quietly poetic lyrical canon through a previous handful of major-label U.S.-issued releases constitutes the band's major rise to distinction, and this life philosophy was crystallized on the cover of this archetypal Golden Earring slog through the human psyche. For *To the Hilt*, Hipgnosis executes an idea put forth by the band's guitarist, George Kooymans, concerning a somewhat hapless detective who lurches from crisis

to crisis, always "to the hilt" but squirming out of it somehow. The theme of impending execution is carried throughout the cover art, which puts forth a number of scenarios (death by train on the front, shark attack on the back, circular saw on the inside). One possible ancillary message is that a harsh world will figure out new and inventive ways to punish you, when all you had been looking for was a patch of human connection—a likely unintended reading, to be sure, but nonetheless a recurring theme through the band's thorny lyrics.

LED ZEPPELIN PRESENCE

SWAN SONG, MARCH 1976
SLEEVE: HIPGNOSIS AND HARDIE

Given the bad vibes kicking around Zeppelin as it became a life force all its own, and given the bad vibes concerning the quality of what is on *Presence* (and the unfortunate personal circumstances of its making), it is fitting that a mystical, creepy sleeve would be conjured. But Hipgnosis pulls it off with its usual sense of mischievous humor, for "The Object" is no object at all, but a hole, a lack of presence; thus the album's called *Presence*. But then the prism's light shifts again, for despite its lack of corporal presence, this hole provides a life force—or does it drain? Clearly, the people

in these pictures (an exhaustive search of magazines from decades back resulted in very few who could sustain the idea of intense focus on this void) can't live without the talismanic benefits of this clip in the time-space continuum. Alas, once inside the album, we find that there might be an object after all, or, more likely, given the love for the puncture, what we have here is a crude souvenir of this thing, an actual talisman, that is much less effective than the intrusive force that reigns over all lives—including, presumably, Led Zeppelin's.

SWEET "GIVE US A WINK!"

RCA/CAPITOL, MARCH 1976
ART DIRECTION: PAT DOYLE
SLEEVE DESIGN AND ILLUSTRATION: PETAGNO

By the time of the masterful *"Give Us a Wink!"* Sweet had found itself clear to issue a proper album worldwide rather than cobbled-together compilations. *Desolation Boulevard*'s "Fox on the Run" and "Ballroom Blitz" had been roller-rink hits from the previous year, and the Sweet members were minor teen-dream stars across North America. Ergo, it was fitting that the follow-up was in possession of a mischievous schoolyard vibe somewhere between Alice Cooper's *School's Out* and the Bay City Rollers. A fancy bit of die-cutting allowed the moptop metalhead to play with his new allowance purchase as he spun such raging rockers as "Action," "Cockroach," and "Yesterday's Rain." Recalls guitarist Andy Scott: "The *'Give Us a Wink!'* album cover came out of a meeting with . . . I think by that time we were using a guy called Joe Petagno, who came up with this idea. There were two or three sleeves, I believe; the one that everybody seems to have is the one where you

pull the eye through the slot and it closes and winks at you. But the other one was . . . you know, the early days when you had those glasses where you nodded your head up and down and they would change? They look like your eyes were open and then closed. They had stuck one of those across the eye in some territories, but it was never that successful. We all said, look, it may be a bit more complex, but as you pull this lever, the eye closing or opening is a much more credible laughable idea." And what of that strange title? "The truth is, in Europe, Mick Tucker was forever asking girls, you know, if you want to come back to the room and everything. And when he used to get knocked back once in a while, which wasn't very often, his next play was, 'Well maybe you could see your way clear to giving me a wank, then?' And they could never say the word *wank*. They always used to say, 'Vat iz diz vink?' So after that, he used to say, 'Go on, give us a wink.'"

KISS DESTROYER

CASABLANCA, MARCH 1976
DESIGN: DENNIS WOLOCH
COVER PAINTING: KEN KELLY

Come the *Destroyer* sleeve, the messaging additional to the visual story of Kiss thus far is this long-desired idea to move Kiss beyond the mortal into the mythical—or, perhaps more modestly speaking, at least into the realm of comic-book heroics. Added to this is something more subliminal: the idea that the guys in Kiss were of stature enough now to be meticulously illustrated rather than merely shot photographically, like any other schlubs. Ken Kelly, illustrator of *Love Gun* and Rainbow's *Rising*, delivers splendidly, portraying each of the band members in some of their very coolest likenesses so far (save for Ace, who's a bit

effeminate!), dancing upon, or more like floating above, an apocalyptic ruin. Additionally, the band's dependable branding logo, presented in fiery red, is framed by Paul's glam right hand and Gene's heavy-metal fist—an apt anchoring and bookending metaphor for the dichotomy we experience in three-quarters of the band's music. Trivia note: Ken had to paint this thing twice, given that the first time around, the label thought the image was too violent, although the main problem was that the band members had recently gotten new costumes; Ken's first cover, known as the "brown" one, depicted the band in its more rudimentary *Alive!* garb.

JUDAS PRIEST SAD WINGS OF DESTINY

GULL/JANUS, MARCH 1976
ART DIRECTOR: JOHN PASCHE—GULL GRAPHICS
SLEEVE PAINTING: PATRICK WOODROFFE

Grand, imposing religiosity might seem audacious for a heavy metal album in 1976, but when the music is this serious, pioneering, and timeless (plus—gotta love it—print ads were touting Priest as "one of the heaviest bands around"), the sound and image work resolutely together, each upholding its end of the regal bargain. Browns, oranges, and purples, skillfully muted, work in concert with the name of the band and the Gothic font in which it's rendered, not to mention the pageantry of the album title. The impression that is created is one of medieval majesty, the theme reinforced on the back cover, where one solemnly experiences song titles like "Tyrant," "Genocide," "Epitaph," and "Island of Domination," which together, in fact, comprise this hugely important metal album's alchemical second side.

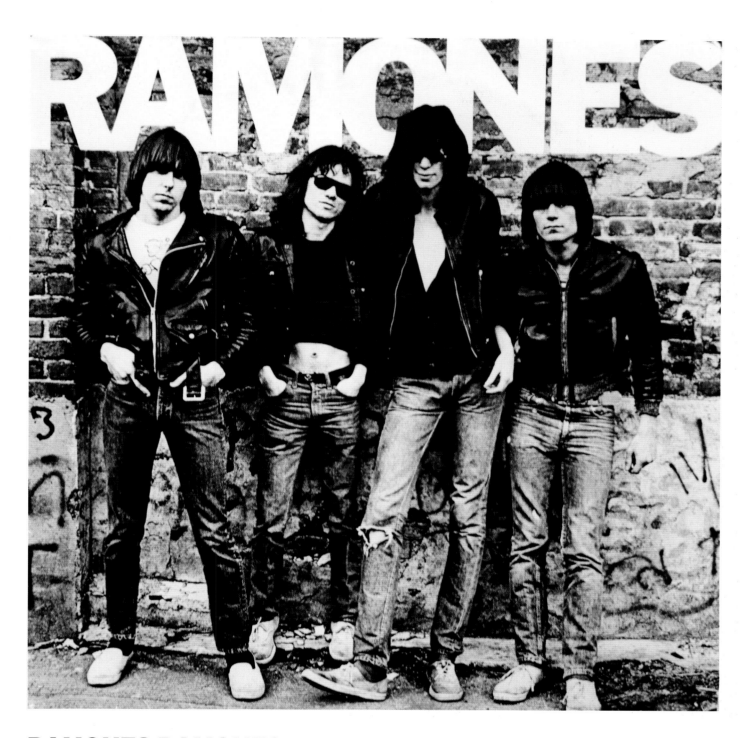

RAMONES RAMONES

SIRE, APRIL 1976
FRONT COVER PHOTOGRAPHY: ROBERTA BAYLEY

Sure, we've got punks in this book, but man, for so many reasons, one might consider the Ramones less as punkers and more as hard rockers, anyhow. But that would be missing the point, which this album cover unassumingly (without care, without emotion) makes, namely, the idea that the Ramones are ill-fitted for any day job or Day-Glo dog tag. Their name is out of the '60s, as is their haphazard arrival at a band uniform. Their hair is neither long nor short; two of them look like '60s rejects from underneath some garage band. And then what of that uniform? Of course it's the antiuniform: merely clothes draped on hoodlums to make it from A to B across the streets of New York (at its worst rotten-Apple time in history)—not punk, not hard rock, maybe even indicative of a time well before both, circa the original postwar motorcycle clubs. Again, whatever fuzzy logic the viewer and listener has worked out for himself upon looking and listening, one constant conclusion, established right here, starkly and without much trying, would have to be that the Ramones confounded categorization.

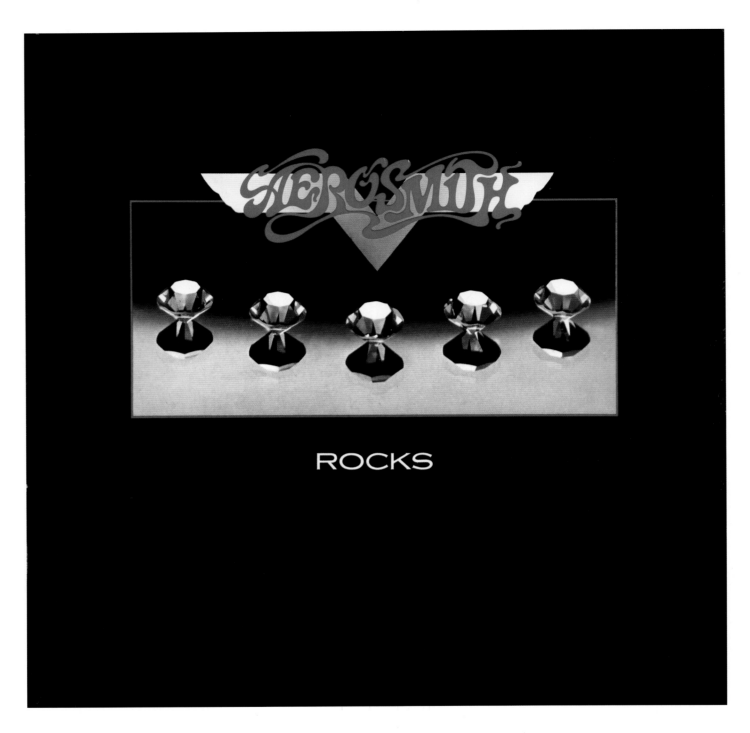

AEROSMITH ROCKS

COLUMBIA, MAY 1976
ALBUM COVER DESIGN: PACIFIC EYE & EAR

Dripping with ostentatious class, the *Rocks* cover (textured, no less) helped catapult Aerosmith into becoming "America's greatest rock and roll band," a label thrown around during the band's golden heyday. This meteoric rise occurred despite a ragamuffin look and occasional shoddy gigs to match. The grime and crime of the actual Aerosmith were tacitly and/or sub-consciously obscured on the album cover by the hard and exacting opulence of what is essentially a jewelry display case stamped with a triumphant logo that any huge corporation would kill for (and probably has). We

see five rocks, one for each member of the band, like a Super Bowl ring (insert snickers here, for they are both stones and ice). But the main joke is the obvious pun that Foghat executed with less of an upper-class ring on its *Rock and Roll* album (technically self-titled) three years previous. An interesting trivia note: print ads for the *Rocks* album featured a gorgeous high-society gal holding the cover, but alas, the background color was white, not black, putting a whole different, almost *A Night at the Opera*–like spin on a young and angry met-alhead's tweaked, upwardly spiraling emotions.

RAINBOW RISING

OYSTER/POLYDOR, MAY 1976
ART DIRECTION AND PHOTOGRAPHY: FIN COSTELLO
PAINTING: KEN KELLY

The award for the most epic use of a rainbow goes to this mighty post-Purple album cover, a strident illustration by one Ken Kelly, man-legend behind Kiss's *Destroyer* and *Love Gun*. A sense of energy and impossible muscle is conveyed by the rising fist, the roiling waves, and the mountain peaks blended into castle turrets. All told, the class of the totality perfectly conveys the medieval, mysterious vibe sought by Ritchie Blackmore and his spellbinding wordsmith, Ronnie James Dio. Notes keyboard wizard Tony Carey, also a medieval enthusiast: "We didn't have an album title. It didn't start off, 'We're going to do an album called *Rising*.'

And then Ronnie sings, 'I see a rainbow rising' in 'Stargazer.' One thing leads to another and another, and we got the cover of this fist coming out of the ocean grabbing the rainbow, which I thought was great graphics. And then inside, a full-page spread of the band, just a black-and-white picture, taken by Fin Costello, if I'm not mistaken. I don't even think there was a Plan B. I never saw any alternatives to it. It's the only cover I ever saw." *Rising*'s sleeve is further enhanced in importance by the album's status as an early prototype of traditional, classical-based heavy metal, a subgenre also known as power metal.

BOSTON BOSTON

EPIC, JULY 1976
DESIGN: PAULA SCHER
COVER ILLUSTRATION: ROGER HUYSSEN

It's hard to look at this cover objectively, given that if you grew up in the '70s, it's an image imprinted on your frontal lobe, pinball-machine color scheme included. But it's kinda cool how there's a bit of a story coupled with the second album, *Don't Look Back*. On that cover, the good people of the guitar spaceship are delicately touching down on a new Eden (where, presumably, they can obsessively construct and deconstruct

recording gear for years on end, unhindered by reality, maybe making another record with the resulting inventions, maybe not). In any event, back on the debut cover, we see that these tech-heads had to escape, en masse, as a guitar army from an exploding planet—a narrative that fits what we know about Boston founder Tom Scholz and his worthy environmental worry (when he's not wielding a soldering iron).

BLACK SABBATH

TECHNICAL ECSTASY

BLACK SABBATH TECHNICAL ECSTASY

VERTIGO/WARNER BROS., SEPTEMBER 1976
SLEEVE DESIGN: HIPGNOSIS
ROBOTS DESIGNED BY GEORGE HARDIE AND ILLUSTRATED BY RICHARD MANNING

The clinical, austere, upper-crust, uncommunicative vibe of the great Hipgnosis cabal turns in a signature piece devoid of human interaction—or, rather, one with quite a touching touch of interaction, but between robots. The title says it all; the scene depicts two robots, strange machines in the night, passing each other on some corporate escalator next to walls of marble. Instead of glances, these two (a round and a square) exchange a love squirt for a laser ray. What's intense is the whole abstract interaction between this scene in muted colors and the music of Black Sabbath at that time, as the band indeed had started to lose their minds, become robots, had somewhat fallen out of favor with their fans as well as their label, and had essentially been in a state of white-knuckle siege. Even the mere idea of using Hipgnosis seems strange for this band, and yet here they are on the receiving end of a starchy, high-art concept as the guys are running out of gas but fast. Mixed feelings, but to be sure, it's impossible to separate this artwork from the band's calcified state of mind in 1976.

TED NUGENT FREE-FOR-ALL

EPIC, OCTOBER 1976
ALBUM DESIGN: PAULA SCHER
ALBUM PHOTOGRAPHY: JIM HOUGHTON

Okay, hands down, this has always been my favorite look on the Whackmaster, namely, slacks, suspenders, a bit of good-guy white, and that '70s 'stache, also worn by my fave hockey dudes, including Derek Sanderson, René Robert, and Rick MacLeish, not to mention, back in the guitar hero world, Frank Marino and Les Dudek. And there he is, so cool you had to show him twice, affirming the life force of rock and roll in a sequence of action shots that gets even better on the back and in the gatefold. "We were recording *Free-for-All* while the retrorockets were still screaming fire on the *Ted Nugent* album," recalls the Tedinator. "Obviously, the whole attraction to my music is the live performance of it. And everybody at Epic Records was so tuned in to that that they wanted that imagery on the cover, me doing the things that I do live, representing that outrage. So we did those photos, and I remember that they weren't

prepared for the numbers that were selling, either, so there were two or three printings, and they had some different fonts." (This last comment refers to the curious variations in the type styles used in different printings and different territories). The one I have, the original, featured thin multicolored lines weirdly incongruent with Ted's coursing life rhythm (but evocative of Aerosmith's *Draw the Line* vibe the following year); the man is much better off with his iconic "autograph" logo splashed on the records before, after, and beyond. Adds Earl Steinbicker, partner of photographer Jim Houghton: "Those would have been studio shots. We also did *Cat Scratch Fever* and the famous shot of Ted bound and gagged in a straitjacket, which I think were just used for promo. *Free-for-All* would have been done in the studio, as we absolutely refused to do live work."

Featuring: Richie Blackmore David Coverdale Glenn Hughes Jon Lord Ian Paice

DEEP PURPLE MADE IN EUROPE

PURPLE/WARNER BROS., OCTOBER 1976
COVER DESIGN: PHIL DUFFY/CREAM
ALL PHOTOGRAPHS: FIN COSTELLO

Mk III–era Deep Purple holds a near monopoly on striking Purple cover art, with this composition smartly working to remind one of the glory of the similarly appointed *Made in Japan* album, but also improving on that record's classy enough but stilted sleeve. In addition, wrapping its arms around Mk III, the graphics incorporate the gorgeous purples of *Burn* as well as the decadent yet elegant new band logo crafted for *Stormbringer*. Finally, the live shot by the celebrated Fin Costello captures the druggy and demonic heat of the band as they white-knuckled it toward an implosion that had already occurred by the time *Made in Europe* was released.

KANSAS LEFTOVERTURE

KIRSHNER, OCTOBER 1976
ART DIRECTION: TOM DRENNON
ILLUSTRATION: DAVE MCMACKEN

Kansas always offered covers of gravitas, although whether the band is hard rock enough to be in this book is up for debate. The debate's over, as we celebrate a sleeve so hopelessly wise and progressive-rocking—the band's aged thinker writing the greatest musical work ever, deep and tormented in thought, that work none other than the *Leftoverture*. And ain't the band's logo one of the yummiest ever, lofted there and elusive between cut glass, copper, and silver, its modernity contrasting the lasting Renaissance feel of

the rest of it? One could imagine this sleeve used for any number of Rush or Genesis (or Saga or Klaatu!) albums—it's that smart and haughty and gracefully blanched. But it's ended up here, reinforced as an illustration of the "part and parchment" Kansas universe by a similar sleeve for a second (and last) hit album for the band, namely *Point of Know Return*—again, delicate, fantasy-flown art applied to the origami rock of America's only progressive band.

THIN LIZZY JOHNNY THE FOX

VERTIGO/MERCURY, OCTOBER 1976
ARTWORK: JIM FITZPATRICK
ARTWORK COORDINATION: JACK WOOD AND SUE DUBOIS
PHOTOS: JOHN PAUL

I'm not sure why the guys keep apologizing for *Johnny the Fox*, citing its rushed creation after the mild-hit status of *Jailbreak*, for the album is a warm and washed humdinger of Springsteen-inspirational Irish hard rock. And it could have no other sleeve; the album's loose conceptual status is reinforced by the slinking, probably winking fox (suggesting the lone wolf, the seducer, the Phil Lynott figure). The cover's rich brown and oranges were matched to John Alcock's plush production, the elaborate (and Doodle Art–ish!) Celtic knotwork echoing the record's timeless epic-saga quality. On the cover's flip side, the band and song titles are soundly, geometrically incorporated into the motif; both front and back add greatly to the mind's coloring of this charming Lizzy spread. "I'd actually done a huge amount of cover roughs," recalls Fitzpatrick. "That one, there was a warrior in the center of it. It had a border, and Philip loved the border, and he said, 'I want that; we'll use that.' And that became the border for *Johnny*

the Fox. But he didn't have a title for *Johnny the Fox*, but we had the border, with the circle blank, literally until twenty-four hours before it was due to go to press, to be printed, and Philip said, 'We've got a title for you: *Johnny the Fox*.' And I thought, 'There's no "Johnny the Fox" in the track list. There's "Johnny the Fox Meets Jimmy the Weed,"' and he said, 'Oh, just give us *Johnny the Fox*; nobody will notice.' So I put [it] in the center, the fox over the city, kind of echoing *Nightlife*. So it was a rush job. I would have much preferred something more elaborate for the center section." And the evil character in the circles around the side? "That was just an idea that came into my head that Philip liked. It's not a personification of anyone in particular. We just wanted something sinister-looking. Celtic borders are inevitably very humorous. It's all intertwined animals, interlinking and getting up to anything you want. But I wanted something a little more sinister and metalish."

KISS ROCK AND ROLL OVER

CASABLANCA, NOVEMBER 1976
COVER AND INNER SLEEVE DESIGN AND ILLUSTRATION: MICHAEL DORET

Designer Michael Doret's done sports logos, food stuff, covers for *Time*, all sorts of things, but the idea for *Rock and Roll Over* came from a combination of his Coney Island youth, a Japanese magazine cover he had recently done, and cheap, stamped-tin toys. Ergo we have a Kiss cover that looks like a Japanese shooting gallery with a tin Kiss top for a prize, one that no doubt shoots sparks. Doret also endeavored to use pure Pantone colors rather than the four-color process. He remarked that the circular nature of it—with no top, bottom, left, or right—simply comes from the title,

Rock and Roll Over. This one is vividly T-shirt–ready, although I must confess that as a kid, I found the crude cartooniness of it when compared with the manly *Destroyer* sleeve helped shape and fuel my denigration of the music within as also more childish. I mean, maybe me and my buds were starting to outgrow Kiss, but the general consensus was that *Rock and Roll Over* comprised a poppier, less ambitious, happier set of songs than did *Destroyer*, and the cover art indeed feels like a provocation, a reminder, a graphic dumbing down—even if it's arguably the more stylish sleeve.

ZZ TOP TEJAS

LONDON, NOVEMBER 1976
ALBUM DESIGN: BILL NARUM
ALBUM CONCEPT: BILL HAM

This is the coolest ZZ Top logo the band ever came up with (a carryover from *Fandango!*), and I've always loved this cover, given its Tex-Mex vibe, the swoopy script for the album title, and those hot, hazy, atmosphere-bending blues. It matches perfectly the laid-back, bugs-a-buzzin' vibe of the album's music, *Tejas* being the band's least electric, most intimate album and a cover prime for pastels if there ever was one. And though not exactly a cover art issue per se, *Tejas* is the first of two covers for the guys that gave you more, this one having a triple gatefold with a thick, card-stock lyric sheet inside.

PAICE ASHTON LORD MALICE IN WONDERLAND

OYSTER/WARNER BROS., MARCH 1977
ALBUM AND LOGO DESIGN: PHIL DUFFY AND JANE LEWINGTON AT CREAM
FRONT COVER: OIL PAINTING BY GRAHAM OVENDEN FROM THE "ALICE IN WONDERLAND" SERIES

This doomed Deep Purple offshoot band beats Nazareth to the punch with the catchy *Malice in Wonderland* title, but hey, both of them cooked up nice sleeves to go with the catchphrase. In any event, I gotta say that it was almost necessary that Ian, Jon, and Tony offer something sharp, given their accounting-firm band name and the general lack of excitement that greeted

their jazz-fusion-confusion hard rock sound. Helping the cause are the arch-funky '70s fonts for both the band name and album name, plus an intriguing color scheme of muted blues, pinks, and purples, punched in the middle by the black-and-white energy of that wordy band name.

JUDAS PRIEST SIN AFTER SIN

CBS/COLUMBIA, APRIL 1977
ART DIRECTION: ROSLAV SZAYBO (CBS RECORDS)
DESIGN AND PHOTOGRAPHY: BOB CARLOS CLARKE

Issued in '77, *Sin after Sin* came at the time of the shift toward metal as a proud, self-aware entity. Signifying that shift, most of this somber, powerful cover could hold any sort of music, but then there's a skull with glowing eyes, and the angry young pup metal listener perks up and takes notice. Like its predecessor, *Sad Wings of Destiny*, most of the image is graceful and magical, its most metal square inch being a skull.

Still, the *Sin after Sin* sleeve may exude even greater rich reserve than that of the previous sleeve, given its muted silvery grays that split the difference between the white for the record title and the concrete gray of the band name, a nice sense of branding happening with the use of the Gothic font featured the last time (although a modern upgrade would be just around the corner).

SWEET OFF THE RECORD

RCA/CAPITOL, APRIL 1977
SLEEVE CONCEPT AND DESIGN: NORMAN GOODMAN
SLEEVE ARTWORK: TERRY PASTOR

Off the Record features a geometric, expertly composed illustration of the drama that was, for so many of us growing up, a needle hitting the groove on a piece of vinyl. We are reminded that deep within that flat-black world live tiny mountain ranges, and that within the valleys, music is made by a passing chunk of diamond scraping the walls of the mountains. Unfortunately, the album stiffed, as did its similarly themed follow-up, *Level Headed*. The U.S. cover of that record featured a squinty-close look at a cassette deck, and I can't help but feel that the cold, lonely, austere, mechanistic vibe

of these two gatefold sleeves (the cover art extended to the back) contributed to this uneasy feeling of an impenetrable wall between band and fan. And the artist responsible for the sleeve? "Norman Goodman," says bassist Steve Priest. "He did the *Level Headed* one, too. It's really pop art—I like it. He was the engineer at the studio where we were recording it, so he just brought his ideas in, and that one looked good to me. I don't believe the painting was any bigger than the album cover. In fact, it was the same size; I used to have a poster of it."

TED NUGENT CAT SCRATCH FEVER

EPIC, MAY 1977
DESIGN: JOHN BERG
COVER PHOTOGRAPH: JIM HOUGHTON
LETTERING: GERARD HUERTA

The yuk-up, of course, is that the priceless look on Ted's face is due to the chest mauling he's getting at the hands of some adoring beauty as she gives him cat scratch fever. But even without the vertical wrap-around back cover, those bulging green eyes say it all: Ted is a wildcat who cannot be tranquilized. Good to see that the autograph-style logo from his solo debut is back, and equally cool seeing it applied to the album title. I also love the coloring: Ted and his frazzled mane backed with a pale blue sky, a color expertly separated and difference-split into the white and darker blue of the cover's text elements. As for the photographer,

says his design firm partner, Earl Steinbicker: "Jim has completely vanished from the face of the earth over twenty-five years ago—even his family can't find him," adding that with respect to his studio's methodology, "We did a lot of work with John Berg and [graphic designer] Paula Scher. They always had a clear idea of what they wanted. You don't bring a bunch of famous people into the studio with no clue as to what you're going to shoot. For the Ted Nugent cover, those red marks were, of course, makeup. Not sure who that was, probably a model, but if I were to hazard a guess, it might have been Jim's girlfriend."

UFO **LIGHTS OUT**

CHRYSALIS, MAY 1977
COVER DESIGN AND PHOTOGRAPHS: HIPGNOSIS

Hawkwind and Pink Floyd each got one, but UFO's got two; namely, these Battersea Power Station sleeves— *Lights Out* followed by *Obsession* themed the band frigid blue, which kinda bled into the live album and *No Place to Run* as well. Anyway, *Lights Out* is typical, classic Hipgnosis, from the extra elbow grease thrown at the type to the no-face photography to the dials, nuts, bolts, and belching steam of all these Battersea doodads. What any of this has to do with the title *Lights Out* is anybody's guess.

THE TUBES NOW

A&M, MAY 1977
ART DIRECTION: ROLAND YOUNG
DESIGN: MICHAEL COTTEN, PRAIRIE PRINCE, AND CHUCK BEESON

Bravely eschewing a now-established vibrant and sensuous logo, the Tubes reinvent themselves graphically, making use of an illustration by the drummer for the band, Prairie Prince, who was inspired by a similar drawing of the Ramones from *Time* magazine. Entitled *Tubes Descending a Staircase* (a play on Marcel Duchamp's *Nude Descending a Staircase*), the shot features the populated band jagged and chaotic, much like the confused signals sent off by their package: crazy visuals, surreal humor, and meticulous instrumental prowess.

HAWKWIND QUARK STRANGENESS AND CHARM

CHARISMA/SIRE, JUNE 1977
DESIGN AND PHOTOGRAPHY: HIPGNOSIS
GRAPHICS: GEOFF HALPIN

Hawkwind has always had its strangely raw and noisy space rock nudged toward classy through its mysterious cover art. *Quark* is their cleanest and classiest yet, offering a classic, characteristic, typical Hipgnosis sleeve of the day, the science fiction and technology theme lining up with *Lights Out* and *Obsession* from UFO as well as Pink Floyd's iconic *Animals* sleeve. "That was photographed at Battersea Power Station," explains Hawkwind flight commander Dave Brock,

"and that's actually Bob Calvert on the back cover in the white coat, sitting there on a chair with a book over his head. That was all taken inside the power station, with all the knobs and dials and stuff. I mean, it looked kind of retro-fifties sci-fi, didn't it? And of course you know what quark strangeness and charm is—molecules that zoom through earth, and through our bodies, no doubt."

RUSH A FAREWELL TO KINGS

MERCURY, SEPTEMBER 1977
ART DIRECTION AND GRAPHICS: HUGH SYME
COVER PHOTOGRAPHY: YOSH INOUYE
DESIGN ASSISTANCE: BOB KING

Shot not in wistfully failing England but actually in equally crumbling Buffalo, the sleeve for Rush's austere '77 classic, *A Farewell to Kings,* makes sense for both places and in the context of the lyric it supports. Rush drummer-lyricist Neil Peart draws unflattering parallels between those in power in kingly times and those in power today. Why a band of reasoning atheists like Rush have got creepy glam puppet man hooked to strings descending from the sky is another matter altogether. Although, when one flips the cover over, lo and behold, there is no puppet master. Well played, Mr. Peart, well played indeed.

BLUE ÖYSTER CULT SPECTRES

COLUMBIA, OCTOBER 1977
DESIGN: RONI HOFFMAN
PHOTOS: ERIC MEOLA
LASER EFFECTS AND PHOTO ASSISTANCE: DAVID INFANTE OF LASER PHYSICS INC.

Hot damn! According to my Top 100 in the back, this is your goodly author's second-favorite (hard rock) album cover of all time and space. Sure, I'll bite, 'cause *Spectres* is a beauty—all glowering yellows and reds, yet old-timey, back to the band's roots in H. P. Lovecraft, the guys looking like detectives or at least book collectors, with Eric particularly inscrutable. The lasers shooting all over the place (acquired at great cost for the live show) add to the otherworldliness of the scene, as does the rearing cat, the hand from nowhere, and the noose under the table. My favorite element, however, is the manner in which the band upholds the tradition of featuring its cross-of-question logo (I just made that up) somewhere on the front of every cover—here tucking it into the lower left within a misty crystal ball oddly placed on the floor next to bowler-hatted Allen.

QUEEN NEWS OF THE WORLD

EMI/ELEKTRA, OCTOBER 1977
LAYOUT AND SLEEVE COORDINATION: CREAM
ORIGINAL ARTWORK: FRANK KELLY FREAS

The jarringly uncharacteristic *News of the World* sleeve has its roots in a sci-fi illustration called *The Gulf Within*, used for a tale of the same name in *Astounding Science Fiction* back in 1953. A robot holding a dead human is pained at having caused such damage with his blunt touch. The band, always in for dramatics, summarily summoned artist Frank Kelly Freas to redo the piece, showing all four Queen members in place of the one dead guy. The result is a vibrant and at the same time retro wraparound image (and attendant inner gatefold) that cleansed the palate and snapped

Queen back to center stage after two sleeves that were stuffy and related to each other, namely, *A Night at the Opera* and *A Day at the Races*. Indeed, there was a tacit refreshing of the band in an era dominated by punk (and punk's attacks on Queen Elizabeth II and the likes of the unapproachable rock band Queen). This change is represented on the cover by a tossing aside of the celebrated Queen logo and the inclusion on the record (like a cyst) of a frenzied, manic punk metal track called "Sheer Heart Attack."

THE DAMNED MUSIC FOR PLEASURE

STIFF, NOVEMBER 1977
PHOTOS: CHRIS GABRIN

Turning the tables on the grimy punk ethic, and quite decisively the yuk factor of their own debut record sleeve, the Damned go all Kandinsky-inspired high art for a second record that is similarly cleaned up—and produced by Pink Floyd's Nick Mason, no less. Colin "Barney Bubbles" Fulcher does a great job of not only squeezing in the band name with high-energy creativity and obscurity but also graphically representing the rambunctious boys in the band (Dave and the good Captain are clearest). And I can tell you from experience (my radar up for the possibility of the next Damned

album being somewhere in my fave record emporium, Strawberry Jams, on this particular trip to Spokane), my pupils summarily dilated as I pulled *Music for Pleasure* from the racks and slowly made out D, A, M . . . I freaked—in fact, jumped and almost hit my head on the old wooden beams—and then as I got home and got to know the record, grew to appreciate the band's Buzzcocks-style left turn into graphic austerity and how it dovetailed with the quiet chugging intensity of the music inside.

NAZARETH EXPECT NO MERCY

MOONCREST/A&M, NOVEMBER 1977
SLEEVE: SMART ART
FRONT COVER PAINTING: FRANK FRAZETTA

How can the hard rocker at heart not love this? Two warriors clashing steel in front of a big multicolored brain. And yet it was always annoying when the music inside didn't live up to the promise of the cover art, at least with respect to delivering those tall-enough stacks of riffs and power chords. In any event, Frazetta delivers the goods here; the further bonus beyond the narrative is the geometric composition, the image's centering, supported by the lower sword's positioning along the horizon line of the brain. "I remember quite a few of our covers, how they came together," muses Naz bassist Pete Agnew. "Every one was from a different person. One of the best, I thought, was *Expect No Mercy*. We saw this calendar when we were up in Canada, at Morin-Heights, when we were doing that album, and we had the song 'Expect No Mercy.' And somebody came over with this calendar with, oh my God, this Frank Frazetta. The actual thing is called

The Dream—that's the name of the painting—and we thought, 'This is great, this is really good.' Although, if you take a look at it, if you see that cover, and I always felt it was very funny, the big devil guy that is standing with the sword, and actually tries to kill the guy in front of him, he's going to take his own arms off, with his horns. Not to be nitpicky here. But we actually phoned up Frank Frazetta, and we got his wife on the phone and we were talking, we told her what we wanted to do, and no one had ever approached Frank about doing album covers, and she said, 'Okay, I'll speak to him.' And I said, 'Well, could we speak to him?' And she said, 'Frank doesn't like phones.' Okay, fair enough. And she says, 'Frank said yes. Use it.' It was just like that. It was, 'Yeah, use it.' So we used it. I thought it was quite a wee funny story, and of course after that, people like Molly Hatchet and a whole bunch of people used Frank Frazetta stuff."

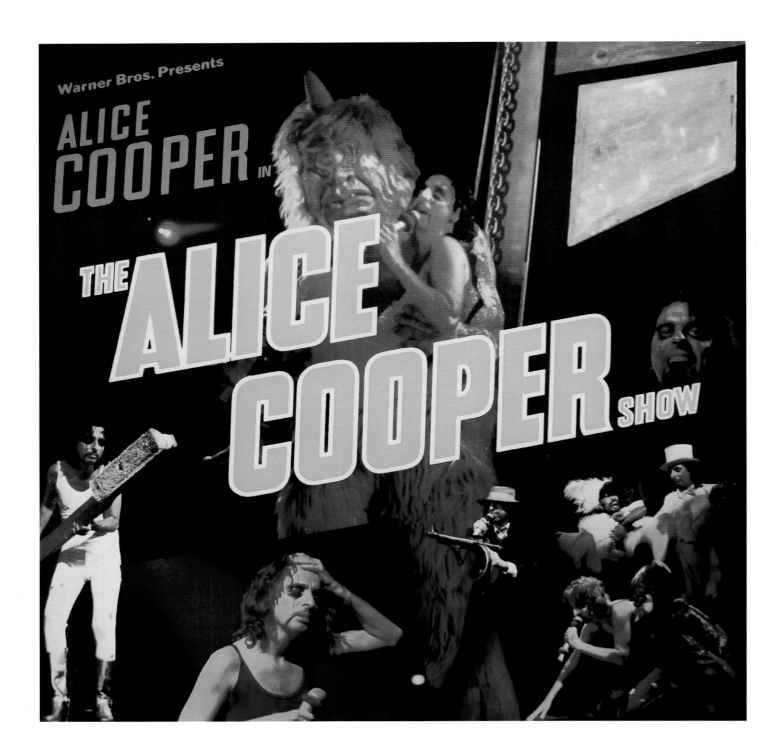

ALICE COOPER THE ALICE COOPER SHOW

WARNER BROS., DECEMBER 1977
DESIGN: RICHARD SEIREENI/ROD DYER, INC.
PHOTOGRAPHY: KEN BALLARD

This album makes a nice movie-vibed tie-in with Alice's greatest hits pack as well as with the '75 Montrose album, the title of which also includes the words *Warner Bros. Presents*. In any event, what's important here is that Alice was drifting into watery singer-songwriter-ville, and this cover reminds the listener in full Technicolor what Alice got famous for—his macabre show of all shows. Top hats, gangsters, the big ol' toothbrush, monsters, that eerie soiled unitard he wears . . . it's all

here as career summation, including—looking ominous and large to the right—Alice's most famous prop of all, the guillotine. Add 'er up, and the reason this works is that it mainlines the message that despite what you might be thinking of Alice 2.0, dis-attached from the classic band, as well as Alice as thoughtful balladeer, he's really still worth seeing on shock rock stages all over America.

STARZ VIOLATION

CAPITOL, 1977
DESIGN: DENNIS WOLOCH
COVER PAINTING: ALEX SIBURNEY

Weirdly similar to Moxy's *Ridin' High* cover, *Violation*'s nonetheless got a memorable sleeve; illustrator Alex Siburney makes amusing use of the band's quintessential '70s logo (sort of Aerosmith crossed with Van Halen and Legs Diamond) with a scene of artful coloring. "At the time, I had stars on my guitar," explains Richie Ranno on the origins of the band's heavily utilized logo, "and some of us wore stars pendants; I guess it was a common thing back then. But Sean Delaney came up with that name, and we thought, 'Nah, it doesn't sound right.' 'What if it has a *Z* on it?' 'Yeah, maybe.' So Sean went to Dennis Woloch, who was the graphic designer for all those Kiss albums, and also a few of our albums, and he said, 'Can you come up with something

for this?' So he got the guy who did the movie *Zardoz*, a well-known artist—he lives in L.A. now. And he came up with this logo, and they gave it to us on a Xerox, about two or three inches wide, and we thought, 'Oh man, that is cool! And that's when we decided on the name right there, with the *Z*. But the concept of *Violation* was a spacey kind of thing. What we told management was that we wanted the Starz logo crashing into the ground, somewhere in some sandy desert, and the door opens and the five of us are getting out. You know, a couple of guys are peeing on the ground; you see them from behind or something. The idea was that we were landing on earth, but they didn't go for it."

THE RUNAWAYS LIVE IN JAPAN

MERCURY, 1977
DESIGN: MASAO OHOGIYA
PHOTOGRAPHY: AKIYOSHI MIYASHITA, WEEKLY HEIBON, AND EIICHIRO SAKATA-APACHE

I love the tough glam look of this arch-'70s sleeve, with the band decked out somewhere between Sweet and *Rollerball* (at a stretch, a precursor to Priest during the *Turbo* era). The threat of metal comes from Joan Jett's studded wristband, not to mention the three big guitars one only becomes aware of when the sleeve is flipped over or unfolded, a process that also reveals the band's wicked platforms. Also so lovely and fit for the heavenly '70s is the typeface treatment, a combination of red, yellow, orange, and lightning (gotta have lightning) breaking up an ethereal whitish blue, a look that feels Japanese, which makes sense, given that *Live in Japan* was very much a Japanese production top to bottom.

THE RUNAWAYS QUEENS OF NOISE

MERCURY, 1977
DESIGN: DESMOND STROBEL
PHOTOGRAPHY: BARRY LEVINE

Falling flat by four-fifths (it featured only lead singer Cherie Currie), the debut Runaways album had a cover that missed out on conveying to the world the band's secret weapon—i.e., its heaviness at the hands of five girls. "The Runaways I loved, because it was the first time I ever encountered a female band," notes photographer Barry Levine. "And they were part of that whole glam thing. [Manager] Kim Fowley was completely out of his mind and tried to take a lot of the credit for this band. He was smart in the way he introduced them to the industry, but this band really had their own perception of who they were and what they wanted to be and how they wanted to write, and they didn't want to be a puppet. They were a street band that were trying to be sexy, but had a hard-core sensuality to them. And that's as far as they wanted to go. They didn't want to be like some of the female bands today or whatever, that sell

pure sex. I mean, they were selling a mixture of innocence, smart innocence, and sexuality. You know what Kim was trying to do. But these girls were rock and rollers; these girls were musicians who wanted to make music, play, and live a pretty rough lifestyle. Lita was an amazing guitar player! Fifteen years old, watching her play . . . and Joan had great presence, great songwriter, and Sandy was a great drummer; I mean, Sandy played like a guy. But PolyGram wanted to work on their sensuality a little bit, and that's why we used poles on the second album cover." Yet all the above was captured in the smoke, the logo, the title, the insistent stares, and the pink, purple, and black motif. However, the cover's main accomplishment was in assaulting the world with this idea of a female hard rock band through a pose that could have been used on a snarling Blue Öyster Cult, New York Dolls, or Dictators cover.

ANGEL ON EARTH AS IT IS IN HEAVEN

CASABLANCA, 1977
COVER ART CONCEPT AND COVER DESIGN: DAVID JOSEPH
PHOTOGRAPHY: DAVID ALEXANDER

"The whole thing with that was to introduce the upside-down logo," says Angel vocalist Frank Dimino. "That's why we went with that idea." And quite an idea it was, set alight by the killer Bob Petrick–designed logo, which indeed read "Angel" quite clearly right side up and upside down. The band is shot in mirror reflection as well, so the whole album cover is the same when turned 180 degrees. Inside the original LP was a two-panel poster that did the same. Vaulting the theme into the stratosphere was an explosion of sumptuous blues and greens shrouding the white-clad

and very photogenic band. The result was an upscale glam image far beyond that portrayed on the band's first two albums, and slyly classier than that of the band's evil Casablanca twins, Kiss. It all made sense, because once inside the sleeve, what we got was an Angel paring down its songs and backing off of the complex metal of *Helluva Band*, opting mostly for pop confection, even if, incongruously, the Eddie Kramer production job represented the dirty opposite of the gleaming-team look on the candy wrap.

LEGS DIAMOND A DIAMOND IS A HARD ROCK

MERCURY, 1977
ART DIRECTION: TIM BRYANT/GRIBBITT!
COVER ILLUSTRATION: VINCE TOPAZIO
ALBUM COVER CONCEPT: MICHAEL DIAMOND

Trying to sell Legs Diamond to unbelievers was always hard once one had to utter the goofy title of this, their penultimate album, but hey, all the album covers rocked. Here the relatively unknown Vince Topazio gives us a tough guy (possibly the Legs of yore) using his Super Bowl–size diamond ring as a weapon, punching through a wall of red steel (hopefully it's not some poor kid's wagon!). This cover always reminded me that all these records in the '70s, even the relative obscurities—despite the fame and fortune some folks rose to—were on major labels, using big-name producers and studios, incurring the same costs as Aerosmith, Ted Nugent, and Rush albums and having the same attention paid to cover graphics. In other words, the hope was there, and subsequently the resources apportioned were roughly the same.

BILLION DOLLAR BABIES BATTLE AXE

POLYDOR, 1977
ALBUM CONCEPT: BILLION DOLLAR BABIES AND PREVUE MANAGEMENT
DESIGN AND ILLUSTRATION: ERNST THORMAHLEN

Billion Dollar Babies was essentially the Alice Cooper band without Alice, hatching one record and then disbanding. Musically, the magic wasn't there, and one suspects the modest pile of albums that got sold had more to do with the sparkle and the shine of the album cover than the wobbly songs Neal, Dennis, and Michael were putting forth. The band's name in lights, as on Broadway, the cockle-warming reds and purples, the big warrior dude wielding a guitar shaped like an ax

(didn't Gene Simmons have a bass like this?)—angry young patrons frankly figured they were in for an actual heavy metal album, instead being served weak-tea generalist hard rock with a glam twist. Still, we can thank the boys for this waxed-and-buffed hot rod of a sleeve, the general idea of the thing soon to be revived by Bobby Barth and his underrated Southern rock act simply called Axe.

THE SAINTS ETERNALLY YOURS

HARVEST/SIRE, MAY 1978
DESIGN: CREAM
PHOTOGRAPHY FRONT: PETE VERNON

To inject some energy and controversy into things, we've massaged a little bit of punk into the equation, and man, putting aside the fact that *Eternally Yours* is in my top half dozen punk albums of all time, it's also got one of the most egregiously squalid, gritty, and urgent punk album covers going—without resorting to anything cheap and obvious. Not only did the band members forget they were posing for a picture, but it seems they didn't take the time or effort to cut their hair, as any good punks should. Leader Chris Bailey

looks particularly sullen about the rules, even dressing upmarket for the stand he's sleeplessly taking. Finally, an additional yet weirdly subconscious touch of the incendiary is achieved by the punctuating place-ment of a red star, which managed to twist the album commie or at least Clash-lefty. The whole vibe of this sleeve—including that star, importantly—reminds me very much of those late-career photos of the New York Dolls in Soviet mode, courtesy of impresario Malcolm McClaren.

BOSTON DON'T LOOK BACK

EPIC, AUGUST 1978
ART DIRECTION: TONY LANE
COVER CONCEPT: TOM SCHOLZ
COVER ARTIST: GARY NORMAN

Boston's ELO-ish "guitarship" was established on the debut, but the second sleeve is better composed, exhibiting depth, featuring nonobvious hard rock colors. In addition, here's Tom participating fully in the golden age of the hard rock logo (yes, hard rock bands tried harder; ask Angel and Starz), emblazoning the front of the rockin' space facility in gold, like a hood ornament or, more in tune with the times, trucker's belt buckle. Note also the hermetically sealed civilization.

URIAH HEEP *Fallen Angel*

URIAH HEEP FALLEN ANGEL

BRONZE/CHRYSALIS, SEPTEMBER 1978
SLEEVE DESIGN AND ARTWORK: CHESS CREATIVE SERVICES
COVER ILLUSTRATION: CHRIS ACHILLEOS

Heep always gave good cover, and here they are, propping up a batch of traditionally structured, generalist rock and roll songs with full-blown fantasy art, quietly proposing an increased gravitas to the sight-and-sound totality. Indeed, if one flips to the back cover and its continuation of the illustration, reads the pedestrian song titles, and feels somewhat "boared," a quick turn back to the front re-pleases through the presentation of a scantily clad female warrior, one who, additionally, possesses an interesting face. This illustration was obviously modeled on a real person of significance. Fanciful type and the oddball choice of yellow background complete this solid fantasy art tour de force.

BLACK SABBATH
Never Say Die!

BLACK SABBATH **NEVER SAY DIE!**

VERTIGO/WARNER BROS., SEPTEMBER 1978
SLEEVE DESIGN: HIPGNOSIS

This stunning image of fighter-jet pilots looking robotic and anonymous, like terrorists, fits perfectly the mood within Sabbath at the time; the band sullen-sounding, uncommunicative, lonely, dreary, and weary with doom. This sense of quiet unease was also the signature of the design house for the project, the famed Hipgnosis, who had captured very much the same vibe the last time out for the band. Note the imagery painted into the clouds and the military type used for the band name—a look that would have been interesting enough to use as a logo, although Sabbath had always somehow been above the idea of resorting to that instrument of quick-and-easy branding.

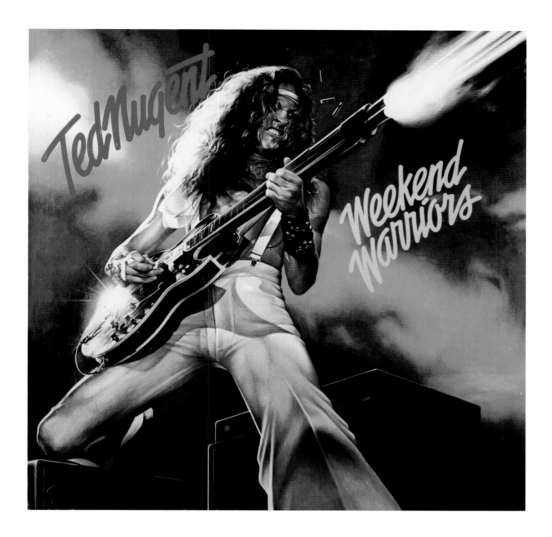

TED NUGENT WEEKEND WARRIORS

EPIC, SEPTEMBER 1978
DESIGN: PAULA SCHER AND JIM CHARNE
ILLUSTRATION: JEFF CUMMINS

A Deadly Tedly album goes Tedinator-illustration-as-Whackmaster for the first time, and, as I say elsewhere, that imagery generally shoots out the spark that a rocker has arrived, that his likeness is worthy of meticulous painting by a creator on par as a peer. And it's a humdinger of a cover, combining so very literally two of Ted's passions: guitars and guns. It looks real metal as well, or protometal, given that 1978 is really the last year before metal would become defined as a complete package, thanks to two phenoms: Judas Priest and the NWOBHM. Plus, hey, this was always a great look for Ted, namely, the white slacks and suspenders, Ted being one of the few rock and rollers of physique to pull it off. Explains Cummins on the laborious birthing of this illustration: "Originally, *Oui* magazine commissioned the Ted Nugent piece for an interview article with Ted. To be honest, at that time, I'd never heard of him! The art editor sent me some pics of Ted playing live and wanted a kind of G.I. Joe thing, with machine-gun guitar, etc. The original artwork was kind of a *4* shaped with the gun end bleeding across the opposite spread, above the text. When Ted saw the published article, he wanted the artwork for his next album cover! *Oui* sent the artwork back to me, and CBS then asked me to 'square up' the blue background. Luckily there was just enough room on the art board to do this. This is all pre-Photoshop, don't forget. Also, they wanted me to add the Fender logo to the amps and make Ted's legs more muscular! Best of all, though, CBS then asked me to 'move some of the hair from in front of Ted's eyes, so that we could see more of his face.' Yeah, like his face would be there waiting to be revealed once the hair was removed! I explained that, as I had based the likeness on a photo provided of Ted, with hair cascading forth, his face beneath the hair didn't actually exist. They sent me loads of Ted photos, and I kind of made it up in the end! Later, the cover art received an award from the Society of Illustrators in New York, and was exhibited at their awards show in the Eagle Gallery—I think it was called—in Manhattan. Ted is currently hanging in *The Vinyl Canvas* exhibition in Hertfordshire, England."

Blue Öyster Cult: Some Enchanted Evening

BLUE ÖYSTER CULT SOME ENCHANTED EVENING

COLUMBIA, SEPTEMBER 1978
COVER CONCEPT: HILLARY VERMONT AND MARY PEKAR
SLEEVE DESIGN: ANDREA KLEIN
COVER PAINTING: T. R. SHORR

The cover of this live album is about as gorgeously executed as any young metalhead could wish for. "T. R. Shorr" (a misspelling—it's the same Todd Schorr who did Starz's *Coliseum Rock*, Peter Criss's *Out of Control*, and AC/DC's *Fly on the Wall*) offers up a simple, traditional Grim Reaper riding a slightly more decked-out, green-eyed horse sporting the BÖC logos as head weapons. The ebony pair thunder through a moonlit desertscape (shades of "Death Valley Nights"?), the scene topped by a formal typeface that invites the listener to some enchanted evening. An interesting touch is that the back cover appears to be the source

photograph for the illustration's desert background. Recalls Schorr: "That was first used as a trade ad, but the group liked it so much they used it as an LP cover and also as a giant stage backdrop curtain for their tour." In any event, BÖC retains its track record of stunning sleeves with the elegant elbow grease even applied to the live albums that come just before (*On Your Feet or on Your Knees*) and after (*Extraterrestrial Live*). Where other managers are content with a blurry concert shot of their band rocking out, not so with the mythmaking Sandy Pearlman and his like-minded literary charges.

MOLLY HATCHET MOLLY HATCHET

EPIC, SEPTEMBER 1978
ILLUSTRATION: FRANK FRAZETTA

Credit Molly Hatchet for the heavy, insistent use of a warrior mascot, a happenstance that would be repeated most successfully in the future within the realm of power metal, starting with Manowar four years hence (for real, maybe six years hence) and living in the modern day most potently through Swedish revivalists HammerFall. "The painting on the first album cover is called *The Death Dealer,* and it's a Frazetta," explains guitarist Dave Hlubek. "We actually came across that in a bookstore in a mall in Jacksonville. Banner Thomas had ordered a book or something, and we went there to pick it up. I happened to go with him, and while he was getting this special-order book he'd been waiting for—he was a big-time, avid reader—while we were waiting to see if it had come in, I so happened to be sorting through some lithograph books. Myself, not much of a reader, but if there's a book with many pictures, then

I'll read it. And there was this Frazetta thing, *The Death Dealer.* We already had our deal with Epic; we were going to come out with the first album, but the Epic art department couldn't come up with anything that looked anywhere near what we were looking for, as far as cover art goes. I know that Nazareth had some cool covers. But they didn't know, or anybody else for that matter, what a Molly Hatchet was supposed to be. So we got that book of lithographs and showed it to our manager. We went ahead and designed the banner to go across it, and I guess he shot it up to New York, to the art department, and he said, 'That's the one.' And so they dealt with the Frazetta people to get the rights to use it, and that's where the story starts. It was a good marriage between the music and the cover art. At that point, I think we were selling albums mostly for our cover art. It was definitely a good marriage."

JUDAS PRIEST HELL BENT FOR LEATHER

CBS/COLUMBIA, OCTOBER 1978
COVER DESIGN: ROSLAV SZAYBO (CBS RECORDS)
PHOTOGRAPHY: BOB ELSDALE

Yes indeed, if you've mischievously cheated and skipped to the back of this tome, you'll see that I've rated the UK edition of this album, called *Killing Machine*, as the greatest hard rock cover ever. (The North American issue, called *Hell Bent for Leather*, replaced the red album title type with orange—inexplicably ruining the whole thing!) It was hard to pick one cover, of course, but this one is certainly magical, vibrating alchemically and with nuclear force between high art and heavy metal—a searing combination so hard to balance. What's not to love, and where to start? Let's begin with the allusions to the lead singer, who, instinctively, we sort of figure this is, given the shades and the hint of metal garb. In any event, one imagines it's a masochistic lover of violent music so aggressive that it might

blind you, his Mona Lisa smile betraying the pleasure and the pain. Moving on, there's the bloody shattered-lens effect, which, if you think about it, is quite strange and quite an obscure idea. "That was done by Roslav Szaybo, from the art department at CBS in London," notes bassist Ian Hill. "He did a couple of them. For that effect with the sunglasses, he actually got an air rifle, and he had dozens of pairs of sunglasses and shot them with the air rifle until he got the right effect. And then he lit it from behind to get all the colors right." Whatever the motivation, there's a futuristic look to the thing, which aptly syncs up with Priest's mining of metal for the future. There's no question that, with this record, the band was at the front edge of metal achievement circa late '78.

QUEEN JAZZ

EMI/ELEKTRA, NOVEMBER 1978
SLEEVE CONCEPT: QUEEN
SLEEVE DESIGN: CREAM

Part of the holding power of the *Jazz* sleeve is its reflection of the sentiment that this was a band constantly reinventing itself. If there had been, essentially, no real sense of surprise or a moving off from the message with any of the first five covers, *News of the World* thenceforth cleansed the palate, and now *Jazz* was doing so yet again—fresher, starker, and razor-sharp. It's black and white with a shocking pink (embossed) "JAZZ" emanating from the sound waves, speaker cone,

reflecting pool—the center of the Queen universe. The band name is repeated ticker tape–like at the top, with a perplexing line of naked girls on bikes along the "fat bottom." Flip over the cover and it's the opposite color scheme with some subtle differences. Still, the overall message is one and the same with Led Zeppelin's: the biggest, boldest bands in the world operate within a rarefied realm completely without rules.

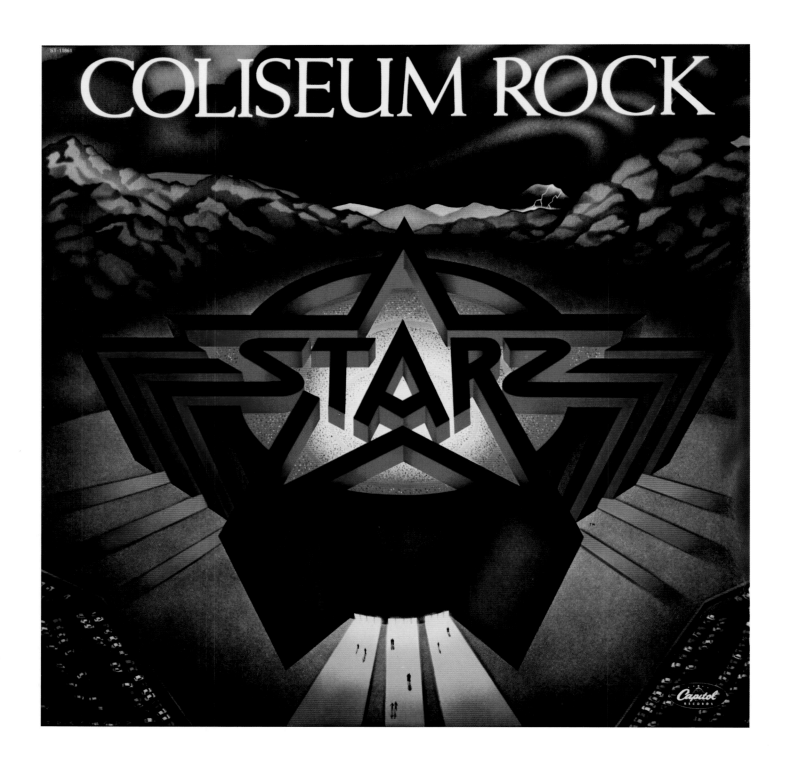

STARZ COLISEUM ROCK

CAPITOL, 1978
DESIGN: HOWARD MARKS ADVERTISING INC.
COVER PAINTING: TODD SCHORR

The front wraps of the entire four-record Starz catalog are about celebrating the band's logo. *Coliseum Rock* is most akin to *Violation*, however, in that the band is trying to do something imaginative (and Boston-like) with it, here creating a massive rock coliseum out of it, where, as we know, Starz is either third on the concert bill or a solid sandwich act. Aspirational, though, isn't it? And also somehow Kiss-like in that the back cover offers nothing additional: a simple replication of the front sleeve, sort of like a repeating blues lyric.

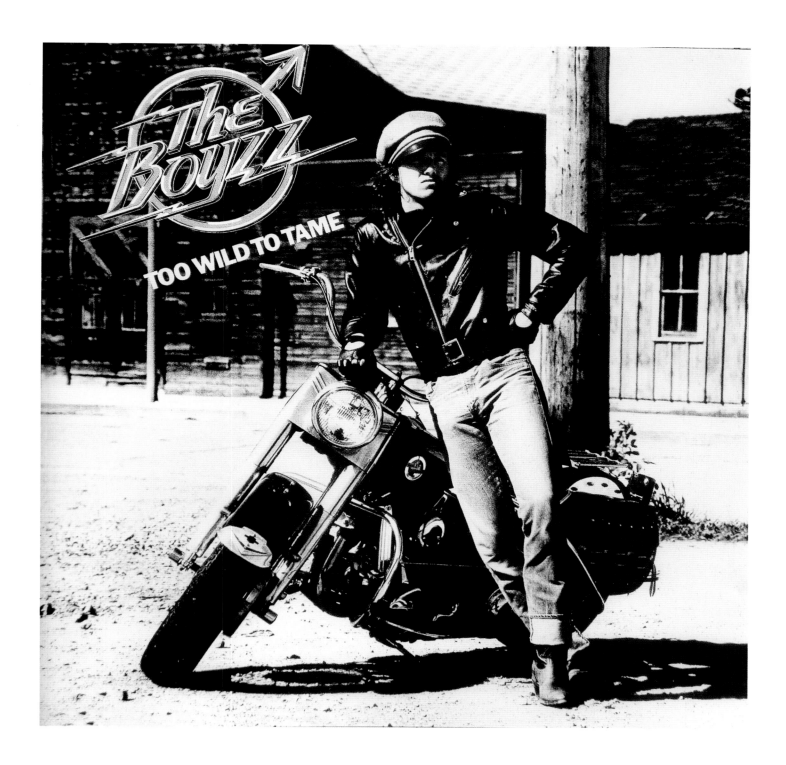

THE BOYZZ TOO WILD TO TAME

EPIC, 1978
ALBUM DESIGN: JOHN BERG AND PAULA SCHER
ALBUM PHOTOGRAPHY: JIM HOUGHTON

A surefire way of prodding a metalhead to dig a rough-and-tumble Southern rock album is to throw in a motorcycle and leather jacket. Over to the back cover, with the band crowding around Dirty Dan and his ride, each of the bad ol' boy(zz) dutifully dressed in the uniform, and the connection was complete, with the band's marginally heavy rock now crossing the line into the range of metal circa '78. The look is a bit tongue-in-cheek, though, not quite real, like something out of a '50s biker-gang exploitation film. The title fits that vibe as well—heck, so does the band's name and its glam connotation. And hey, the logo's grilling itself upon the international symbol for male, so don't get any funny ideas, or we'll be swinging some pool cues upside the head, neck, and chest area.

NAZARETH NO MEAN CITY

A&M, JANUARY 1979
SLEEVE DESIGN AND PAINTING: RODNEY MATTHEWS

The esteemed Rodney Matthews (of Magnum, Eloy, and Diamond Head) turns in a decisively heavy-metal sleeve for what would be Nazareth's most guitary and belligerent album since *Hair of the Dog*, another album featuring a sleeve of nasty disposition. "We based *No Mean City* on a book that was written about razor gangs in Glasgow," notes Manny Charlton. "That's where the title track came from, and then we handed it to Rodney Matthews, who's a fantastic artist that we liked, and we said, 'What can you do with this?' He then came up with the sleeve and we were just gobsmacked—it was awesome." Adds Rodney, fleshing out the tale: "According to the brief given to me in 1978 by the band for *No Mean City*, the album was influenced by the novel of the same title. The book concerned the hard times and gang warfare rampant in Glasgow, Scotland, during the depressed years of the '20s and '30s. Nazareth had come across my calendar for 1978, [entitled] *Wizardry and Wild Romance* (Michael Moorcock–inspired images), while recording the album in Switzerland. As my art style was thought to suit requirements, the Nazareth manager invited me

up to the Isle of Man to meet the band and work out design details. We settled on the concept of a menacing character in a dark landscape to be drawn in the fantasy genre. I later presented two pencil sketches, one of which was accepted without alteration. The razor man became affectionately known to the band as Friendly Fred and went on to appear on publicity, including T-shirts, badges, mirrors, press, and concert programs. For many years, I have seen new renderings of Fred sprayed on trucks and cars, mostly in the U.S. The image also sold well as a poster but is now out of print. Because of renewed demand, I am about to publish new *giclée* prints for sale on my Web site store. Fred lives on!" The garish and monster-mashed illustration Matthews created would presage Iron Maiden's Eddie; both in turn would create a visual vibe that would usher in the NWOBHM. Of course, as history would have it, Eddie, comparatively, would carry much greater resonance, given that Nazareth never came to reinforce this sword-and-steel directive musically or visually, choosing to de-emphasize the hard rock for many years to come.

BAD COMPANY DESOLATION ANGELS

SWAN SONG, MARCH 1979
COVER DESIGN AND PHOTOGRAPHY: HIPGNOSIS

Bad Company doesn't have the best track record with album covers, and at face value, this one isn't particularly remarkable, either. But it gathers moss like a rolling stone, given that it's a Hipgnosis joint and that Bad Co. are one of the rare Swan Song acts besides Zeppelin and that the sleeve reminds one of that band's *Presence* packaging. *Presence* was all about a poked black hole in which absence takes on a presence. Here, what we experience is pure absence, as if a selective nuclear warhead had blown away bits according to some rule, leaving other bits exactly as they were, one bit still working on a car.

MOTÖRHEAD OVERKILL

BRONZE, MARCH 1979
COVER ILLUSTRATION: JOE PETAGNO

Okay, I'm now reliving the sense of excitement I felt seeing this thing for the first time, staring out of the racks as a new release I had been anticipating after being soiled by the band's first smutty album. It was at this point that Motörhead became actualized, the atom-splitting album cover being the main reason, along with the fact that the band was on a bigger, better label, namely, Bronze. But what a stunner of a

sleeve; the mysterious and surly Petagno creates a stylized version of the Snaggletooth that frankly has yet to be surpassed, though the field of competition has always been strong. With the logo in light blue and the album title brilliantly splattered and split with a blood trail, the masterpiece that is the *Overkill* cover is many a Motörheadbanger's favorite.

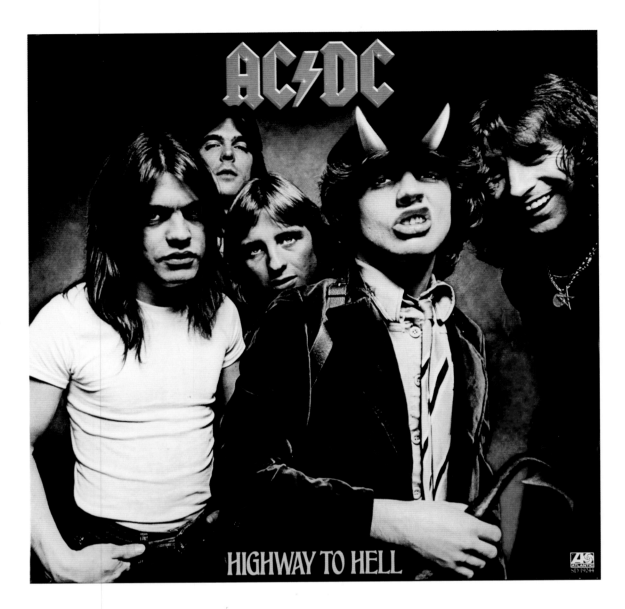

AC/DC HIGHWAY TO HELL

ALBERT/ATLANTIC, AUGUST 1979
ART DIRECTION: BOB DEFRIN
PHOTOGRAPHY: JIM HOUGHTON

Van Halen, Foreigner, Def Leppard, and AC/DC are the first names that come to mind for big bands consistently turning in bum sleeves. But maybe that's a bit unkind to the last of those, given that the band's plethora of Angus-centered presentations at least manage to crack a smile. And so *Highway to Hell* is the most egalitarian of the band's covers, offering up a hairy and lovable band shot, a photo-illustration montage, with the joke being either the horns and tail on Angus or the fact that Bon Scott's hair never looked that good. Prodding and provoking the finger-waggers, Scott is shown wearing a pentagram necklace, and he seems quite pleased about it, or, perhaps, pleased with the fine work done by his hairdresser. But my favorite area of the surface is covered by three faces sporting expressions that reflect guys who are unemployed, loitering, pretty vacant, and punk rockers. Indeed, in some of its guises,

disguises, songs, and stances (back in '76, anyway), AC/DC could pass for a punk rock band, and somehow that spirit prevails on the pop-culture staple that is the *Highway to Hell* sleeve. Recalls Earl Steinbicker, partner of photographer Jim Houghton: "That front cover was a shot from the sessions for the previous album, which you can tell if you compare it to the back cover of *Powerage*—same session. I always cringe when I see that hand holding the tail. I thought it looked so stupid. That and the horns were added in later, obviously. The back cover was actually the session that we were going to use for the front. We took them to a highway that was closed for construction, over on Long Island, and took some pictures, but they just never looked dramatic enough. But yeah, great guys, AC/DC, very quiet and polite. I just remember them being so thrilled to see New York City for the first time."

LED ZEPPELIN IN THROUGH THE OUT DOOR

SWAN SONG, AUGUST 1979
SLEEVE: HIPGNOSIS

Not that they knew that this would be the last Led Zeppelin album, but for *In Through the Out Door*, Hipgnosis pulls out all the stops, turning in its most elaborate concept yet, arguably across all acts. Moving from in to out, the record is housed in a black-and-white heavyweight inner sleeve that contains spots that turn various colors with the application of water. The inner sleeve is housed in a conventional album cover that contains no type save for the spine (an occasional Zep tradition). The front and back of that cover consists of a sharp yet sepia-toned barroom scene, rich of narrative—but six different views of this scene were commercially available in the shops, the

views corresponding to the perspective of six different characters in the bar looking at the man seated directly at the bar burning a piece of paper, identifiable as a Dear John letter only by the remnant rendered in black and white on the inner sleeve. According to designer Storm Thorgerson, the "wiping clean" effect slashed once across the sleeve was to signify the band's idea that the music on the album is Zeppelin with "a lick of fresh paint." Finally, the aforementioned three parts are housed within a fitted paper bag so one couldn't divine which of the six sleeves one would end up with. Helpfully, the bag was stamped with the band name, album title, and even song titles and label information.

FOREIGNER HEAD GAMES

ATLANTIC, SEPTEMBER 1979
ART DIRECTION: SANDI YOUNG
FRONT COVER PHOTO: CHRIS CALLIS

Foreigner, unfortunately, became known for bafflingly drab album sleeves, but *Head Games* was almost like one of the band's hit songs: unremarkable upon inspection but "catchy," hard to get out of your head, instantly recognizable from a distance. Is the scene sexist? We'll let Lou Gramm deal with that. What's unarguably admirable about the sleeve is the hand-tinting of the photo and the expert echoing of these colors in the title and band name text. "We got clobbered for that album cover," recalls Gramm. "The cover was submitted for us, and it was basically about a young girl sneaking into the boy's bathroom to wipe her name and telephone number off the wall. And the expression on her face looks as if she's been caught. Now, other people saw

that cover and suggested she was in there sitting on the urinal. Not so. It doesn't even look that way. And other people had a lot of other things that they saw, all of which were not true. We basically tried to make it cute, and just a little bit questionable. And we were banned at radio stations in Boston. We had women's groups calling big stations saying that they were going to make a big stink at city hall if we didn't pull that song and that album off rotation. I don't know, I don't think it was really worth the problem that it got us into for just trying to be a little funny. I've seen many, many things that were so much more blatant and disgusting, and I don't know what. And this was just a little cute; that's all. And it started World War Three."

CHEAP TRICK DREAM POLICE

EPIC, SEPTEMBER 1979
DESIGN: PAULA SCHER AND STEVE DESSAU
PHOTOGRAPHY: REID MILES

Do the math: Cheap Trick pushed their duality shtick (two pretty boys, two clowns) about half the time, but we're all happier when everybody's on the cover. Here the band dressed as "dream police" (a pretty heavy concept for a pop metal alum, if you think about it) for a geometrically composed, comfortably white and wispy cover that almost feels like a reprise of *Heaven* *Tonight* (or the narrative's next frame or scene, i.e., casual clothes into uniform), visually and philosophically. And in that spirit there was always this tendency to pair *Dream Police* with that record, and to pair the first two (*Cheap Trick* and *In Color*), and then onto a break with the new decade and no more pairing.

LIVE IN JAPAN
PRIEST IN THE EAST

JUDAS PRIEST UNLEASHED IN THE EAST

CBS/COLUMBIA, SEPTEMBER 1979
PHOTOGRAPHY: FIN COSTELLO

Shot in a sleepy, granny-friendly town hall in England and not, as would be suggested, unleashed in Japan (ha! for emphasis, we're showing you the Japanese version), the cover for Priest's first and best live album announces a new metalness and personableness for this band, given that it's the first (and, as it turns out, the only one) of the band's covers to feature a photo of the Birmingham bashers. "Just fell into it, really," says bassist Ian Hill of the band's newfound leather-and-studs image so prominently runway/runaway–laid for the sleeve. "We were wearing all kinds of things: velvet, satin, denims, a whole eclectic look at one point. I think one day Rob walked in wearing a leather coat, a biker jacket, and we thought, 'Gee, that looks pretty good,' and we all got one. I think it was as simple as that. I

think we just fell into it. It fit perfectly with the music we were playing." Indeed, the new look signaled a clear identification with heavy metal that would carry Priest to the top. It was a unified look, save for a perennial spot of red fancied by Glenn Tipton, also established right here. The *Unleashed in the East* sleeve also helped establish the overtly gay look that Rob would adopt to match his reality, although curiously, this was never glommed on to and/or discussed; Rob, for the most part, stayed well in the closet for decades to come. The shot of K.K. is as metal as it gets, and the fact that Les Binks, the band's mystery-shrouded (and best-ever) drummer, cannot be seen—well, he had been quietly purged from the band by the time this photo was staged.

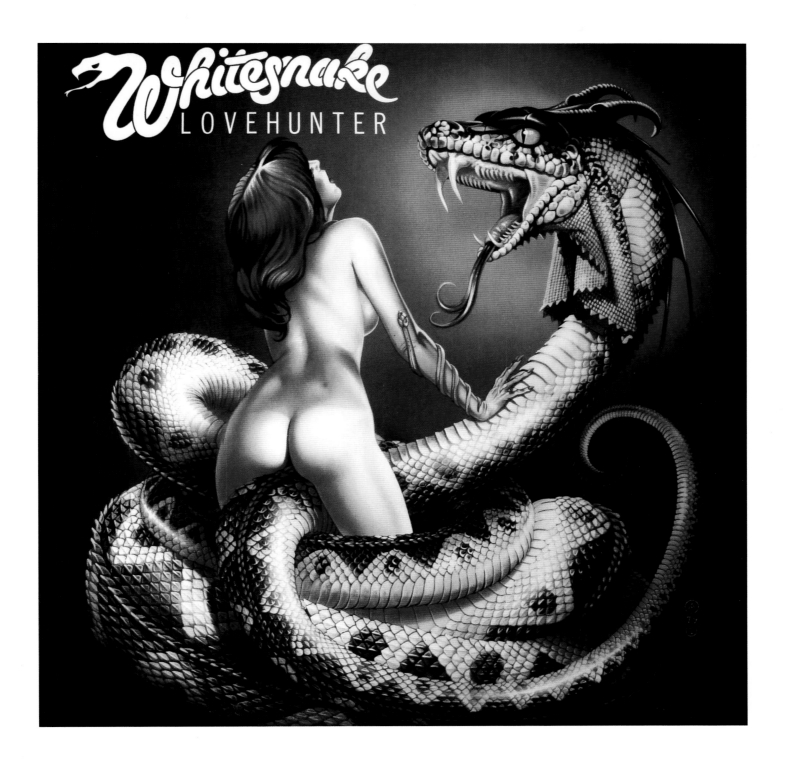

WHITESNAKE LOVEHUNTER

UNITED ARTISTS, OCTOBER 1979
ART DIRECTOR: JOHN PASCHE
ILLUSTRATION: CHRIS ACHILLEOS
LOGO: JIM GIBSON

I drew this full-size in blue pen on my math Duo-Tang back in grade twelve, although, truth be told, I was too reticent to include the beefy gal. Sure, it's a bit naughty, but that's Coverdale's thing, a dirty-dog message throughout the catalog. Still, it was always a bit annoying how David denounced metal and rocked only halfheartedly, and then gave us garishly NWOBHM-ish sleeves like this corker. But even if the music was on the slightly stodgy side, one could muse, impressed, on the way the band's logo was a simplified version of the richly appointed snake of the illustration, and on the fact that both were, indeed, white snakes. I mean, nothing else to look at, is there?

MOTÖRHEAD BOMBER

BRONZE, OCTOBER 1979
SLEEVE ARTWORK: ADRIAN CHESTERMAN
WAR-PIG LOGO: JOE PETAGNO

Unfairly maligned as an album, *Bomber* nonetheless sported a sleeve everyone could agree upon as flash and even a tad humorous, given the visages of the terrible trio manning this most awesome of bombers as it strafes, well, its own fan base, really. Motörhead's music and a face full of lead was pretty much the same thing. As illustration goes, one couldn't find a piece more skillfully rendered, heightening the scene with burgundy and blue text. Brilliant. "I was given the commission on a Friday," recalls Adrian Chesterman, "and I suggested we all meet on the Saturday at midday to discuss the cover, as I was only given a few days to illustrate this and I had to crack on with it. They looked a bit pissed off to have had to get up that early. They had the title but not much else, so I suggested a dramatic angle on a diving bomber, and they all seemed to like the idea. Philthy Animal didn't say anything at all but sucked noisily on a can of Special Brew. Lemmy suggested it should be a German bomber, as 'the bad guys make the best shit,' which I couldn't argue with. Fast Eddie seemed to go along with it all. We agreed on a Heinkel one eleven, as the glass nose and underslung gun turret would give me more places in which to put the boys. I bought a little Airfix model, put it together, and sprayed it black. I then shot it with dramatic lighting, and this gave me excellent reference from which I could execute the airbrush illustration. I painted it in black and white first, as this gives maximum drama, and then tinted it with color later. I added Joe Petagno's Snaggletooth logo in a kind of chrome effect where the swastika would have been. Lots of searchlights and explosions and a detaching bomb flying towards the camera completed the drama. I took passport-sized pics of the boys all looking mean. Lemmy curled up his lip and perfectly looked the part, and Phil just had that expression permanently, so he didn't have to try hard. Eddie wasn't overjoyed at his 'girlie-looking hair,' but overall Motörhead were ecstatic about the final illustration. It proved to be so popular that they subsequently made the famous forty-foot lighting rig in the shape of the bomber for the tour. It was one of the most famous album covers I've ever done, so my mum had the original artwork on the wall of her sitting room. She was very religious and would have the Methodist circle over after church on a Sunday. So there would be Lemmy and Philthy Animal snarling out of the picture with the vicar sipping tea underneath."

ZZ TOP DEGÜELLO

WARNER BROS., NOVEMBER 1979
ALBUM COVER: BILL NARUM
PHOTOGRAPHY: GEORGE CRAIG

After a long absence to (ahem!) sort a few things out, ZZ Top comes back with a brighter, snappier version of the hoedown that was *Tejas*. Poetically, accurately, the visuals respond, with ZZ bringing the zippy, hot Mexican graphics, three bullets through a flag, smoke and toke through a skull, gorgeous yet playful type framing the scene. Throwing in a little extra, the sort of "official"

cover is augmented by a copacetic inner sleeve with a shot of "the lone wolf horns," as they're labeled, and an outer wrap—wrapping papers, as it were—teasing with a crude pastel version of the skull that would blaze beneath. All three pieces are of the same slinky, thin card stock, but combined, they hold their own.

CREAM RECORDS, INC. CR-1010

LEGS DIAMOND FIRE POWER

CREAM, 1979
CONCEPT: MICHAEL DIAMOND
DESIGN: JOHN C. LEPREVOST
ILLUSTRATION: JIM DEESING

"America's Deep Purple" is back, now kicked down the stairs off Mercury and onto a label called Cream. But that doesn't mean their album covers have to suffer; Legs brings back his thug, identified only by his black leather glove and massive diamond ring, reaching across the scene and shooting, yes, a diamond gun, under the watchful gaze of the band's newly diamond-cut logo. Turn the cover over, and one gets a lesson in ballistics, namely, that a diamond gun shoots diamonds.

THE GODZ NOTHING IS SACRED

MILLENNIUM/CASABLANCA, 1979
ART DIRECTION: PHYLLIS CHOTIN
PHOTOGRAPHER: LEN KALTMAN
GRAPHICS: GRIBBITT!

Here's a case where the wrapper builds manic expectation. Alas, hope of heaviness is dashed once inside, as Eric Moore and Co. actually get poppier on record number two versus the rumbling blue-collar debut. But we can all bask in the smoke, oil, and roil of the album cover. The Godz present and represent their ties to bikers and biker culture in a formation that reminds one of Priest's *Unleashed in the East.* Flip over the cover and the band is hanging with some babes, looking badass after a hard ride. Says Eric, with reticence: "Whether we're close to any biker organization or not, I was in a club when I was a lot younger, and it will go unmentioned. You know, I ride. All the guys in the new band ride. The second album cover was all us. On the back cover, that bar's in Bayonne, New Jersey, and that's a shot from a video that we shot—one of the first videos that was ever done. The only one I had ever seen done was I saw Todd Rundgren make one, because we were

in the same studio. And when I wasn't producing, I would watch him do this video stuff because I thought it was fascinating. And we used the *60 Minutes* film crew, their bus and everything, and of course the video disappeared after a short couple of times. I've never even seen it. Casablanca never paid the bills to *60 Minutes,* so the band ended up paying it. That's the way it's always been. On the front cover, I'm second from left, and that's Bob Hill on the far right—the other blond guitar player. I was in three different bands with him and roommates with him for almost ten years. We got along really good, but he left. It's just that you wake up in the middle of the night and something seems wrong. And you realize that you got on the freeway going the wrong way. You've got a stoned driver who doesn't even know he's on the wrong side of this freeway, and after a couple of things like that, Bob said 'bye."

RUSH PERMANENT WAVES

MERCURY, JANUARY 1980
ART DIRECTION AND GRAPHICS: HUGH SYME
COVER CONCEPT: HUGH SYME AND NEIL PEART
PHOTOGRAPHY: FIN COSTELLO, FLIP SCHULKE, AND DEBORAH SAMUEL
COVER GIRL COUTURIERE: OU LA LA
COLOR COLLABORATION: PETER GEORGE

So much about this Hipgnosis-like Hugh Syme symphony of a sleeve is admirable, from the elegant type for both the band name and the title through to all the visual puns. And let's get to those, shall we? Okay, the core photo is of Galveston, Texas, getting hit by a hurricane in 1961, accompanied by waves breaching the seawall. That's none other than artist Hugh Syme across the street waving. The eerily oblivious model on the cover has her dress waving around, and her hair style is a wave. And there's a chunk of newspaper waving around in the strong winds as well, its permanent headline in error, reading "Dewei Defeats Truman," 'cause the *Chicago Tribune* objected to "Dewy Defeats Truman." I'm not sure why that would bother them, or why going with Dewei would placate them!

JUDAS PRIEST BRITISH STEEL

CBS/COLUMBIA, APRIL 1980
DESIGN: ROSLAV SZAYBO
FRONT COVER PHOTOGRAPHY: R. ELSDALE

The *British Steel* cover is considered one of the most iconic in the annals of heavy metal, often topping polls of this sort of thing, sending metalheads back to a nice neat year and early in it, when metal could be said to have kicked off a similarly tidy ten-year golden period for the loud and proud. The occasion was the ignition of the NWOBHM, and the Roslav Szaybo design chosen for the band's sixth album graphically celebrated this first of defined metal flankings. The razor blade could be said to be—and, indeed, was fleetingly interpreted as—a salvo against the punks that the new metalers were sending to extinction, or at least to the knobby and knotty realms of postpunk. A metalhead's leather-and-studded hand (reaching out of the cover and presumably out of some sort of bad music mire) was literally taking back the steel, emblazoning it tattoo-style with the jagged name of his band and their NWOBHM-approximate motto, *British Steel*. Our metalhead martyrs himself, making himself one with the movement, as fans did, by letting the steel slice into his hand. Indeed, blood was considered as an addition to the blade, but that idea was deemed too garish, too extreme of a martyring. "*British Steel* came out as sort of a lighthearted joke," comments bassist Ian Hill, "because there was a huge steel company in Britain called British Steel, and we couldn't come up with a title, and they were on strike at the time, and I said, 'How about British Steel?' as a bit of a joke. Everybody laughed a bit, and then the giggles died down, until they realized, you

know, that sounds pretty good. You couldn't escape it in the Midlands. In the eighties, things were starting to wind down a little bit, but when we were growing up as kids, they called it the Black Country for a very good reason. I mean, there were foundries, factories, coal mines, you name it, everything in probably, I don't know, thirty square miles between Wolverhampton and Birmingham and everything in between. And it was very, very industrial—you would go to school, and you would go past three or four foundries, spring works, all kinds of things. British Steel ended up as . . . I think the government bought everything out, the different steel companies, and nationalized it as British Steel." Any legalities to using the title? "No, I don't think so. Not a peep out of the company. In fact, not long after that, they went bump anyways." Adds Hill with a laugh, "We might have had something to do with that, I don't know." In truth, Judas Priest was already too long in the tooth to be said to have participated with relish in the NWOBHM and its firecracker demographic, but all its hard work had indeed been validated by it, the band members becoming respected elders to the young pups who were firing on more cylinders. Still, the image was perfect for rock T-shirts, given its striking sculpted look and a convenient fade to black. It graphically illustrated, and not without pain, the dedication of a rambunctious and pimply new metal army to their very own form of British Steel.

BLACK SABBATH HEAVEN AND HELL

VERTIGO/WARNER BROS., APRIL 1980
ART DIRECTION: RICHARD SEIREENI
COVER ILLUSTRATION: LYNN CURLEE
LINER ILLUSTRATION: HARRY CARMEAN

The *Heaven and Hell* cover art embodied the quiet malevolence that seemed to follow Ronnie James Dio around wherever he went. It's a classy sleeve for a band used to classy sleeves, and yet something about this illustration feels a little bit too commercial, in tandem with the bright, immediate songs on the record. Still, it's a brilliant concept, a mischievous poke at society that any young metalhead could appreciate, and an image primed for T-shirts. It was indeed revived twenty years later, when the Ronnie version of the band would reform under the name Heaven and Hell. "That's Lynn Curlee," says Sabbath manager at the time, Sandy Pearlman, "the guy who painted the cover for *Agents of Fortune*. I didn't actually discover him. My wife is an artist, and she was exhibiting at an art museum in Southampton, and he was exhibiting there, so I came in to see her exhibit because it was all set up, and she says, 'You've got to look at this guy's paintings—they're just amazing.' And they *were* amazing; it was 1976 that I got his number and hired him immediately to do the cover for *Agents of Fortune*. And when I took over

Sabbath, I said, 'You know, there's an artist who I think can really nail what you're doing.' And this painting, as I recall, existed already, and they just bought it. I could be wrong, but I think that this was off the shelf. But the Cult has been very lucky in its cover art, so I transferred that off to Black Sabbath, kind of in exchange for getting Martin Birch to produce for Blue Öyster Cult, and you know, Martin did a great job on *Fire of Unknown Origin*." Commented Ronnie James Dio (in an interview with me, years before his death from cancer in May of 2010): "I'd like to get the original painting that was used for that—that's the one I love. In fact, I did try to buy it, but it wasn't for sale. But I thought that was absolutely magnificent, one of the best pieces of art I've ever seen. To me, it referred so much to the title, *Heaven and Hell*, and to the song I wrote for that. I would assume it would be at Warner Bros., because that's where it was bought, and I'm sure that's where it stayed. They weren't about to give it up. I think we all tried to get it. I know Geezer tried to get it, but likely they said no to him as well."

IRON MAIDEN IRON MAIDEN

EMI, APRIL 1980
FRONT COVER ILLUSTRATION BY DEREK RIGGS
ARTWORK BY CREAM

The power of the first Maiden wrapper derives from the idea that, looking at it, you had no doubt that what you'd be getting inside would be nothing but heavy metal. No apologies—in fact, pride in that. This was the underlying emotional magic and excitement of the NWOBHM, that there would no longer be dancing around the issue, no shyness at shock or speed or fantasy lyrics or the casting out of ballads—unless, of course, they were about death and dying. I've interviewed many a heavy metal star who felt exactly the way I did when I first lifted this from the import bins: assured that this would be $8.98 that would not go to waste (domestic issues were $6.98 and $7.98). Once having played it, I understood the coded affirmative message that somebody was making music directly for me, the new breed of metal fan, and that somebody

wasn't making records containing a high percentage of heavy music with no deliberation or awareness of how it got there or, for example, what was special about the fast songs over the boogie ones. "The cover that was the first Iron Maiden album, that was already finished," recalls the legendary creator of Eddie, Derek Riggs. "I had done that a year and a half previous to Maiden forming, basically. They had only been together about six or eight months, and I had that picture in my portfolio for about a year and a half. And I did it for various reasons. Anyway, I had an agent at the time—they were supposed to be a good agent, although I never got any work out of them—and they kept it for a few weeks, then gave it back to me and said, 'Look, we don't think this is very commercial.' So I went off and sold it for about twenty years."

BLUE ÖYSTER CULT CULTÖSAURUS ERECTUS

COLUMBIA, JUNE 1980
COVER DESIGN: PAULA SCHER
FRONT COVER PAINTING: RICHARD CLIFTON-DEY
BACK COVER PHOTOS AND INNER SLEEVE PHOTOS: COURTESY OF THE AMERICAN MUSEUM OF NATURAL HISTORY

BÖC was set back on its heels after the commercial failure of its *Mirrors* album, yet, bravely, the band soldiered on in a heavier direction, working with producer Martin Birch and then wrapping this dark collection of nonsingles with a sleeve featuring an anachronism of a monster that clearly couldn't make it up the evolutionary ladder—not the message you would want to send to your record company. The illustration is a preexisting, quite famous Richard Clifton-Dey painting

called *Behemoth's World*, but tradition is maintained, through the band's Kronos logo appearing in its smallest guise yet, roughly added to the fuselage of the retrorocket sent for unmanned observation of this massively improbable feature-creature. Flip over the cover, and inside joke and archaeology collide through references to Stalk-Forrest, Diz-Bustology, Professor Victor Von Pearlman, Stony Brook, the Underbelly Institute, Oaxaca, and the Horn-Swooped Bungo Pony.

TYGERS OF PAN TANG WILD CAT

MCA, AUGUST 1980
DESIGN AND ARTWORK: CREAM
PICTURES: PETE VERNON

There were all sorts of exciting records spilling into the import bins during the magical NWOBHM, but none visually captured the frenzy so much as the debut from the Tygers. The crowning point of the movement was that it was indeed a movement, an army, a patriotic flank for metal, and the bold visual of a tiger head shot was our version of the python on *Killer* or, er, both a cobra and a panther, as proposed by Southern hard rockers Blackfoot. Like Iron Maiden's Eddie (another strong contender for explosive image of the day), the Tygers' bloody-fanged tiger gave notice that the music inside would not disappoint, that it couldn't be anything but heavy. "Well, it was just very strong," muses vocalist Jess Cox. "We were shown a few pictures, paintings, from a company called Cream, and that just jumped out—it was just a phenomenally powerful

image. It's an instantly recognizable image, and I still see patches and things of it now." Adds guitarist Robb Weir: "The first album cover is, for me, quite ground-breaking, really, inasmuch as it says what it does on the tin. The band's called Tygers of Pan Tang—it's a snarling tiger's head, very colorful—and the album is called *Wild Cat*, and that's what this creature is on the front; it's a wild cat. It's going to jump out and rip your head off, hopefully while you're busy listening to the music." Enhancing the expertly brushed feline is a regal deep-blue backdrop and the iconic Japanese-style Tygers logo font, which alone gives a clue as to the allegiance of this band with the NWOBHM, considering the amusing number of rising-sun T-shirts British rockers would be wearing over the brief four-year run of this inspiring metal age.

THE MICHAEL SCHENKER GROUP THE MICHAEL SCHENKER GROUP

CHRYSALIS, AUGUST 1980
ART DIRECTION: PETER WAGG
COVER DESIGN: HIPGNOSIS
PHOTOGRAPHY: HIPGNOSIS/ROB BRIMSON
COLOR PRINTS: MAINTIDE

I'm not sure whether the concept of Herr Michael being examined for brain-wave activity (and more, but that's undoubtedly what first comes to mind for any of his fans) is a demonstration that Schenker was able to laugh at himself and his reputation for being mentally unhinged. In any event, one sensed that kind of maturity as portrayed in this sleeve. It's cool that his hot nurse has brought along a fruity cocktail to calm him for his examination, a test that indeed has something to do with his guitar playing, if the scene played out on the back cover is to be trusted.

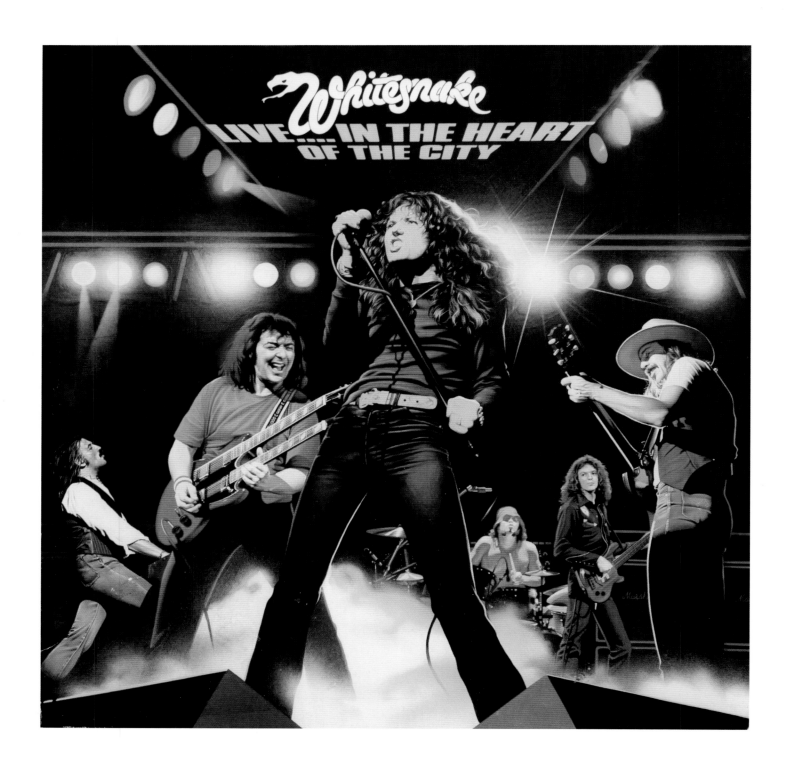

WHITESNAKE LIVE . . . . IN THE HEART OF THE CITY

UNITED ARTISTS, NOVEMBER 1980
COVER PAINTING: JEFF CUMMINS
DESIGN: SHOOT THAT TIGER!
ART DIRECTION: JOHN PASCHE

A bluntly obvious Whitesnake choice might be the lascivious and shocking *Lovehunter* wrapper from the previous year, but there's something heroic and personable about this one that struck more at an emotional level, subtly kicking the band up a notch. The composition evokes Judas Priest's *Unleashed in the East*, or even *Alive!* from Kiss, but the idea of going with

realistic illustration makes the band seem somehow more important—you know, worthy of portraiture. Unfortunately, like live albums from the familial Purple and from Rainbow, the sum total of the music inside didn't rock out nearly as hard as do the guys on the front (Bernie Marsden even going so far as to unleash upon us a piercing solo from a double-neck).

PAT TRAVERS BAND CRASH AND BURN

POLYDOR, 1980
COVER ART: MARK PATERNOSTRO
ART DIRECTION AND DESIGN: BOB HEIMALL (AGI)
PHOTOS: STEVE JOESTER AND BILL CRUMP

Crash and Burn was perhaps no better a sleeve than its two "sunny-era" predecessors, *Heat in the Street* and *Live! Go for What You Know*, but it was the last, and it was positively feverish. What we see is the curvature of the earth, smoky hot, or perhaps the sun smoldering—the perfect image for Pat's recent run of sun-dappled stadium rock, red-hot and funky. The band's goofy,

intrinsically '70s logo further cranks up the thermometer, as does the yellow title text. Proceed to the back, and it's a reinforcement of the celebrated live-album vibe all over again, indoctrinating one to the fact that you pretty much couldn't picture this band playing anything other than outdoor festivals fried by sunburn.

NAZARETH MALICE IN WONDERLAND

A&M, 1980
ALBUM DESIGN: AMY NAGASAWA
FRONT AND BACK COVER PHOTOS: BERNARD FAUCON

A sleeve that Hipgnosis or the Blue Öyster Cult would have been proud to have had in its portfolio, I'm sure, *Malice in Wonderland* features a bunch of eerily robotic, doll-like, and frankly Aryan-looking children of privilege loaded on fine booze and not much food, spinning records and burning down the hillside. It's certainly another one of those situations where a sleeve is inextricably linked with the music inside; here Nazareth shifts upscale, toward Pink Floyd graphically, ditching

the warriors and monsters as well as their hard-rocking logo, and then doing pretty much the same sonically, polishing their sound with Jeff "Skunk" Baxter producing. "I have no idea where that image came from," comments Pete Agnew. "That's really kind of a freaky cover, isn't it? Gives me goose bumps, having all these mannequins. And it's mainly really, really young people. Kind of creepy—I was never very relaxed with that one."

RUSS BALLARD BARNET DOGS

EPIC, 1980
GRAPHICS: ANGLOGRAPHIC
ILLUSTRATION: BARNEY ALDRIDGE

Ex-Argent guitarist and all-around Roy Orbison look-alike Russ Ballard wasn't committed to rocking out on the main, but *Barnet Dogs* is pretty electric and up-racket, as is its nasty and brutish sleeve, which feels like a sequel to Nazareth's *Hair of the Dog* with a little *No Mean City* mixed in for atmospherics. Violent typeface supports the imagery, which also carries the vibe of trouble at the venue, which actually looks like it's been torched.

QUARTZ STAND UP AND FIGHT

MCA, 1980
DESIGN, ILLUSTRATION, AND 15-MINUTE DAGGER BY CREAM

Hard to separate my passion for this cover from the fact (!) that *Stand Up and Fight* is the finest NWOBHM album of all time. Okay, while yer gasping at that, bask in the mighty, stark, and direct Viking imagery at hand—and reflect that, as illustrated through the sleeve of the first Maiden album, or the first coupla from Saxon, the headbanging draw of the NWOBHM was the idea that these bands were the first who were proud to be metal, and sent those signals through their coded cover arts.

Also cool about the Quartz jacket is that it ratcheted up, subconsciously, the class level of a band that, in photos, came off as dated, pub-rocking, definitely not mighty, and not even all that metal. Simply put, Mike, Malc, Mick, and Dek did not look like this Viking vanquisher about to clock his victim, no doubt with a hearty "Death to false metal!" followed by a drinking horn frothed with mead.

GAMMA 2

ELEKTRA, 1980
PACKAGE DESIGN AND ART DIRECTION: MICK HAGGERTY
COVER PHOTOGRAPHY: MICK HAGGERTY AND JEFFREY SCALES

This smart and sassy Hipgnosis-like sleeve by Mick Haggerty won *Playboy* magazine's album cover of the year award, and it's no wonder, given the thoroughly righteous image of some sharks slicing their way through someone's backyard (the operative word being *slicing*) and a garden hose that becomes (improbably) severed as the two beasts make their way toward what is identifiable as a man entangled with a woman on a chaise longue. In addition, the big band logo at the top is a consistent carryover from the debut, as is the album title, the first one being called *1*. The back of the sleeve continues the motif, with the cardboard being ripped open to reveal the locations of the tracks on the first-rate classic hard rock album enclosed. "For the addition of the man's hand," explains Haggerty, "we have the Rolling Stones to thank, and their depiction of a woman chained to a billboard on Sunset to promote their album *Black and Blue*. The predictable furor of women's groups and their threats of boycotts, while music to Jagger's

ears, scared the less-than-brave hearts at Elektra, who originally insisted that there be a man *and* a woman both lying on the chaise, which would have looked incredibly stupid. Last-minute negotiations persuaded them to agree to the hand, and to Ronnie's dismay, I added the cigarette to at least give it a little post-coital edge. I'm glad that the animal rights folks were not protesting that week. or I might have had to change the sharks into moles. Working for Ronnie was an artist's dream. For all three Gamma covers, the phone would ring, and Ronnie would just give me dates. Then a few weeks later, I would present him with my best shot; he loved them all, and just pushed them through Elektra. Remember, this was years before marketing departments had any say in imagery, and we were free to invent visuals that attempted to be challenging and incongruous and to not just pander to market stereotypes. I'm proud of all of these packages."

APRIL WINE

THE NATURE OF THE BEAST

APRIL WINE THE NATURE OF THE BEAST

AQUARIUS/CAPITOL/EMI, JANUARY 1981
DESIGN AND CONCEPT: BOB LEMM PROMOTIVATIONS
COVER PHOTOS: ANDRZEJ DUVEL
COORDINATION: VIRGINIA DUVEL
TONAL SEPARATIONS: MOE DINH

There have been mostly goofy sleeves for this Cana-dian act of many styles over its forty-year history, but, sweetly, commercial success, heaviness, and rockin' visuals coincide and collide right here on *The Nature of the Beast*. At the top, we get the most popular ver-sion of any sort of April Wine logo, somewhat Fastway-like, actually. Then, in matching fiery reds and blacks, we're hit with a blurry image of a guitarist, artfully,

convincingly, with a tiger head. Sadly for the metallur-gists, Myles Goodwyn and crew rocked somewhat acci-dentally, and the records tended to get progressively poppier from here on in. The lesson? Rock out, show it on your sleeve, and your public will respond. *The Nature of the Beast* hatched a handful of minor hits, but, more important, it launched the band's two heaviest songs ever, namely, "Future Tense" and "Crash and Burn."

IRON MAIDEN KILLERS

EMI, FEBRUARY 1981
FRONT COVER ILLUSTRATION: DEREK RIGGS

In philosophical alignment with the album's bolder, sharper, more purposeful music, the *Killers* cover leered and sneered beyond Maiden's frantic and youthful debut through the image of an Eddie who looks less the malnourished victim and more the embodiment of revenge—the revenge of rock over punk, perhaps, a viewpoint that would make Steve Harris chuckle, to be sure. Explains Derek Riggs: "I had the idea for the *Killers* cover, and I mentioned it to [lighting designer] Dave 'Lights' [Beasley], and he had run off and talked to [manager] Rod [Smallwood] about it, who had said they were doing another album and they wanted to use Eddie again because he was quite popular. So I just went ahead and painted it. The band didn't take much notice at all. Occasionally, when they came across the paintings, they would go, 'Oh, that's cool,' and they just went off. Those streets are where I used to live in London. It's not exactly the block of flats I used to live in, but it's close enough. That would have been my flat with my cat in the window. But I didn't have a black one. I had a tortoiseshell and a white tabby, and the tortoiseshell was called Cat Black the Wizard's Hat, and the tabby was called Magus Matter, Guru Master of the Universe. The building is not quite right, either, because where I lived, the one in the end only had two layers. It was a funny block of flats, but great, actually. It was in Finchley in North London, and it was an old decrepit block of flats, desperately in need of repair. And it was set back off the road in a gap, so nobody could ever find it because there were trees growing up all the way around. There were houses here, houses here, houses there, there was a road that went like that, and the block of flats was in the middle, trees all the way around it, so you couldn't see it from the road. There was just one long driveway that went in, and one long driveway that went out the back that nobody ever used. And all the trees had grown up and the grass had gone completely apeshit because nobody had ever tended it. It had a caretaker, and he was fighting a losing battle, I think. They had what turned out to be allotments in the back, which had gone completely wild. And somebody had built a swing in a tree. So it was like living in the countryside in the middle of London; it was great. Except the roof used to leak all the time. I used to put pots and pans of different sizes and you could play tunes. The woman upstairs, she had a hole in her roof, apparently. And snow used to settle on her floor, and it used to melt and drip through the ceiling. So winter, I would have quite a wet kitchen. I kept the kinky sex shop and the Letraset. That's actually a joke. Rub-on letters—that crap people use—they got them from a company called Letraset, Letraset instant lettering, so I just took the logo off and used that. They blew this cover up in Virgin Records in London, about twelve foot square, and they stuck it in their window. They got some guys who projected it onto wood, and he painted it, and it was bloody fierce, actually, quite awesome. You would walk down the street, and you had this twelve-foot Eddie looking at you, which was like, 'Whoa.'"

KROKUS HARDWARE

ARIOLA, MARCH 1981
LOGO BY BEAT KELLER

Swiss boogie metallers Krokus did a fine job of brand identification through the stamping of most of their records with a mighty logo that serves as a precursor to Metallica's and many other pointy and bannerish embellishments. Also stamped here is the title of the album, *Hardware*, in a manly font, hovering above a forged-in-fire shot of metal being made. All that's missing is Anvil's anvil, and—ahem—music that lives up to the hot sparks and molten steel. Krokus still sounds like a wobbly AC/DC at this early point in their happy-go-heavy career. Cool covers as well are *Metal Rendez-vous* and *Headhunter*, but it's *Hardware* that really . . . er, as I say, oversells the band.

TYGERS OF PAN TANG SPELLBOUND

MCA, APRIL 1981
SLEEVE CONCEPT AND DESIGN: TYGERS OF PAN TANG
FRONT COVER ARTWORK: NOEL JOHNSON
PHOTOGRAPHS: RIK WALTON
BUNGED TOGETHER BY CREAM

Tacitly demonstrating the shift from the punky vocals and the attendant musical scrub of the band's feisty debut, the Tygers suggest for us a new class, this Roger Dean–like sleeve arriving in time to represent the band's upscale vocalist, Jon Deverill. As well, the boys had made the shift to a major label, so it seemed reasonable that everything should become a bit rich, including the guitar riffs, now the domain of soon-to-be superstar John Sykes. "The second cover we got

up in the Northeast," recalls Robb Weir. "I think we ran some kind of competition, and that was one of the entrants that was sent in, if my dodgy memory serves me, and then everyone quite liked it." The deep blue of the debut gives way to a muted blue, and if not for the presence of a tiger, as laid-back as he is, the *Spellbound* sleeve would have been suitable for use on a progressive rock album.

BLUE ÖYSTER CULT FIRE OF UNKNOWN ORIGIN

COLUMBIA, JUNE 1981
SLEEVE DESIGN: PAULA SCHER
FRONT AND BACK COVER ARTWORK: GREG SCOTT

Meticulous and mystically minded illustration genius Greg Scott turns in one of his finest here, cooking up for the boys, finally, an actual "blue oyster cult," an army of vaguely lizard-like beings possibly on their way home after a BÖC concert, but probably not. Color, composition, and depth create a symphony for the senses, within an image that efficiently sends the marketable message that this is a mysterious and complex band and that smartly balances science fiction, fantasy, conspiracy theory, and ritual under the umbrella of a cool night sky.

HAWKWIND SONIC ATTACK

ACTIVE/RCA, OCTOBER 1981
ART DIRECTION: ANDREW CHRISTIAN
ILLUSTRATION: JIM MOUNTJOY

Look, we saw this with Budgie, another Active/RCA act—this idea of an old hard rock bird band sharpening their graphics and their sound to complete with the bedheaded NWOBHM crowd. Ergo, there goes Hawkwind with an electrified logo (tapped from Budgie's *Power Supply*?) supporting a mystical winged contraption that is equal parts Van Halen, Aerosmith, and Egypt.

The title smacks hard as well, with epicness added by the whole thing taking place way up in the clear blue sky. Netting out the dubious pontification, this cover frankly suckered me into buying *Sonic Attack*, because I thought it was going to be way heavier and NWOBHM than it actually is, no matter how valiantly it tries.

RUSH EXIT . . . STAGE LEFT

MERCURY, OCTOBER 1981
ART DIRECTION, GRAPHICS, AND COVER CONCEPT: HUGH SYME
PHOTOGRAPHY: DEBORAH SAMUEL

What Sabbath does through illustration on *Live Evil*, Rush manages through photography, namely, the idea of referencing past work within the design for a live record. Sabbath was about the songs on the album; Rush draws upon images from the album covers, namely, the model from *Permanent Waves*, the formally dressed *Hemispheres* guy (previously an illustration), and the owl from *Fly by Night* (ditto). On the wraparound back cover is the naked *Hemispheres* man, the *Farewell to Kings* king, and the *Moving* *Pictures* movers, moving a picture of the *Caress of Steel* cover; behind them, a *2112* logo. Finally, in the bottom right corner is a stamped logo making use of the type from the debut album. The back's a jumble, but even without the backstory, the front actually makes for a very nice sleeve. The tricolor type picks up on elements in the photo; the red alludes to my favorite portion of the piece: the old baseball-style rock T-shirts worn by the band's jolly-looking security.

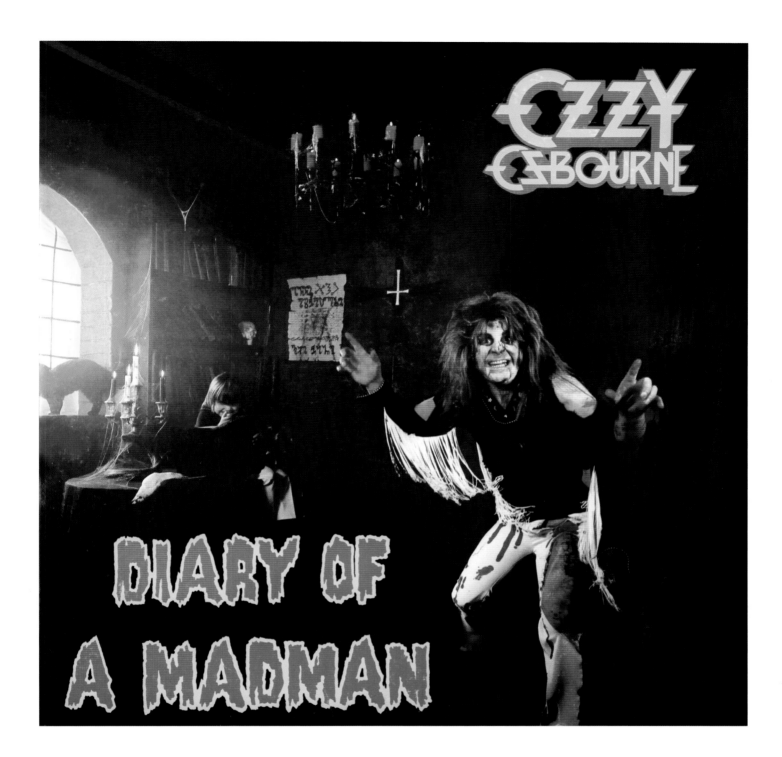

OZZY OSBOURNE DIARY OF A MADMAN

JET, NOVEMBER 1981
DESIGN: STEVE "SKULL" JOULE
SET: ERNIE SPRUCES/DENISE RICHARDSON
PHOTOGRAPHY: FIN COSTELLO AND TONY HARRISON
MAKEUP: CHERYL HUBBARD

Okay, not the most upscale sleeve, but there's something amusingly demented about the *Diary of a Madman* cover that captures perfectly Ozzy's dizzying rise to the top; much of it is based on musicianship and dynamic songs, but much of it also centered around the drinking and drugging and showmanship and urge to please of the shredded, incredulous figure doing . . . what? Signaling a touchdown? No, he's just going, 'Boo!' and rather pleased with himself for not flubbing the line. Anyway, the hastily assembled scene of garish horrors is mercifully drowned out by the blaring-car-horn type—a welcome distraction as we put on the record and discover that the music inside is no joke whatsoever.

THIN LIZZY RENEGADE

VERTIGO/WARNER BROS., NOVEMBER 1981
PHOTOGRAPHY AND DESIGN: GRAHAM HUGHES
TYPOGRAPHICAL DESIGN: GARY WARREN

Flags have always stirred the metalhead's blood, all the way back to the days of Blue Öyster Cult and perennially through Bruce Dickinson's waving for Maiden. Here, Thin Lizzy plants one—actually, turn to the back and it's four, one for each member—reasserting the band's reputation as regal, aristocratic, above the fray, thoughtful, and literary with its hard rock. Not much of a splurge, but a splurge nonetheless, in Vertigo's choice of metallic gold ink for type on the front and back, making the band name and album title proudly prominent and equal. Anyway, why this sleeve succeeds is the support it gives the music; this is the band's classiest visual tied inexorably to the band's plushest, most poignant collection of songs.

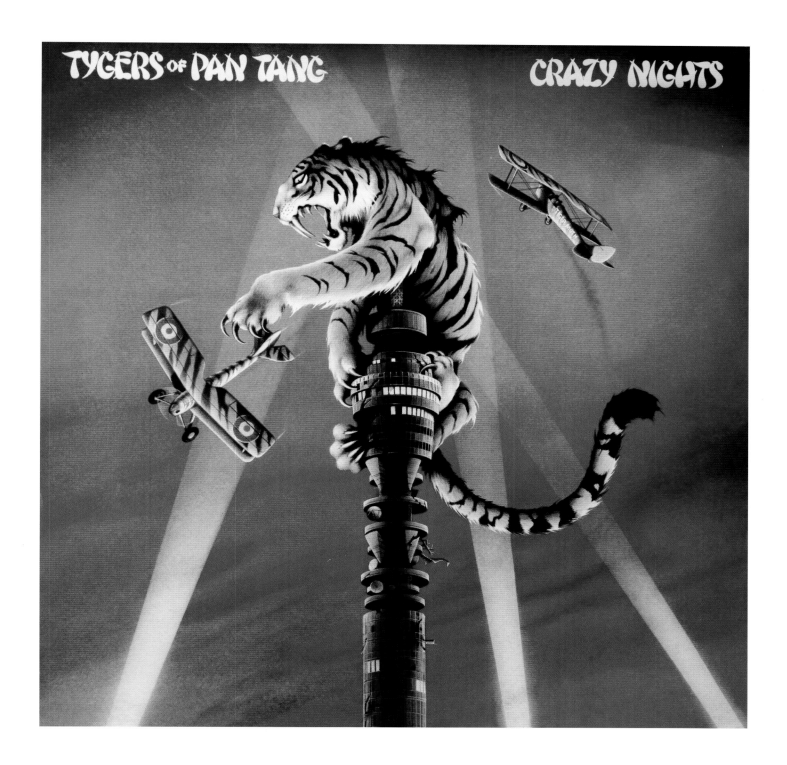

TYGERS OF PAN TANG CRAZY NIGHTS

MCA, NOVEMBER 1981
SLEEVE DESIGN, ARTWORK, AND LAYOUT: RODNEY MATTHEWS
PHOTOS BY RIK WALTON

This into-the-red production values for the Tygers' third album is underscored by the new heat applied to their sleeves. *Crazy Nights* would be the last—and arguably the best—of the Tygers' sleeves, three in a row now being illustrations incorporating a wild cat. "*Crazy Nights* is one of my favorite pieces of artwork, really, and I wish I had the original painting," reflects guitarist Robb Weir. "That was done by Rodney Matthews, the

guy who did a lot of the Magnum art as well. All he was told was, 'The band's called Tygers of Pan Tang, the album's called *Crazy Nights*—what do you think?' And he came up with this fantastic parody of King Kong, but obviously instead of a great big ape, it's a great big saber-toothed tiger at the top of the post office tower in London, fighting off Tiger Moths. It's just awesome, really a fantastic piece of artwork. I love it."

BUDGIE NIGHTFLIGHT

RCA, 1981
SLEEVE DESIGN: ANDREW CHRISTIAN AND A.D. DESIGN
ILLUSTRATION: DEREK RIGGS

The significance of this one, other than the fact that it's a flashy bit of metal illustration, is that it's an early and rare non–Iron Maiden picture from Derek Riggs, the creator of Eddie and all the early Maiden sleeves. *Nightflight* finds Derek carrying on the band's tradition of sticking its absurd budgie namesake into weird situations; this time our embattled bird scopes out the grounds surrounding a pyramid-type structure, no

doubt looking for like-minded refugees from Hawkwind and Eloy album covers. As teenagers, we'd stifle a bit of a snicker at this pilot's phallic firearm, but other than that, there weren't many laughs, for this convincingly heavy metal-looking cover unfortunately wrapped a Budgie album that was surprisingly bereft of kerranging power chords.

MAGNUM CHASE THE DRAGON

JET, MARCH 1982
SLEEVE DESIGN AND ARTWORK: RODNEY MATTHEWS

Magnum wasn't so much heavy metal or even hard rock, but was at the hardish end of neo-prog and was actually one of the links between Rush on its way to Queensrÿche and Fates Warning, not to mention fellow Brits Marillion. The deft skills of Rodney Matthews helped magnify their mystery, though, aiding prospective fans down a path away from the churlish AOR material and toward the fantasy stuff, the songs that had folks thinking that guitarist Tony Clarkin—writer of everything—was as wise as a wizard. As well, with NWOBHM going strong, association with the distinctive Matthews and his spiky fantasy realm made commercial sense, given his work with Praying Mantis, Bitches Sin, and Diamond Head.

SCORPIONS BLACKOUT

EMI/MERCURY, MARCH 1982
COVER DESIGN AND ARTWORK: GOTTFRIED HELNWEIN

A killer sleeve—all metalheads love it, as they do the album. The extra layer to do with its krautrockish cover is that, even though it's a self-portrait by stratospheric Austrian conceptualist Gottfried Helnwein, it in fact looks very much like Scorps guitarist and ersatz leader Rudolf Schenker, one supposes proposing what it's like to rock out to one of the band's more manic panics, perhaps, say, "Virgin Killer" or "Dark Lady." Shocking, direct, and freshly sky blue for you.

SCORPIONS BLACKOUT

SRM-1-4039

THE RODS WILD DOGS

ARISTA, APRIL 1982
ART DIRECTION: MAUDE GILMAN
COVER ART: LES EDWARDS, YOUNG ARTISTS

I'm sure the Rods' three-headed dog would make a mess of the two-headed toddler of Van Halen's *Balance*, but that's a battle for a parallel time and space we'll never experience. In any event, scrappy upstate New Yorkers the Rods, unfortunately, rarely got graphics this violently metallic, the hapless heavyweights usually winding up with presentations too aligned with their no-future blue-collar metal. Fact is, I'd bet that this red, raw, and rabid wrapper is 10 percent or 15 percent of the reason most Rods watchers consider *Wild Dogs* the band's best album. Punk-rock type adds to the mauling, plus the tidy parallel between the canine Hydra and the fact that the band is a power trio.

BLUE ÖYSTER CULT EXTRATERRESTRIAL LIVE

COLUMBIA, APRIL 1982
COVER AND INSIDE ILLUSTRATIONS: GREG SCOTT

Man, even the way the text is presented, including the "BÖC," which picks up on the way the band name was configured in their last (hit!) album—very cool. And this, in fact, is the style Greg Scott moved into as he transitioned into a major gallery artist (i.e., meticulous monochromatic drawing). But back to the sleeve: *Extraterrestrial Live* is a narrative continuation of the *Fire of Unknown Origin* cover. Fascism, spaceships, road cases—it all swirls and whirls out the other end of the mind that is manager Sandy Pearlman, human

computer at the heart of the narrative Ö'cult that, in fact, was born well before the first album, thence woven through songs on every album forward. It is more than fortuitous that Sandy found Greg, for within a trio of albums there, Pearlman (and those interested within the band) could actually peer into snapshots of this verdant alternative reality, one that was hitherto text-based and, for some plotlines, only existing in Pearlman's head.

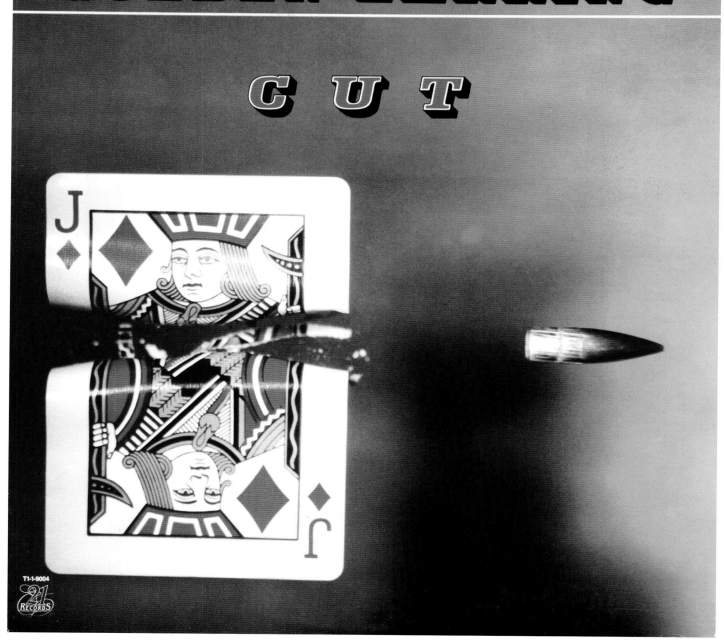

GOLDEN EARRING CUT

CAPITOL/21/MERCURY, AUGUST 1982
PHOTOGRAPHY (FRONT): HAROLD G. EDGERTON
LETTERING: KOOS O

And yes, doing the math, these Dutchmen could be fairly hard-rocking quite regularly. In any event, *Cut* features the band's second and last hit in "Twilight Zone," and it also features a cool image of a bullet slicing through a jack of diamonds—an amusing twist on the title and likely a challenge to (ahem) execute, given that the card is impacted at its edge. In the video for "Twilight Zone," this idea was reproduced, representing the killing of the spy figure, with the bullet cutting through the card a shade lower down. Six years later, the BulletBoys, on the sleeve for their self-titled debut, reprised the idea, also with photographer Harold Edgerton, using the same blue background, same type of bullet, but a different victim: an apple.

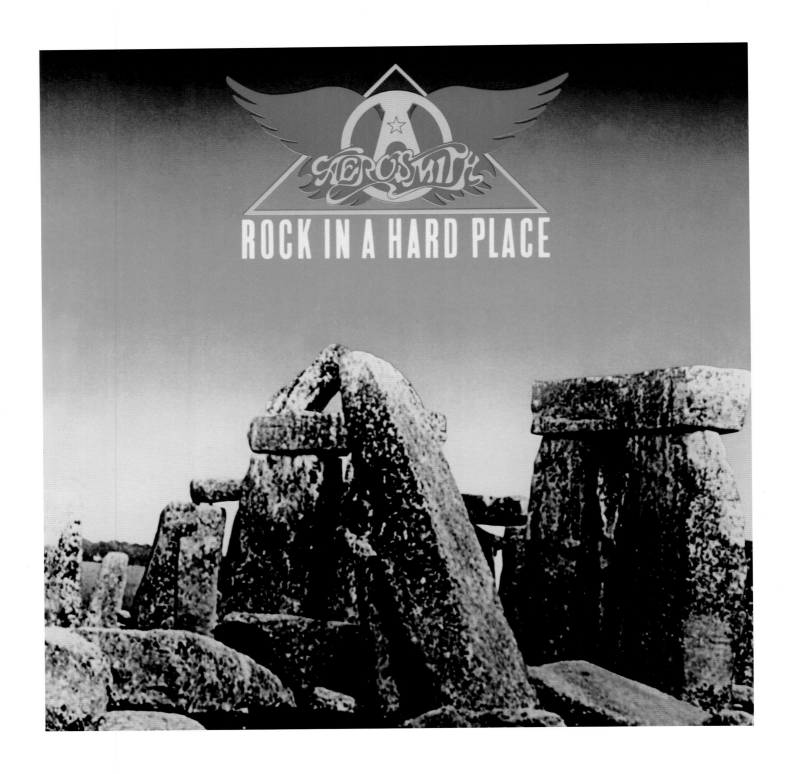

AEROSMITH ROCK IN A HARD PLACE

COLUMBIA, AUGUST 1982
PHOTOGRAPHY AND VISUAL DIRECTION: GERARD ROZHEK

Draw the Line and *Night in the Ruts* were both black-and-white and frankly a little standoffish, and in between, *Live Bootleg* was just horrible. And so the appeal of the *Rock in a Hard Place* sleeve is that it invites the fan back to the fold, proposing a T-shirt–ready image, one that is immediately discernible, understandable, likable enough, and even offering a little chuckle. Actually, if you think about it, this is the fourth (and a half?) studio album in a row offering a visual pun. I dunno—the subconscious vibe of the thing is that Aerosmith was okay with being considered part of the metal community.

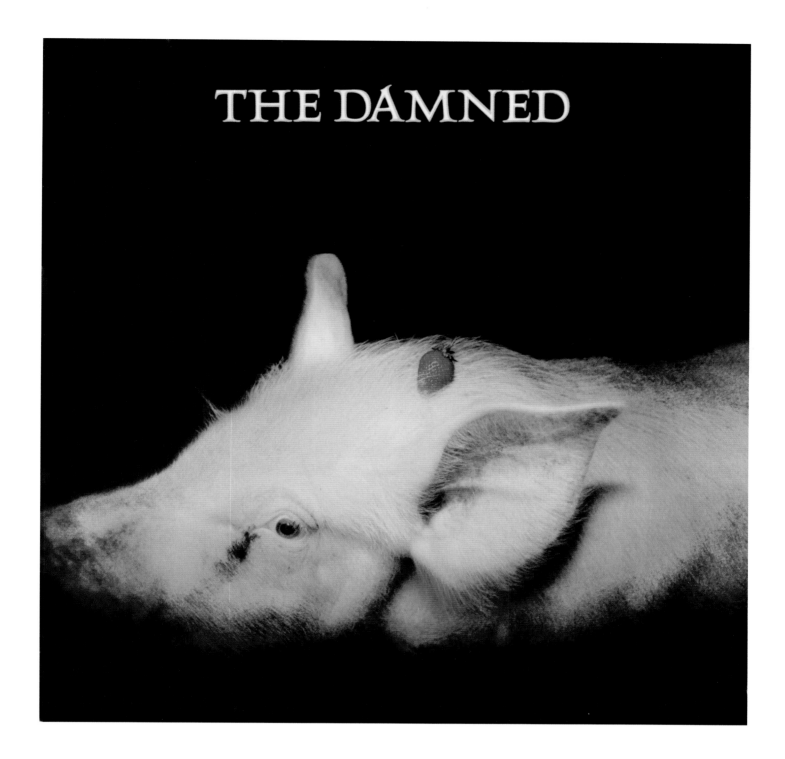

THE DAMNED STRAWBERRIES

BRONZE, OCTOBER 1982
COVER: LINDA ROAST, DAVE VANIAN, AND MARTIN POOLE
PHOTOGRAPHS: NIGEL GREERSON

It's well known that the good Captain Sensible is a vegetarian, which I suppose is why he signed my copy of this record with a speech bubble containing the words "Captain won't eat me." In any event, this stunner of a sleeve, quite amusing given its title, places one strawberry on a piglet's head, and then on the back cover shows the cute porker backed into a corner, surrounded by squashed strawberries. The only text on the front is the band's name—so is the piglet damned? One would certainly think so, given the ominous, shadowy lighting of this iconic photograph. Note: early limited editions featured a strawberry-scented lyric sheet.

VENOM BLACK METAL

NEAT/COMBAT, NOVEMBER 1982
ARTWORK: MAGDA

The *Black Metal* sleeve acted as a refinement to the original: the silver-on-black motif somehow caused intensified unease, as did the dropping of the pentagram for an intimate meeting with the band's leering goat. Just as the album would become the classic statement of the entire Venom catalog, so would this less obvious but altogether more frightening image. Notes drummer and designer Abaddon: "For *Black Metal*, we had a little bit more time and thought put into it, and the demon's face on the front, that came from some other people putting input in, and we kind of developed the Goat of Mendes idea away from the pentagram. It was still a shock—it's kind of like the Motörhead shots of the time. You thought you knew who it was, when you'd go into a record store or merchandise store, and you'd see the big *Black Metal* head, and you know who it is, and then everybody started talking about black metal and, 'What is black metal?' And it came out of a journalist talking to us. I think *Kerrang!* had something like Bon Jovi on the front cover, and he said, 'We don't understand it. We don't understand your music; it's very, very different.' And he said, 'Is Venom a heavy metal band?' And we said, 'No, if this is heavy metal . . . if this is what they think about what heavy metal is, how can we be heavy metal?' And we said, 'We're death metal, thrash metal, speed metal, black metal,' and all these things, they've never been heard of. And he said, 'Wait, wait till I write all this down! What was the last one?'" Flip the sleeve over, and, weirdly, Venom manages to disturb by using a motorcycle as a prop—it's a stretch, but stay with me: I remember my first impression being the tie-in between Satanism and no shame for the pursuit of earthly riches. Adds Abaddon of that shoot: "Yeah,

that was a time when I was interested in photography and in design, this kind of thing, and Cronos had shown that he wanted to do something with this girl-in-a-cave type of look, and this pentagram on the floor. And I said I was going to do something with dogs, so I had the dogs and kind of a castle thing. And I suggested . . . I had a friend who had a Goldwing, so, 'Why don't we do something with a motorbike?' with a big backline, kind of a Judas Priest–type thing. And Mantas is a huge Judas Priest fan, so he took one look, and he said, 'Yeah, that's great.' And although the three photographs are completely different, they all kind of sum up an aspect of Venom. You had the denim-and-leather look with the guitars and the backline and the Judas Priest motorbike. On my photograph, I had my hair across my face so you couldn't see who I was, and that led kind of to the black metal thing, where you can't see people's faces. And also the way Venom was written, where it kind of folds inside itself, a lot of people said, 'You can't read the word *Venom*.' And I said, 'Yeah, but you can tell what the logo is. You can tell that it's Venom's logo by looking at it.' And if you look at black metal bands now, you read the logo, and part of the mystique is that you can't read the logo. It's got a lot more extreme now, but it's taken from that first step, from that first single cover, in fact. So we were kind of putting stuff out there which was . . . I wouldn't say subliminal, but it would be the look of a whole kind of genre—other people took aspects of it and took it to the next logical step." A final note on Venom: the knotwork logo of the band could read as *demon*, a bonus feature that would be revived by Ronnie James Dio for his Dio logo.

Y&T BLACK TIGER

A&M, 1982
ART DIRECTION AND DESIGN: CHUCK BEESON
ILLUSTRATION: JOHN TAYLOR DISMUKES

Expected, but staunchly metal and indicative of the contents, the *Black Tiger* sleeve pairs up nicely with that of the band's next one, *Mean Streak*; both exploded with color, both used the same logo and framed vibe, and, more important, the band got the metal messaging right for the first time. The tiger was a big thing back in the day (think Blackfoot's *Tomcattin'* and the Tygers of Pan Tang's debut, not to mention a Canuck obscurity by the name of Hanover Fist). Y&T gussied theirs up with steely appointments and an intriguingly Japanese color scheme.

BUDGIE DELIVER US FROM EVIL

RCA, 1982
SLEEVE DESIGN: ANDREW CHRISTIAN
FRONT COVER PHOTOGRAPHY: GERED MANKOWITZ
COLORING AND ARTWORK: SHOOT THAT TIGER!

Dispensing with the birds behaving like humans, Budgie chooses for what would become its swan song (until reunion) a stunning image that belied the seriousness of some of the (underrated) songs inside. The swoopy, gloopy Yes-like logo perseveres to the end (gotta dig that!), and it's a quixotic touch to go with sentence-style capitalization for the title. It is said that Budgie leader Burke Shelley's newly born-again Christian status informs this record, and if it does, it's mainly in the sleeve, but delicately so, even Zen-like.

DIAMOND HEAD BORROWED TIME

MCA, 1982
SLEEVE CONCEPT: SEAN HARRIS
SLEEVE COORDINATION AND MECHANICAL ARTWORK: CREAM
ILLUSTRATION BY RODNEY MATTHEWS

Hapless management and a diva of a lead swooner constricted the movement of this band that should have been. The press, in fact, compared it to Led Zeppelin, although this had more to do with potential than boots-on-the-ground evidence. Still, there was a raw magic to Diamond Head, and the palpable yet vague feel of future flourishing is metaphorically foretold through the plush appointment of Rodney Matthews to paint a sumptuous wraparound sleeve of fantasy claptrap, the image vaulting Diamond Head into the ranks of the seriously examined and examinable. A far cry from the band's debut, which came in a plain white sleeve and was sold at gigs, *Borrowed Time* nonetheless musically didn't live up to the exotic stoner landscape-with-storyline that Matthews proposed upon the punters.

QUIET RIOT METAL HEALTH

PASHA/CBS, MARCH 1983
ARTWORK: QUIET RIOT
ART DIRECTION AND DESIGN: JAY VIGON
PHOTOGRAPHY: SAM EMERSON AND RON SOBOL
ILLUSTRATIONS: STAN WATTS

Part Alice Cooper, part Iron Maiden's Eddie, part slasher movie, the *Metal Health* album cover succeeds due to the mascot-ness of the rock-crazed inmate on the cover. Who is he? Is it Kevin DuBrow, the man with the leonine roar and thinning mane? Is it one of a new breed of millions of headbangers, born overseas (as the phrase *bang your head* was), deep within the NWOBHM, and now transplanted to L.A.? What it turned out to be was money in the bank, as *Metal Health* became famously known as the first heavy metal album to hit number one on *Billboard*, eventually selling six million copies worldwide. "I had my art director design the cover," says band producer/Svengali Spencer Proffer. "Kevin and I and Frankie brainstormed, putting a guy in a red leather straitjacket, in a padded room, so he could bang his way out. And we put a hockey mask on him so he wouldn't just be a guy in the band. He would be everybody. He would represent the kids, who I thought—because I was living in L.A., and I saw how active the

metal scene was—I thought that would represent all the kids who wanted to bang their heads. And we took something from the album cover into the video to the audience: that mask. It became a great merchandising piece before a lot of these merchandising ideas came about. So we thought that was pretty cool. In fact, the mask, and the kid who caught the mask in the first video, 'Metal Health (Bang Your Head),' was the kid we used to lie in the bed, and we put that mask behind his bed as a crucifix, because he worshiped the mask, in 'Cum on, Feel the Noize.' We serialized the videos. And a lot of people got that connection. When we finally put out 'Cum on, Feel the Noize' after 'Bang Your Head,' it was taking us to gold album status; it really started to spread." The masked metalhead would be used periodically throughout the band's career but never in such a memorable pose, smartly muted colors, and never with such remarkable results as on this rough and rugged, hair-metal-exploding debut.

KISS LICK IT UP

CASABLANCA/MERCURY, SEPTEMBER 1983
COVER PHOTO AND PHOTOGRAPHY: BERNARD VIDAL
PHOTOGRAPHY: BRUCE DAVIDSON

A cover like this means nothing for anybody other than Kiss, but yeah, it's history in the making, as Kiss unmasks starkly, in regular clothes on a white, brutally neutral background. Heck, even the logo is keyline black on white. And surprise, even Gene looks pretty good, although he has to hide much of his face behind tongue to get there. Vinnie Vincent foreshadows his hard out-falling with the band, showing up for the shoot in distracting pink. Additionally, the cover ekes out a win because the album was a swaggering winner, hauling Kiss back from various types of taint toward surprising (and frankly underreported) status as one of the first big acts of the L.A. hair metal era, the band's inbred New Yorkness notwithstanding.

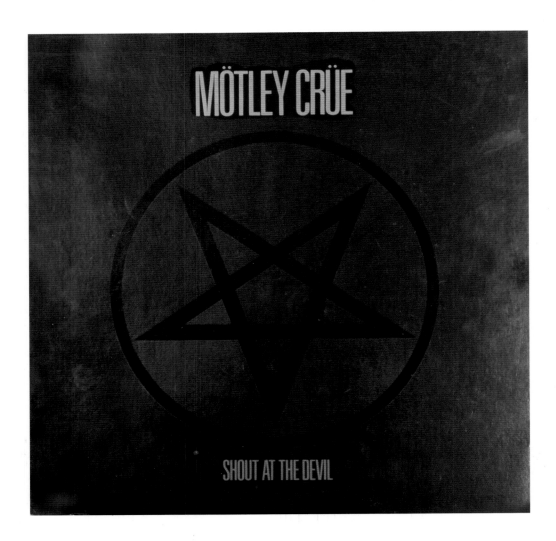

MÖTLEY CRÜE SHOUT AT THE DEVIL

ELEKTRA, SEPTEMBER 1983
COVER DESIGN: BOB DEFRIN
COVER ART CONCEPT, COVER PHOTO, PHOTOGRAPHY: BARRY LEVINE

Trust Nikki Sixx and his Mötleys to capitalize without substance on the whole Satanic-panic craze of the '80s, in which heavy metal played a big part. Sure, there was Venom and Mercyful Fate, who were quite serious about it, but more invasive were Ozzy, Maiden, and the Crüe. Of the three, the rotten-to-the-core Mötley actually vibed most Satanic, and the simplicity and stupidity of the *Shout at the Devil* cover seemed to say it all: "We have nothing here, we're blacker than black, and if you choose to stare into this void and find anything to hang your witch's hat on, well, you'll be damned just like us." "That was Nikki," recalls Mötley Crüe "image consultant" and photographer Barry Levine on the band's haphazard, spontaneous Satanic image. "That's what he felt he was about, and what his audience was, where his music was at. You know, and for Nikki, that was real. That was all Nikki." Sure, it was Nikki, but Nikki turned out to be more image than dogmatically devilish. "When I found Mötley Crüe," continues Levine, "it's funny, they had just come off their first album, *Too Fast for Love*; they were still a glam band in L.A.

that was basically the 'it' band of the moment, okay? Their look was, you know, the glam, ratted hair, the torn T-shirts, the torn jeans, the high boots, just whatever they could put together. They didn't have any money. They hadn't really received national recognition, unless it was to that hard-core glam-rocker type of audience. I just saw, like, a young Kiss, but a Kiss that had more of a punk attitude. But Mötley, basically, was one up on Kiss. They were just a different generation that would try to incorporate theatrics in a punk way, based on no money." Which made its way to the gatefold of *Shout at the Devil*, as well as to the iconic videos from the record, a look that Barry Levine calls "*Road Warrior*—if you look at it carefully, you know, the shoulder pads, Vince's outfit, it was heavily influenced by *Road Warrior*—postapocalyptic." So as it turned out, the cover gave you very little (like *Back in Black* before it and the self-titled *Metallica* much later), and then open it up—bam! There's the Crüe living the Satanic life-style in the scariest way possible: plundering the earth purely for pleasure and personal gain.

THE MICHAEL SCHENKER GROUP

BUILT TO DESTROY

THE MICHAEL SCHENKER GROUP BUILT TO DESTROY

CHRYSALIS, SEPTEMBER 1983
COVER CONCEPT: MICHAEL SCHENKER
ART DIRECTION: JOHN PASCHE
COVER PHOTOS: JOHN SHAW
COVER MODEL: CAROLINE DODD

In the previous record, Michael was foisting his trusty Flying V over a spewing volcano, but now things have turned dark for the troubled genius; Herr Michael throws a tantrum over one of his crazy girlfriends (and there have been some doozies). Sadly, drama and trauma have been constant companions in Michael's life, so a smashed Mercedes seems par for the course. Perhaps the good half bottle of wine these crazy kids have got left will help mellow out the situation.

MERCYFUL FATE MELISSA

ROADRUNNER/MEGAFORCE, OCTOBER 1983
COVER ART: THOMAS HOLM/STUDIO DZYAN

It's hard to separate this chilling image from the fact that the music enclosed was so advanced and professional (and this from an unknown Danish band producing, on a shoestring, their debut album) that even a pagan heathen atheist would swear on a Bible that the hand of Satan was upon the multitrack masters, guiding the recording in exchange for the five souls that compose Mercyful Fate. The witness to the majesty of the *Melissa* album is therefore unsurprised to see such a powerful yet ethereal and elusive portrayal of Satan on the front cover and is racked with the uneasy feeling that this band knows what he looks like and has felt the stare of those hollow red eyes. In other words, the cartoony Satans of infinitely lesser heavy metal album covers, well, those are in fact childish imaginings. The real thing must (and does, according to King Diamond and probably Melissa herself) howl with unspeakable horror, as depicted within this rare firsthand portrait of the devil himself.

BLUE ÖYSTER CULT THE REVÖLUTION BY NIGHT

COLUMBIA, OCTOBER 1983
DESIGN: JOHN BERG
ILLUSTRATION: GREG SCOTT

Scott had actually hoped that the more ambitious and mystical back cover image would have been used for the front, but there's a certain quiet power to the one that's used, given its tie-in with the title and that one of the band's many thematic areas is biker culture, an element addressed on two of this record's songs. As is traditional, there's always a BÖC "Kronos" logo; on this cover, it's on the lower right, next to a subscript

12, representing the fact that *The Revölution by Night* is the band's twelfth album. In any event, a narrative through the Greg Scott sleeves has been maintained (this is his last of three), with the Dobermans on the inner sleeve a carryover from the live album and the robed figure on the live album a carryover from *Fire of Unknown Origin*.

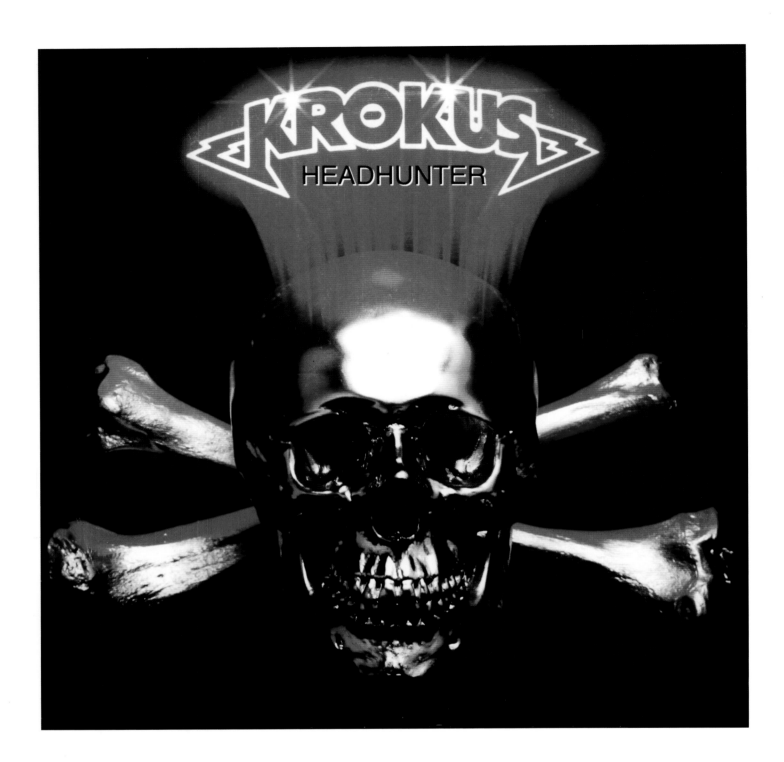

KROKUS HEADHUNTER

ARISTA, NOVEMBER 1983
ART DIRECTION: DONN DAVENPORT AND HOWARD FRITZSON
DESIGN: KROKUS
FRONT COVER PHOTOGRAPHY: STEVE JOESTER
BACK COVER PHOTOGRAPHY: JOHN KROHNE AND TOM BARTLETT

The Swiss boogie metalers of Krokus have always branded themselves well through their cover art, only occasionally straying from the structure of their red banner logo over a simple yet effective T-shirt–ready image. *Headhunter* adhered to this plan. The band went with a mean-looking metallic skull and crossbones to match the increased metal quotient of this particular batch of songs, which were a little more technical and less AC/DC-ish due to inspiration gained when touring with Judas Priest. The cover theme is carried smartly over to the back cover, where each band member is photographed head-on, as half face, half skull.

VANDENBERG HEADING FOR A STORM

ATLANTIC, 1983
COVER DESIGN AND PAINTING BY ADRIAN VANDENBERG

Sure, we stuck the band's third and last record, *Alibi*, in here as well, but hey, we're suckers for melodic, Schenker-like guitarists from Holland who also paint their own album covers. Love the way the band's pointy, chrome-plated logo itself looks like a shark, and also the way the dominant blue sky forces identification with the band's eponymous debut album, itself blue and featuring the same logo. In fact, that record consists of little more than the logo, subconsciously leading one to position *Heading for a Storm* as an improved cut above—added value, as it were. It's certainly a few strata o'er and above anything from that other shark band, Great White, or, for that matter, the other "berg" band, Chris de Burgh.

AXE NEMESIS

ATCO, 1983
ILLUSTRATION: H. D. MICHAEL

Wise doodlers say never paint the text right into the painting, and most of them don't, which makes the commitment to do so both fresh and noble and actually quite artistically pleasing, when you do happen to see it. The rest of this is pretty cool, too, down a goofy metal pathway; Axe brings back the ax-guitar from the previous album cover and gives it to a new guitar tech, an alien dude who could presumably work security for the band as well.

GRIM REAPER SEE YOU IN HELL

EBONY/RCA, 1983
SLEEVE DESIGN: GARRY SHARPE-YOUNG

There's a sense of Maiden magic to this image, the idea that the contents of this wrapper could be nothing but unapologetic heavy metal, and that once the happy customer finds himself headbanging along, the image will only bolster the experience, drawing him into a landscape that will become the subconscious backdrop of every cloak-and-dagger track of thunderclouded doom. "I was paid a camera for the Grim Reaper *See You in Hell* cover," recalls Sharpe-Young, who died in 2010 at the age of forty-five. "In those days, Ebony Records would farm most of their cover art out to me. I had no idea about money back then, so the head of Ebony Records, Darryl Johnston, would say, 'What do you need?' We would work out the cost, and that's what I got! When I started to ask for real fees, the work dried up! Which is why I didn't do the second Grim Reaper cover; I'd started it when the payment issue became a deal-breaker. There's a story with this cover. I was doing three covers for Ebony at the same time, I remember, all on the typically tight last-minute deadline. Darryl phoned late one evening to say, 'I'm sending

a motorbike courier round to get the Grim Reaper cover.' Trouble was, I had only just started it, and I had my girlfriend's birthday party to go to that same night. Ebony insisted it had to be ready, so I spent the early hours of the morning on it, no sleep. The paint was still wet when the courier arrived, and the painting was not finished. I asked the guy to wait for an hour, but he said he'd get the sack! There was supposed to be a whole city in the background—and notice how the reaper's scythe is matchstick-thin? The logo was missing, too. I got one copy of the album—and loved it. The music was always the most important thing for me. Soon after, Grim Reaper scored big in the U.S.A. I remember getting sent all those photos of metal fans with my Grim Reaper artwork tattooed on them. There was even one guy with his whole back tattooed with the *See You in Hell* cover. I sent him a letter back, saying he really ought to get the tattooist to make that scythe handle thicker. Credit to them, when Grim Reaper signed over to RCA, they asked me to do their third album cover, *Rock You to Hell*. Now, *there's* a story."

ACCEPT BALLS TO THE WALL

LARK/PORTRAIT, JANUARY 1984
COVER IDEA: DEAFFY, WITH SPECIAL THANKS TO A. JANOWIAK
DESIGN: JEAN LESSENICH
PHOTOS: DIETER EIKELPOTH

If Rob Halford was first off the mark to infuse gay imagery into heavy metal, Accept soon followed, but with a sass and a wink of the eye fully unintended. In truth, one almost attributes the mixed signals due to a pronounced English-as-a-second-language effect, although, hey, this was photography, not poetry. In any event, the *Balls to the Wall* cover was an exercise in unexpected class for metal so early in the game. Cliché fantasy illustration and the like begone, for here was high-fashion photography with a twist of Berlin in the '20s: an amusing visual quote of a risqué album title (with a walloping metal anthem to match) and then a complete lack of text, reminding one of Zeppelin. "*Balls to the Wall* was called the first gay metal album," says an incredulous Stefan Kaufmann, drummer for Accept at the time, with a laugh. "Then it was about the Berlin Wall, and nobody cared about reading the lyrics. It was actually about minorities, that's it. For example, 'London Leatherboys' was about punks or bikers or whatever, enjoying their life. They're normal people; they just look different and they behave different. But they're normal people, another minority. And 'Love Child' was about gays, true, but it's basically about people who

are suppressed." As for the cover? "We had this guy with his leg. Actually this guy was fiftysomething years old, and he was a boxer, and he had those two wooden balls in his hand. Of course we knew it was going to be controversial, but we never thought about the gay connotations. We were just thinking we'd get in trouble because of *balls*." Adds he of the shriek, lead singer Udo Dirkschneider: "As soon as we had that title, that was it. But the front cover, I had nothing to do with it. It was an idea of the management. And yes, a lot of people were thinking now we were a gay metal band, but it had nothing to do with that." Fueling the fire was an enclosed two-panel poster of the band, arms locked in unity, and, er, naked. "Oh, that was a horrible situation," exclaims Udo. "This picture took nine or ten hours, the whole day to get the lamps in the right position and all that stuff. It was very heavy going." It all adds up to a puzzling idle pastime of fun and games and snickers and pointing—time that can be passed productively, given that the sound track to such chicanery just happens to be one of the greatest heavy metal classics of a very competitive decade. As it turned out, *Balls to the Wall* would be the band's only gold record.

VAN HALEN 1984

WARNER BROS., JANUARY 1984
ART DIRECTORS: PETE ANGELUS, RICHARD SEIREENI, AND DAVID JELLISON
COVER ILLUSTRATION: MARGO ZAFER NAHAS

Van Halen, unfortunately, shot blanks with most of their album covers, but everyone digs this one, and indeed it's hard to separate the sunny atmosphere of songs like "Jump," "Panama," and "Drop Dead Legs" from the sky blue and soft skin of this sleeve. It's also hard not to pair this one up with Black Sabbath's *Heaven and Hell*, on which angels are depicted smoking and playing cards. Comparatively apt however, the Sabbath image is a little heavy and formal, whereas this one's rife with

the boyish mischief of David Lee Roth, even though it's Eddie who is the naughty chain-smoker in the band. Nice touch rendering the *1984*, the official title of the album (see spine and back), as *MCMLXXXIV*, both left and right of the band name, giving the sleeve the look and feel of a magazine cover from the '50s, a sentiment reinforced by both the soft airbrush style Margo uses for the scene and the actual face and hairstyle of the puffing preschooler.

MANOWAR HAIL TO ENGLAND

MUSIC FOR NATIONS, JULY 1984
DESIGN: FRANK CANGELOSI
ILLUSTRATION: KEN LANDGRAF

Oddly, at the time it didn't seem like a big deal, but decades later, as it turns out, Manowar really has its fingerprints all over the invention of Viking metal, epic metal, true metal—whatever you want to call it. *Hail to England* is considered by many to be the band's best album, and it's definitely the band's first good album cover, establishing the Warrior and an over-the-top illustrative image the band would use from here on in: bulging muscles everywhere, wenches looking for a piece of that power base, those into false metal to be vanquished by all men who "play on ten." "We wanted to present the strong image," recalls guitarist Ross the Boss. "We wanted to be bigger than life, kind of like what Kiss did. That's why we went and got Ken Kelly, who did *Fighting the World*, and he's been doing all the covers ever since. But the *Hail to England* cover was done by the Marvel Comics guy, Ken Landgraf. Personally, I love that cover." Adds Ross on the message behind the energetic and conquering image, as well as the album's attendant title: "It was kind of difficult for the band, and with the record company and everything, and so once we put out *Battle Hymns* and *Into Glory Ride*, we were getting an extreme amount of press from England. I mean, they were really, really behind the band. *Kerrang!*, *Sounds*, all the other

magazines, they really liked the band and they were giving us a lot of great press. So we figured, we wanted to go to England and start there, and that's what we did." Expanding on the band's visual influences, Ross says, "*Conan the Barbarian* . . . the first movie didn't come out until '82, so we were actually before that. Also Roman mythology, Norse mythology, comic books, Thor—we kind of figured out that nobody was really doing anything like that. I mean, you had Judas Priest that was leather, denim, studs, and we kind of wanted to be separate from that. So once we started getting our footing, it was definitely sort of sorcery and epic. In fact, the word *epic*, we didn't even think of that—that title was sort of given to us: 'the band that makes epic songs.'" About the emphasizing of this image, confirms artist Ken Landgraf, "Ross the Boss and the bass player, Joey, saw some work I did for Jon Mikl Thor called 'Rock Warrior.' They called me up and came to my studio. We discussed the cover idea, and I made two sketches. I tried to create a brutal yet heroic image of a barbarian warrior that would reflect the heavy metal sound of Manowar; they approved of one of them, and then I drew and colored the cover using watercolor. I gave them the original artwork as a gift."

DIO THE LAST IN LINE

WARNER BROS., JULY 1984
ART DIRECTION: STEVE GERDES
ORIGINAL CONCEPT: RONNIE DIO AND WENDY DIO
ILLUSTRATION: BARRY JACKSON

The band's demon mascot, affectionately known as Murray, is back. Last time around, he was drowning a bespectacled man of the cloth, but now he's being more efficient, lording over a peopled scene of hellish destruction, flashing the horns, although the chains are on, as per the subtitle of "Egypt," the geography of which this scene somewhat resembles. "You've got this devil figure with horns," commented Ronnie James Dio, "and he's supposed to scare everybody, and you could call him Beelzebub, but I thought it was funnier than hell to call him Murray. I had come from Sabbath, and there was that dark presence there. I was supposed to be the Prince of Darkness at some point, not that I was, but that's the perspective people see you from, especially when you're with a band called Black Sabbath. So it made sense to carry on with that image. It wasn't meant to paint me or the band as evil people, any more than the name Black Sabbath was designed to paint them as evil people, which they weren't, and which we aren't. But it made sense to carry on with that theme. It

was a popular theme at that time; it was an acceptable theme, you know, 'They're pretty evil, aren't they!' And we thought it was kind of sensible to carry on with our monster, our guy we call Murray, who on the first album was drowning the priest and, of course, he's the central figure on *The Last in Line* as well. I'm very involved in the cover art process. I think that what is on the cover is going to be representative of how I think. If it's going to be silly and stupid, then I don't want it. I don't want people to think that of me. I have a lot of control in that department. We tried to reflect what the albums were about. That made it seem like the normal progression, as it should have been. It was easy." Illustrator Barry Jackson, who soon moved on to movie work, painted this scene entirely in acrylic after receiving a briefing from Ronnie about having the stricken minions marching toward the Murray figure. Instead, Jackson has them essentially tormented in situ. It should be noted that Jackson is also the deft hand responsible for ZZ Top's *Afterburner* and *Recycler* sleeves.

METALLICA RIDE THE LIGHTNING

MEGAFORCE/ELEKTRA, JULY 1984
COVER CONCEPT: METALLICA
COVER DESIGN: AD ARTISTS

The main triumph of this illustration is the epic power of the band logo at the top of the sleeve, the authoritative encyclopedia-like Metallica name rendered in stainless steel so shiny it glows—or glowers. Come *Master of Puppets*, strings would descend from the logo unto the scene below, and here, lighting does much the same, energizing a floating and empty electric chair. And yes,

leaving the chair empty elevates the class level of this cover; Metallica perhaps understood that sticking some headbanger dude or criminal in the hot seat could only be a losing proposition, distracting from the logo, the electric sky, the empowering "ride the lighting" concept, and the first-rate thrash enclosed.

HANOI ROCKS TWO STEPS FROM THE MOVE

CBS/COLUMBIA, AUGUST 1984
COVER DESIGN, DESIGN, SLEEVE DESIGN: SIMON CANTWELL
PHOTOGRAPHY: HIRO ITO

These ragamuffin Finns are the unsung heroes of the hair metal scene, essentially the influential glam link between New York Dolls and Guns N' Roses, Axl being a notable and vocal fan. The cover bleeds glam drama and decadence, as well as the menacing thuggishness of Sweet, Johnny Thunders, and, yes, Twisted Sister. Bedraggled star Michael Monroe, pretty vacant of stare, betrays the band's hard living through sunken cheeks and a certain self-destructive streak in a devil-may-care attitude toward any disruption his skinny androgyny might cause. "We were just influenced by a lot of people," notes Monroe, "from Little Richard to the Alice Cooper band, and we just thought that part of the rock and roll thing was, being an entertainer, to play live and perform, and it's nice to have something to look at, too, right? So a little extra makeup and something colorful and nice to look at, but still, in our eyes, the music and the attitude were more important than anything else. But on top of that, the look goes

along with it: a little bit of everything. So, first of all, we grew up in the '70s with bands like the Alice Cooper band, Mott the Hoople, Faces, Stones, and maybe that affected us a little bit—obviously, quite a bit. But we were also into '50s rock and roll, and then the punk thing was really influential for us. So we used to wear creepers and teddy boys, the drape jackets, and punky stuff, too, and we mixed everything up. I always wanted to encourage people to be individuals, to be themselves, and with some people, they just look better in a T-shirt and jeans and short haircuts and look ordinary. Not everybody would look cool having a big blond hairdo and tons of eyeliner; nothing suits everybody. So everybody had their own style, and that's cool. Not everybody has to look the same—quite the opposite." Tragically, what should have been the Hanoi rocket to the top turned out to be a full stop after the car-crash death of drummer Razzle, a partying passenger in a car driven by a similarly lit-up Crüe frontman Vince Neil.

MERCYFUL FATE DON'T BREAK THE OATH

ROADRUNNER/COMBAT, SEPTEMBER 1984
COVER ART: THOMAS HOLM/STUDIO DZYAN

Half the fright factor of this cover, scaring the bejesus out of messed-up adolescent punk metalheads, comes from King Diamond's overt, willful, almost lustful brand of Satanism. Here Thomas Holm achieves as much through a conflagration of eerily happy yellow, the flames engulfing a first-rate depiction of Satan, as if fire is the air he breathes. Of course, it adds to the situation when we incorporate the horrific knowledge that King is dead serious. In retrospect, Mercyful Fate's second and last album before he goes solo (and before reunion) black-marks the man and band at the height of their powers.

FASTWAY ALL FIRED UP

CBS/COLUMBIA, 1984
ART DIRECTION: SIMON CANTWELL
COVER DESIGN: JO MIROWSKI, TORCHLIGHT, LONDON
ILLUSTRATION: CHRIS MOORE

It's a long story, but Fastway was supposed to include UFO's Pete Way, making it more of a supergroup than it turned out to be. Still, you had ex-Motörhead guitarist Fast Eddie and Humble Pie drummer Jerry Shirley in the ranks, plus a young unknown with much promise, Dave King, on vocals (now doing quite well with Flogging Molly). The band's second album evoked the commercial and creative promise of the firecrackin' debut by again making use of the band's distinctive retro logo as well as that record's overbearing black-and-white checkerboard motif. Stakes were raised by sticking a violently fire-spitting drag racer in the middle of the scene, a heat-stroked image to support the swell title of the album, which, sadly, was detectably less fired up than the exciting debut from a year previous. Recalls illustrator Chris Moore: "As far as I can remember, the entire band, which I think was some ex-members of Motörhead, came down to my little cottage in Hawkhurst, and they arrived in a really big seven-series BMW about two hours late. There was a knock at the door, and this guy with long hair said, 'Hi, I'm Fast Eddie,' to which I replied, 'You're not that fast 'cause you're two hours late!' It makes a good anecdote. They were really nice, and we chatted about what they wanted. They said that the title was based on a dragster race term for when a dragster car has its tires set alight with fuel to increase grip for the acceleration—they say it's 'all fired up' and ready to go. The theme of the album was drag racing. I think I suggested a few ideas, and one was that we have a close-up of the side of a car to display the title of the album as a decal. I had lots of books on cars, and we pretty much decided there and then what the illustration should be. They didn't stay long, and I slotted the job in later that week and started to produce a few roughs, but we settled on that treatment from the off, really. I did the nice chrome ram tubes for the carbs and the exhausts and even did the tires folding up the way they do; it all made for a nice airbrush treatment. It might have been nice as a gatefold album, so we could have had more of the car on the other half of the sleeve, but that never materialized. I think they were quite pleased with the end result. I did the painting in shellac-based inks, I think, or possibly Liquitex acrylics, which I changed to at around that time. The artwork would have been on Crescent board and probably half up from the finished printed size, that is, eighteen inches by eighteen inches. I have no idea where the actual painting is now. In those days, you were lucky to get a high-profile artwork back from the record company; it usually got nicked. It's probably worth a bit now!"

KICK AXE WELCOME TO THE CLUB

PASHA/CBS, AUGUST 1985
ART DIRECTION AND DESIGN: HUGH SYME
PHOTOGRAPH: DIMO SAFARI

A minor record in the U.S. metal scene but a strong seller back in Canada, Kick Axe's second album came wrapped in a cover that tried to elevate the level of discourse beyond hair metal clichés, much like the restrained and bluesy songs inside. The surreal scene is the effort of Hugh Syme, celebrated for his work with Rush. Says label head Spencer Proffer: "Kick Axe had a lot of dimension and color. I heard some ballsy Pink Floyd elements in Kick Axe, and the Beatles, and Queen, being my favorite bands of all time. Through CBS, who the band was signed to in Canada, I met Hugh Syme,

and Hugh designed that very bizarre cover, in very much the Hipgnosis school of album art, that Pink Floyd look. I just thought he was so visionary, and I ultimately relocated Hugh Syme to Los Angeles. He became the art director for Pasha, until David Geffen hired him away for more money, to be the art director for Geffen. But Hugh is still the finest graphic art designer I know in the music and media world. I mean, he designed some of the biggest covers in the history of the business. I give Hugh a lot of credit; I think he's a genius."

IRON MAIDEN LIVE AFTER DEATH

EMI, OCTOBER 1985
SLEEVE CONCEPT: DEREK RIGGS AND ROD SMALLWOOD
SLEEVE ILLUSTRATION: DEREK "R.I.P" RIGGS
SLEEVE DESIGN: STEVE "KRUSHER" JOULE
SLEEVE PREPARATION: ARTFUL DODGERS

Live after Death features what most fans concur is Derek Riggs's most skilled Eddie painting, the man's often primary-color palette disciplined down to a challenging blue and yellow and remarkably very little in between. Eddie himself looks tough and mean and surging with energy as he snaps chains and moves earth, creating enough friction in the process to cause flame. The iconic Maiden logo is rendered in simple outline yellow. The album title is in yellow as well, framing a powerful scene, one that wraps around to the back, at which space and place Derek gets to crack his wee visual jokes, the favorite being a little scribble of a cat, with halo, guarding a tombstone of the scribbler himself. "The tombstone on the front with the Lovecraft quote, I just put it in," notes Riggs. "They didn't have any say in it. My suggestion for the title of the album was *Let It R.I.P.*, as in 'rest in peace.' But they didn't like that, because it had wit and intelligence. I thought it was quite good, because it's something they never do, 'rest in peace.' Iron Maiden . . . get a life. It's not going to happen, you know? On the back, you've got Live with Pride on one of the tombstones; that was a slogan that was going around for live music or something. They

asked me to put that on there. There were a lot of things against disco and lip-synching in those days. The cat is from way back—that goes right back to *Killers*. Because it was an alleyway, it was an alley cat. So the cat was floating around for years, and I just stuck the halo on him and made him look sinister because, 'What's that all about?' Well, it's not about anything, really; it's just a cat with a halo. I'm good at making things look unusual and sinister. There's this idea I came up with: to get people's attention, you've got to get people to look at something and wonder what it's about. And the best way to make people wonder about something is to do something a little bit weird. It's not there because it's great, deep, and meaningful. Its total reason for being there is to make you go, 'What's that there for?' That's all it's there for. That's its total reason for existence. To make you stop and go, 'What's that all about, then?' The rose on the grave; 'Here Lies Derek Riggs, R.I.P.' I killed myself. This 'thank you' on the gravestone . . . do you know what that's about? 'Thank you' on a gravestone: it's the Grateful Dead! Here lies Faust in body only, because Faust sold his soul to the devil. Part of him is missing."

FATES WARNING THE SPECTRE WITHIN

METAL BLADE, OCTOBER 1985
ARTWORK: THIRD IMAGE: IOANNIS

Ioannis's spacey, quietly ornate sleeve for *The Spectre Within* went a long way toward branding Fates Warning as a new breed of metal band, one that dealt in progressive rock traditions, an idea previously discussed on any larger scale only with respect to Rush and, more adjacently, Queensrÿche. "In terms of style," says Ioannis, "I can always say wholeheartedly, unashamedly, that I always was a huge Roger Dean fan. So obviously, my early '80s covers, you can definitely tip the hat to Roger Dean. I mean, I had to figure out half the techniques I was doing for this one. I painted with acrylics and airbrush and ink and stuff. I more so thought I was going to do comic book covers and things like that. I

had prepared this huge story for *Heavy Metal* magazine, which was pretty popular in the early '80s, and in fact it had to do with the character on the cover of *The Spectre Within*. We put a whole story forward, and I did a whole series of paintings. This big massive science fiction concept . . . we were going to turn it into a board game, the whole kit and caboodle. But what happened was, when I started doing all these bands for Brian Slagel at Metal Blade in the mid '80s, a lot of these covers with the paintings had already been done for the story. Brian would look at them and go, 'Okay, this would be perfect for Warlord; this would be perfect for Liege Lord.' I think I did all the Lords."

ZZ TOP AFTERBURNER

WARNER BROS., OCTOBER 1985
ART DIRECTION AND DESIGN: JERI MCMANUS
ARTWORK: BARRY JACKSON

The heavy marketing lift was performed one record back with *Eliminator*, but *Afterburner* sports the much more pleasing cover: ZZ Top's '33 Ford coupe (a.k.a. the Eliminator) transformed into a souped-up space shuttle, which was an appropriate image, given that the music inside was a slicker, more futuristic rehash of the tunes and tones from its predecessor. The revived ZZs thus squeezed even more mileage out of their rolling rock prop, beyond the videos and T-shirts, and it was transformed—much like Iron Maiden's Eddie, who morphed to suit the vibe of each record at hand. Sales of *Afterburner* were similarly out of orbit, at five times platinum. "I illustrated both *Afterburner* and *Recycler*," notes artist Barry Jackson. "The *Afterburner* album

cover was hand-painted in acrylics three foot by six foot. It was agreed that Warner Bros. Records would fly me to Houston to present the art to the band. When I got on the airplane, the art was too big to fit in an overhead bin or under my seat. The flight attendant then took me to the coat closet, where, once again, the thinly wrapped artwork was too big. The flight attendant then told me the artwork would have to go down with the luggage. In a panic, I unveiled the *Afterburner* art and begged to him that it can't go in luggage! This was art for ZZ Top's next album! The flight attendant then put the art in the cockpit with the pilot, and we flew to Houston. True story."

HELLOWEEN WALLS OF JERICHO

NOISE/WARNER, DECEMBER 1985
COVER DESIGN: EDDA KARCZEWSKI AND UWE KARCZEWSKI, HAMBURG
FRONT COVER CONCEPT: WEIKATH
BACK COVER CONCEPT: WEIKATH/LIMB
LAYOUT: L+Z GRAFIK-DESIGN

Helloween's first album and album cover are pretty much pre-pumpkin mascot, if one excuses both the debut EP's pumpkin-hatching supposition and a second weak attempt as viewed on this record's ridiculous back cover. For that reason, the *Walls of Jericho* sleeve is actually easier to take seriously than future pumpkin-dominated dishes, even if the protagonist looks a bit like a nongreen Eddie of Arabia. And what's he doing? Well, Helloween, getting the story wrong, has this robed monster traipsing across the desert and then knocking down the walls of Jericho with his fists, whereas in the biblical tale, the destruction was caused by an overpowering sound that, granted, the guys kind of address on the back cover.

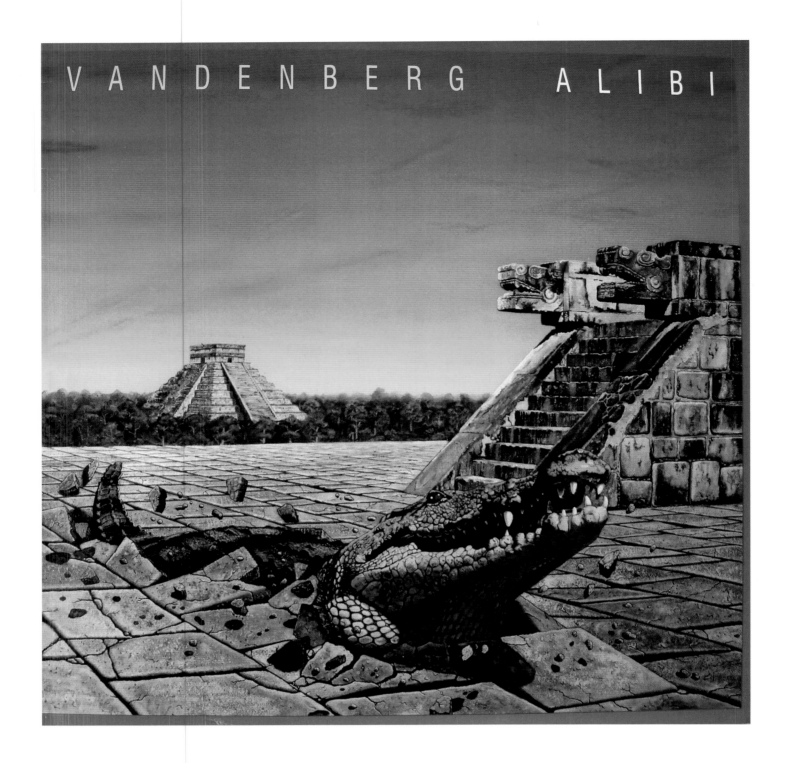

VANDENBERG ALIBI

ATCO, 1985
COVER PAINTING: ADRIAN VANDENBERG

I also went for the similarly themed *Heading for a Storm* (that one featuring flying sharks) from this underrated Dutch melodic metal act, but this one's a more skillfully executed painting. Plus, I dig the fact that the illustration is by none other than the leader of the band, guitarist Adrian Vandenberg, who chucked it all, after rising to the top with Whitesnake, to become a gallery artist. As I say, the *Alibi* cover reminds one of the *Heading for a Storm* cover, and both contain evocations of Gamma's *2*. The bonus is a pleasing geometric composition and nice type choice and placement, but the real icing is the Euro-tinged hair metal music it's wrapped around. Think I'll play it right now.

TROUBLE THE SKULL

METAL BLADE, 1985
COVER MASTERPIECE: GARY DOCKEN

Fire-and-brimstone Christian metal smothered in doom is the order of the day when Trouble plugs in and tunes down. *The Skull* is about as bleak as it gets, the apocalyptic lack of hope captured on the stunning cover image. It's hard to describe what's going on in this bad biblical acid trip. Are we skyclad and electrified or crucified to the ground? And is that Jesus or Jimi? In what is fully comprehended as sky, there's a face in the mist,

and buried within what could be either earth or nasty weather is a skull—*The Skull*, one assumes—the one referenced in the wicked type skulking in the lower right corner of this bad, bad scene. And then in the upper left, in crude and troubled white, is the band's logo, complete with stylized cross *T*, a symbol, one surmises, of the band's particularly morbid take on religion.

METALLICA MASTER OF PUPPETS

ELEKTRA, MARCH 1986
COVER ART CONCEPT: METALLICA AND PETER MENSCH
ILLUSTRATIONS: DON BRAUTIGAM
PHOTOGRAPHY: ROBERT ELLIS AND ROSS HALFIN

The *Master of Puppets* cover further shifts Metallica away from lurid thrash imagery and lifts its band's class level away from the pack of rockscrabble speed fiends nipping at their tails. *Kill 'Em All*'s sleeve was practically hard-core, and *Ride the Lightning* had an electric chair, but now we pay our respects at somber rows of white crosses, quietly manipulated by puppet strings descending from omnipotent hands behind the band's iconic and mighty logo. The Don Brautigam illustration combines the prevalent thrash themes of war and government manipulation; the picture is gorgeously possessive of both depth and striking color sense, given the contrast between the pure white of the crosses and the multiple rich shades of brown both above and below.

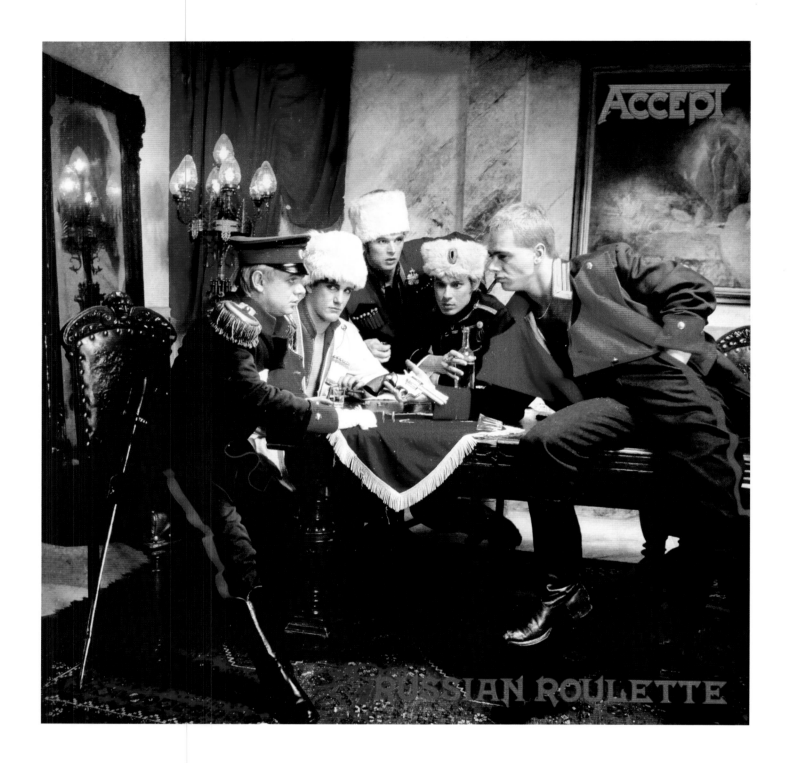

ACCEPT RUSSIAN ROULETTE

RCA/PORTRAIT, APRIL 1986
COVER IDEA, CONCEPT, AND REALIZATION: DEAFFY
COVER PHOTO: DIDI ZILL/BRAVO

Metal Heart is arguably a better album, but with a crap cover. Thankfully, Accept bounces back with a plush sleeve of pomp and circumstance, dressed up to the nines as Russian military elite and, more important, playing the part convincingly, from singer right down to lowly drummer. Bassist Peter Baltes has explained how the set piece was used to reinforce the antiwar themes of the album; the band extends the discussion,

depicting war as the ultimate game of Russian roulette. But yes, there are the classic facial expressions, the setting, the gun—throw in the title, and elaborate tales full of dramatic dialogue start crowding the mind of any given angry young Teutonic metal lover. Flip to the back cover, and your mind proceeds to imagine any number of second chapters.

MCA-6188

BOSTON THIRD STAGE

MCA, SEPTEMBER 1986
COVER: CHRIS SERRA CONCEPT, JOHN SALOZZO FINAL ART

If crafting a righteous guitarship weren't enough, tech wizard Tom Scholz now looks to expand his fleet. "The *Third Stage* pipe organ spaceship was the result of my wanting a spaceship with a giant pipe organ," explains Scholz. "A contest was run at a local Boston art school, and then the winner's drawing was painted by an airbrush artist. Then the original drawing was put on the sleeve for the album jacket. The photo that it sits on is a NASA shot, one of the early ones. And the layout was done on my living room floor with the old pasteup-style letters and all that, by me and my wife at the time, Cindy." Sure, the *Third Stage* cover is not the pinnacle of creativity, but it was a nice change of pace from the garish and obvious covers screaming the tropes of hard rock smack at the height of the hair metal years.

SLAYER REIGN IN BLOOD

DEF JAM, OCTOBER 1986
DESIGN: STEPHEN BYRAM
ILLUSTRATION: LARRY W. CARROLL

Political illustrator Larry Carroll launched quite the relationship with Slayer through this disturbing, high-minded, and painterly depiction of hell. Again, as with *Master of Puppets*, the effect was to turn thrash upscale, although Slayer, in comparison to Metallica, decided on a hard left turn into shock, so much so that Def Jam's distributor, Columbia, wouldn't distribute

the album (Geffen doing the dirty deed instead). But as testimony to the power of Carroll's paintings, the cover shocked on more of an intellectual level than because of any bluntly understandable poke—like, say, the sleeve he'd fiendishly devise for the band's *Christ Illusion* album twenty years hence.

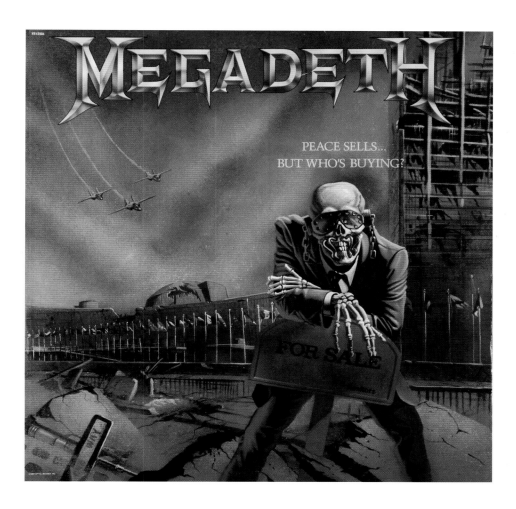

MEGADETH PEACE SELLS . . . BUT WHO'S BUYING?

COMBAT/CAPITOL, NOVEMBER 1986
ALBUM DESIGN AND COVER ILLUSTRATION: EDWARD J. REPKA
COVER CONCEPT: DAVE MUSTAINE AND ANDY SOMERS

Dave finally gets ol' Vic Rattlehead the way he wants him, thanks to the deft and detailed illustration work of one Ed Repka. But it's not all gratuitous monster making, with Vic being used to make a statement about, well, the complicated and cheeky title, posing as a suited Realtor hawking nothing less than the United Nations building, which, unfortunately, has been bombed into oblivion. But let Mustaine explain: "David Ellefson and myself and our agent at the time, a guy named Andy Summers, had got together in New York. We were in Manhattan, and actually across the street from the UN building. I don't know why we were there, but we were there. And we were talking about the album cover, and the fact that the first record was ruined by Combat, and how they ruined the artwork on that, didn't even do it. And just how important it was for me to get the artwork right this time. And we talked to this guy, this artist, Ed Repka. Andy and David and I went out to go get ribs at a place called Wylie's. And over the course of the period of talking, I said that I would like it to be the UN all bombed out, and then somebody said this and somebody said that, and then we would

have airplanes coming in and a 'for sale' sign, all these things, and it all germinated from that meal with Andy Summers. It was pretty straight from the get-go. I wasn't really a big artist at the time, and you've got to remember, this was twenty-five years ago. I've learned a lot since then about artwork and T-shirts and album covers and stuff like that, but at the time, it was my first real proud moment. We had a lot of T-shirt artwork he had done—we basically got ideas from comic books and stuff like that. But as soon as that thing came out, it could become real. That was the beginning, and you know, we've had a lot of great success with it. We've had managers who've said they don't want him. He's been taken off of album covers, we've had the logo changed, record labels saying that we need to change it up, but no, that was the beginning, and it's been a really successful look for us." Indeed, as history would have it, the record label had on their paint-spackled hands another marketable visual, essentially a follow-up mascot to Maiden's Eddie and Marillion's jester, both merchandise boons for acts that, like Megadeth, were working for Capitol/EMI.

FATES WARNING AWAKEN THE GUARDIAN

METAL BLADE, DECEMBER 1986
SLEEVE DESIGN AND ILLUSTRATION: IOANNIS/THIRD IMAGE

The *Awaken the Guardian* cover, courtesy of this book's contributor, Ioannis, charts a continuation and compositional improvement over its sister sleeve, that of preceding album, *The Spectre Within*. It has the same color scheme but with the band name and record title adhering to the disciplined blues as well. And then Ioannis turns up the jets, creating an even more quietly bizarre realm for Fates Warning and its protracted epic tales. Recalls Ioannis: "A memorable moment for me, as it was the first cover that I art directed and designed by myself. Up to that point, I would just knock off a painting or logo and send it to the record label. Mick

Rock once again did the band photos for very little money (God bless him!). It involved three paintings: the front, back, and the inside, which I since have lost. The art is a continuation of the character from *The Spectre Within*. The band was under a lot of pressure, as was I. The deadlines were tough; things were being done up to the last minute. At first, the band was not that responsive to it, but ten years later, talking to Jim, the band's leader, he told me it was their strongest cover, judging by the fans' reactions all these years. The fact that it was also an amazing album helped."

THE CULT ELECTRIC

BEGGARS BANQUET/VERTIGO, APRIL 1987
SLEEVE BY KEITH BREEDEN (FOR AI)
ART DIRECTION: STORM THORGERSON
FRONT/BACK COVER PHOTOGRAPHS: ROBERT ERDMANN/STYLED BY RENEE BEACH

Electric surprised everybody, with the Cult jettisoning their hard, Gothic, U2 thing for a beeline attempt at AC/DC. They lightened up on their pretentious cover art as well, although the image is still oddly Goth, even if it's Goth mixed with . . . American Indian? Frontier woodsman? Whatever the messaging—and even if there isn't any—this sleeve is bold of composition, featuring a soft and cozy band photo dominated by huge, spiky, symmetrical lettering, all in organic browns and blacks; frankly, quite at odds with the starkly unexpected music enclosed. Maybe that's part of the ambush.

SAVATAGE HALL OF THE MOUNTAIN KING

ATLANTIC, SEPTEMBER 1987
COVER ART: GARY SMITH
ART DIRECTION: BOB DEFRIN, GARY SMITH, SAVATAGE

Okay, standard heavy metal illustration, but first off, it's executed deftly, far better than the tossed-off average, as evidenced in the various treatments of the marble architecture within this hall o' metal, as well as in the lack of breakdown or degradation in even the smallest detail. But the main deal here is the messaging—that Savatage is back after a near-disastrous capitulation to commercial demands with *Fight for the Rock*, seen in that record's novelty cover tunes, its photographed sleeve, its Twisted Sister–dumb titling. Can't get more metal than *Hall of the Mountain King*, other

than re-creating that hall in airbrush, reigned o'er by a muscle-clad king with electric fingertips, creating magic while an impish jester looks on (flip to the back, and one discovers that Mr. Mountain King is in fact conjuring the band itself). Also in force is Savatage's modern, steel-slashing logo, back for a third time, perched upon a record that was indeed a robust return to the Gothic power doom of the band's debut, its EP, and much of *Power of the Night*, even if that record's cover, metal as it is, didn't quite say Savatage like this one.

ARMORED SAINT **RAISING FEAR**

CHRYSALIS, SEPTEMBER 1987
ART DIRECTION: MIKE DOUD
COVER CONCEPT: ARMORED SAINT AND JOE VERA
COVER ILLUSTRATION: RICHARD KRIEGLER

Armored Saint turns in its best and most epic illustration on *Raising Fear*, picturing a giant armor-clad, devil-horned warrior smashing through the crust under (presumably) Los Angeles. Kriegler's illustration features a dramatic sense of depth and a particularly mean sky, upon which hovers a fiery-red band logo that picks up succinctly on the colors of the molten mess below Armored Saint's sprawling hometown, a city summarily ruined by glam metal.

DOKKEN BACK FOR THE ATTACK

ELEKTRA, NOVEMBER 1987
DESIGN: REINER DESIGN CONSULTANTS
FRONT COVER ILLUSTRATION: DAVE (THE KNAVE) WILLIAMS

Not a ton of deep meaning here, but given the dearth of good hair metal covers (oh, I tried to find some), Dokken's spiffy, royal blue and orange *Back for the Attack* sleeve stands out. The fact is, Dokken was always a cut above, and this record in particular went through so much anguish between Don and George that you'd have to applaud its heft and its expensive sound and its overall heaviness away from hair. As for the art, the class of the thing carries over to the back, where the muted medieval backdrop is overlain with black-and-white woodcut-type line images of attacking birds and dogs.

OZZY OSBOURNE NO REST FOR THE WICKED

EPIC, OCTOBER 1988
ART DIRECTION AND DESIGN: THE LEISURE PROCESS
PHOTOGRAPHY: BOB CARLOS CLARKE

Look, Ozzy covers are mostly pretty goofy, but this one sort of propped up the music, which is, I suppose, one of the useful things covers can accomplish from time to time. After the fake blood of *Diary of a Madman*, after *Bark at the Moon*'s wolfman, and then with *The Ultimate Sin* being a bit of a dud both musically and visually, here was Oz photographed again, and then with some degree of class, surrounded by demon girls, the old Gothic logo and title text, a snakeskin sleeve, and

sumptuous copper tones. Okay, back to that first comment. The upscale look of the thing reinforces the fact that musically, this is a locked-down, serious, heavy, expensive-sounding record. Seriously, a schlocky illustrated sleeve in primary colors might have undermined what turns out to be a studious examination of the music (at least around these parts) and a subsequent assessment of *No Rest for the Wicked* as a worthy dark horse of the catalog.

GUNS N' ROSES GN'R LIES

GEFFEN, NOVEMBER 1988
CONCEPT, COVER ART CONCEPT: GUNS N' ROSES
ART DIRECTION AND DESIGN: DEBORAH NORCROSS
DESIGN: LESLIE WINTNER
PHOTOGRAPHY AND SLEEVE PHOTO: DOUG HYUN, JACK LUE
PHOTOGRAPHY: ROBERT JOHN, GENE KIRKLAND

Sure, the *Appetite for Destruction* sleeve is iconic, but *GN'R Lies* is a cheeky piece of art, especially in its color scheme of red, black, and tan—a muted palette on which to throw lurid headlines that help hype the band members as the bad boys they were. An interesting wrinkle is that a couple of politically incorrect headlines wound up replaced for the CD issue of the album,

a strange echo of what happened with *Appetite* and its original rape scene. There are also a couple of ties to John Lennon's *Some Time in New York City*, mainly in look and vibe, but also in that both records are half live and half in studio. Taking care of business, the design makes sure each guy gets a photo, and the song titles are smartly utilized as headlines.

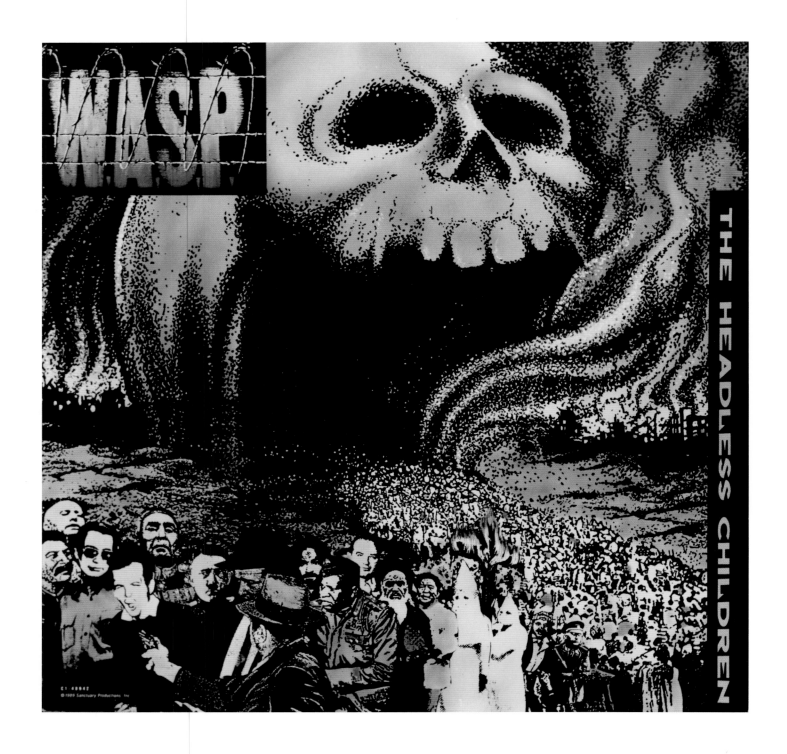

W.A.S.P. THE HEADLESS CHILDREN

CAPITOL, APRIL 1989
DESIGN AND ART DIRECTION: KOSH

Blackie Lawless is a thoughtful guy, so it's no surprise he would eventually turn up the jets, put aside all the fire-and-brimstone props, and hit us with something a little more traumatic on a visceral level. *The Headless Children* was that record—a loose concept album lurking behind a grainy cover, essentially black and white and then tinted in orange and pale, war-torn olive. The scene depicts what appears to be the mouth of hell opening up and vomiting forth a parade of all the nastiest oppressors the planet has seen through history, as well as Lee Harvey Oswald and his killer, Jack Ruby (does Blackie believe Ruby is in hell?). The album turned out to be a high point for W.A.S.P., and no doubt this button-pressing, hair metal–denying cover played a big part in Blackie being taken seriously for the first time.

BADLANDS BADLANDS

ATLANTIC, MAY 1989
ART DIRECTION: BOB DEFRIN
DESIGN: ANTHONY RANIERI
PHOTOGRAPHY: ROBERT MANELLA

Forget Kingdom Come—that band was child's play. Nay, yea, and verily, Badlands was the new Led Zeppelin, or at least all that Whitesnake at its very best through all incarnations tried to be. Jake, Greg, Eric, and that sadly deceased legend, Ray Gillen, created a debut album of fire and passion and torrid blues metal that loomed large enough to be presented with a cover image like this, a simple band shot, 'cause the band stands tall. Reinforcing the stripping of corporate rock baggage back to wood, wire, and flesh is the use of sepia tones plus the portrayal of the band's Wild West name in wide-bodied, attendant brown. Anytime a cocky concept like this is fronted, the idea is that the music speaks for itself, but since you ask, here's a picture of the guys making it. Of course, then the music has to speak volumes, which *Badlands* does, timelessly and unadulterated.

NIRVANA "BLEACH"

SUB POP, JUNE 1989
DESIGN: LISA ORTH
PHOTO: TRACY MARANDER

One of the dirtiest and doomiest and most primal of grunge classics, Nirvana's debut record took on cover art that reinforced that dark vibe. The cover photo features the band in full hair-flyin' flight, but shot in negative form and not by Charles Peterson but by one Tracy Marander. Perched above and below are the band name and title in the now-iconic retro font seen on countless T-shirts. *"Bleach"* appears in quotes, although no one remembers the title or refers to the record that way. It's interesting as well that the band is presented as a four-piece, with the quite metal-looking Jason Everman on guitar and the soon-to-be-replaced Chad Channing on drums.

FATES WARNING PERFECT SYMMETRY

METAL BLADE, AUGUST 1989
ART DIRECTION AND DESIGN: HUGH SYME
COVER PHOTO: SCARPATI
CONCEPT DEVELOPMENT: HUGH SYME/STEPHEN HIBBARD

Through *Perfect Symmetry,* progressive metal stalwarts Fates Warning was leaning commercial, honing its craft, looking for that next level—an expansion beyond a close-knit cabal of obsessive, pocket-protector fans. Just as he did with Dream Theater and even Megadeth, Rush legend Hugh Syme shows up as the visual actualizer of these sorts of sentiments; with Fates Warning he bestows upon the band his usual austere, clinical, peculiar view of things. For the front and back of *Perfect Symmetry*, he gives us six shots of the same assembly-line codger who checks out little Venus de Milo statues as they float by on a conveyor belt in a sad, lonely, and not particularly well-lit factory. There's also a stamped FW-5 in view, to reflect the fact that this was the band's

fifth album. Comments guitarist Jim Matheos: "All of us being huge Rush fans, it was just a huge pleasure and a blast for us to work with these guys who worked with our heroes. [Note: the album is produced by Terry Brown, another longtime Rush alumnus.] I love Hugh's artwork; he's done some amazing things, and it was just a pleasure to get him in there. He came from that kind of Hipgnosis school—those were the album covers back in the day that I thought were brilliant. He takes a different angle on things that wouldn't necessarily be the first thing you think of. With *Perfect Symmetry*, you had to think about it once or twice, because it was very nonmetal; there's a little bit more thought put into it."

SOUNDGARDEN LOUDER THAN LOVE

A&M, SEPTEMBER 1989
COVER DESIGN: ART CHANTRY, BRUCE PAVITT
PHOTOGRAPHY: CHARLES PETERSON

I could have picked *Screaming Life* or Mudhoney's *Superfuzz Bigmuff* just as easily, but the power of these like-minded covers is in the visual representation of a ragged punk-stormed form of obscure metal called grunge. The blurry, black-and-white, usually face-obscured motion of Charles Peterson's iconic photography captures perfectly what these bands were like live in the late '80s, which is essentially a drunken, punkin', virulent type of hard rock that we may as well call heavy metal, 'cause it absolutely sounded darker, sludgier, and more dangerous than anything coming out of L.A. at the time. "It seemed like a natural fit," reflects Peterson. "It comes from my interest in classic music photography, but also, at the time, photographing these bands in small clubs, all they really had access to shooting, or could afford to shoot, was black-and-white. So there were economic factors there, too. And a big part of it, of course, was that I grew up with these guys, from about eighteen on—Mark Arm I met in college, Kim Thayil, Bruce Pavitt, and whatnot—and so I guess to a degree at the time, you are going out to see your friends play. It was just an extension of punk and hard-core combined with a renewed interest in some of the darker aspects of classic rock—the Stooges,

Blue Cheer, Alice Cooper, and things like that—that sort of got a little overlooked, with an emphasis on Zep. Soundgarden is an interesting one because they straddled a lot of worlds. In a sense they were just as pseudometal as somebody like Mother Love Bone or early Pearl Jam, but there was more of a raw edge—kind of off doing their own thing—that made them a little more authentic. Kim, Hiro, and later Ben . . . they weren't out wearing scarves and tie-dyed shirts and headbands; they weren't trying to look the look. They were just being themselves." So there's Chris on the cover of *Louder Than Love*, caught bare-chested in working-man's jeans, hair a-flyin', caught up in the hypnotic yet savage (yet slide-ruled!) music of the crack band behind him. The hurried effect is underscored by an almost afterthought *Soundgarden* stripped down the side, black on orange, with no album title in evidence until the back cover. What falls out is this idea that the grunge bands were too cool to care about album covers and that marketing is anathema, even if what ironically occurred, mostly within the idea and sanctum of Sub Pop, was one of the strongest textbook cases of "scene" branding in the history of rock and roll.

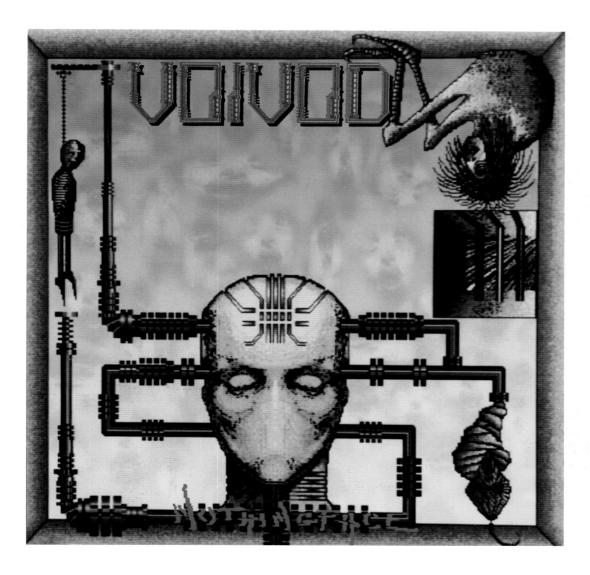

VOIVOD NOTHINGFACE

MECHANIC/MCA, OCTOBER 1989
ART DIRECTION AND DESIGN: IOANNIS/THIRD IMAGE/STEVE SINCLAIR
COVER CONCEPT AND ARTWORK BY AWAY

All of drummer and illustrator Michel "Away" Langevin's sleeves add to his creation of an action-packed, sci-fi world view, mostly of blues and purples, often peopled by freak-forces that are part man, part machine. *Nothingface* is no exception, and, what's more, it's one of the Quebecois's most artistically pleasing covers, given the framing, the geometry, and the intellectual heft of the central Nothingface character and its portraiture on this smart sleeve. The album's twelve-panel booklet offers further one-panel shot-shocks from Michel, and on the booklet's flip side is a full band poster with the guys placed in an apocalyptic future by none other than this book's contributor, Ioannis. As to the front cover art, Michel figures that it took him about three months to produce. "Each time before that and some after, as well, I probably spent about three months doing the art. It probably took me the same time to do this, including the booklet, as the other albums, but I found it much easier to do. The only problem was to

transfer from these old computers. I sent disks to MCA in New York so they could make the booklet, and this was much better than sending the paintings, but still they had to go to a place where they had to transfer everything with better PCs, and this was extra money." With respect to all those pipes on the cover, Michel explains, "It's related to the fact that I was starting to use a computer a lot more—on *Nothingface*, it's all computerized. To make pipes and metal-looking things with the computer graphics really made sense right away. I really wanted to make good use of it, so I thought I would draw a logo made out of pipes and put a lot of machinery and pipes on the drawing also. And those characters . . . the concept represents split personality. And the faces behind the characters, all distorted and stuff, were to make good use of early experiments with layering in of pictures. But the drawings directly relating to the songs are mostly on the back cover or in the booklet."

ZZ TOP RECYCLER

WARNER BROS., MARCH 1990
LOGO AND ILLUSTRATION: BARRY JACKSON
ART HOSTESS: KIM CHAMPAGNE

Barry Jackson gets called back, turning in a more ambitious, dark, and dense painting that depicts the band stylized flat to the point of looking like playing cards. Either Dusty or Billy is presenting a new car (Jackson's made them dead identical) while overshadowed by a cliff side of discarded vehicles reaching up to the sky.

On the back cover, the mountain of cars abruptly stops, taken over by a thin strip of what looks to be (recycled?) metal cacti, before the resumption of drab tenement civilization in night heat. It's a gorgeous use of color and light from Jackson, who manipulates a restrained yet unusual palette of mainly orange and blue.

IGGY POP BRICK BY BRICK

VIRGIN, JUNE 1990
DESIGN: J. GERDES
COVER ILLUSTRATION: CHARLES BURNS
ART DIRECTION: MELANIE NISSEN

Brick by Brick is a collection of songs that offers a jittery worldview of America in decline. Too bad about the plush corporate sound of the thing and the swanky session players. But hey, it was a surprise gold album—very weirdly, Iggy's first. Still, *Brick by Brick* proves for those still paying attention that Iggy's intense and literary lyrical skills, and the cover art by celebrated comics illustrator Charles Burns (see Art Spiegelman's

Raw, as well as Burns's work for Sub Pop), support the loose theme of the record by offering a nighttime vision of an imploding city (something between the cuts "Butt Town," "Neon Forest," and "Home") crammed with all manner of half-human freaks, stressed, goofing around, and otherwise out to get by (or get one over) till dawn sends them back underground for recharging.

JANE'S ADDICTION RITUAL DE LO HABITUAL

WARNER BROS., AUGUST 1990
COVER BY PERRY AND CASEY
PHOTOGRAPHED BY VICTOR BRACKE

Shocking with yet a third album cover, Perry Farrell and the rest of the funk punk alternative metalers of Jane's Addiction liked to push buttons, here portraying both male and female frontal nudity in fearsome threesome configuration, but through the harm-diffusing lens of not-so-realistic illustration. I think what got folks up in arms even more was the undercurrent of Santeria to the thing, Perry being a practitioner; the band was subsequently pressured into offering both a near-plain-white version (including the band name, title, and article 1 of the First Amendment of the U.S. Constitution!) and this cover, pretty tame by today's standards. Still, whatever one's take, it was good to see some creativity injected into the mix after so many years of rote hair metal cover comix, Jane's Addiction being one of the first and loudest slayers and naysayers of all that nonsense.

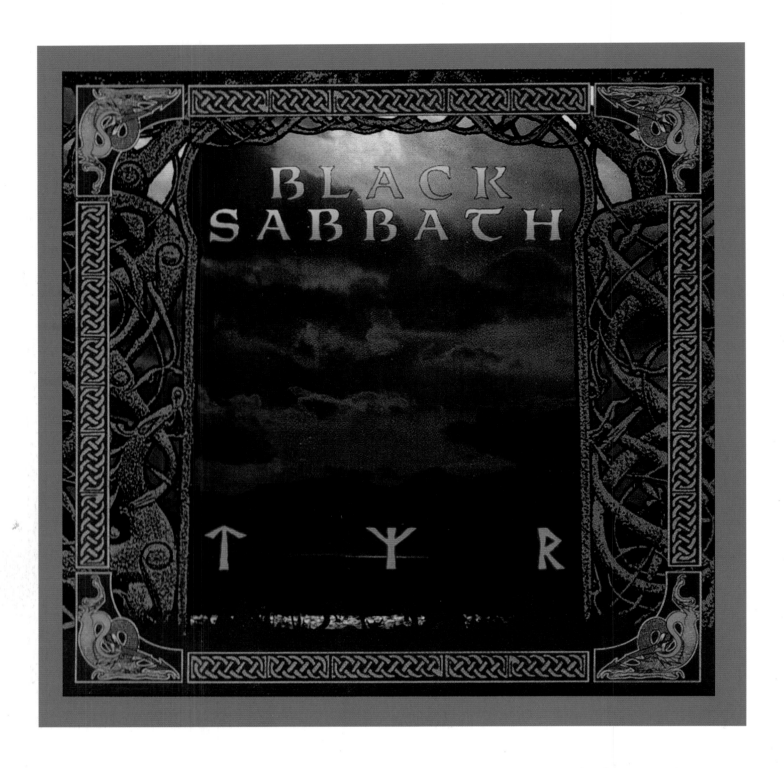

BLACK SABBATH TYR

I.R.S., AUGUST 1990
ARTWORK AND DESIGN: SATORI
PHOTOGRAPHY: ANDIE AIRFIX

Is Black Sabbath a cross between Norwegian black metal and the Thin Lizzy of *Johnny the Fox*? It's a flippant comparison, but the sleeve certainly conjures those leaps of logic. Sabbath (improbably) proposes half a concept album about Norse mythology, attempting to wrap the ruse in verdant Celtic knotwork. The tilt goes to black metal, however, given the doom of Sabbath's ponderous riffs all over this sludgy affair, coupled with the unequivocally stormy skies that anchor the middle of this first good sleeve for the Sabs in . . . nine years?

MEGADETH RUST IN PEACE

CAPITOL, SEPTEMBER 1990
COVER CONCEPT: DAVE MUSTAINE
COVER ILLUSTRATION: EDWARD J. REPKA

Just preceding *Rust in Peace*, the album *So Far, So Good . . . So What!* was both a musical and visual trip-up for the drug-hoovering Megadeth, so it was inspiring to see Vic Rattlehead back in a suit, taunting punters to pony up some dosh for an album that would emphatically not disappoint once brought home and slapped on the turntable of death. Once more, Ed Repka is called upon to paint Vic as the devil in the foreign policy details; here our suited grinning jackal

takes on numerous files, including nuclear war, aliens, and one-world-government conspiracy theories. The overt politics of Megadeth's covers and Megadave's lyrics worked in synchronicity with the band's white-knuckle chops to help garner the band a reputation as a thinking man's thrash act. That reputation served as a fortunate corrective balance against the drug-fueled punch-ups and other personal shortcomings poking holes in the private lives of this embattled bunch.

ACKNOWLEDGMENTS

Special thanks to our intrepid editors and handlers, namely, Barbara Clark and Barbara Berger, and all sorts of behind-the-scenes folks at Sterling we'll never know, as well as to my album cover co-maniac, Ioannis, and brotha George!

Thanks also to the photographers and illustrators who stepped up with illuminating words of wisdom to accompany their works of art, most pointedly Ernie Cefalu, Adrian Chesterman, Jeff Cummings, Roger Dean, Bob Gruen, Mick Haggerty, Ioannis, Barry Jackson, Michel Langevin, Barry Levine, Rodney Matthews, Chris Moore, Charles Peterson, Derek Riggs, Mick Rock, Todd Schorr, Garry Sharpe-Young, Earl Steinbicker, and Drew Struzan.

The writing of *Fade to Black* was fueled by the inspiration of several unsung musical masters, namely, American Dog, Adrian Belew, Chroma Key, Francis Dunnery, Fozzy, the Ghost, Grootna, Nick Lowe, These Trails, and Trader Horne.

—M.P.

Special thanks goes out to the following people, without whom this book would not have been possible: Martin Popoff, Barbara Berger, Barbara Clark, and all the staff at Sterling Publishing.

I also thank my brother, George, for helping put it all together, and Thomas Valentino, for all his legal help. I also deeply thank the following collectors, who helped me track down the classic album covers in this book: the greatest heavy metal radio jock of all time, Peter Sotere; Denny and Theo Somach; and the Classic Rock Society of America.

Thanks also to Lawrence Ciolino (a.k.a. Larz Metal), Bob Briar and everyone at Cutler's Record Shop in New Haven, Connecticut, Doug Snyder at Replay Records in Hamden, Connecticut, and the great Mike DiBiase.

—I.V.

ABOUT **MARTIN POPOFF**

Martin Popoff has been described as the world's most famous heavy metal journalist. Unofficially, he has written more record reviews—7,900 at last count—than anybody in the history of music writing. He has written thirty-six books on hard rock, heavy metal, and classic rock, served as the editor in chief of the Canadian metal magazine *Brave Words & Bloody Knuckles*, and has contributed to many other publications, including *Guitar World*, *Lollipop*, *Goldmine*, and *Record Collector*. He has also written numerous band bios and liner notes for major record labels. Popoff (www.martinpopoff.com) lives in Toronto, Canada.

ABOUT **IOANNIS**

Ioannis created the cover art for more than 170 albums by some of the most legendary bands in the music industry, including the Allman Brothers, Deep Purple, King Crimson, Uriah Heep, Blue Öyster Cult, Styx, Bon Jovi, Johnny Winter, Quiet Riot, and Lynyrd Skynyrd. He also designed the brand identity for Loud & Proud Records, moogis.com, and THINK Televisual Network, and has collaborated with Bob Weir. Additionally, his works have been featured in many magazines, books, and exhibitions worldwide. Ioannis lives in New Haven, Connecticut. See more at www.dangerousage.com.

APPENDIX 1
Martin Popoff's Top 100 Hard Rock Album Covers of the Vinyl Age

Bravely and boldly ranked is the only way to go for something fun, fun, fun like this, so here you go, baby! I really got a kick out of doing this list, first because of the ranking, which is always a blast for an obsessive list guy, but also because I get to show my cards on some things that were perhaps not in the book for various reasons (okay, I even leaned this way a bit, for variety's sake), including the fact that the picking was a collaborative effort with my man Ioannis, who knows a bit about album covers! And there were things we were trying to do with covering the whole history of hard rock album covers, as well as not wanting to go too obscure. So yeah, here's the place where I get to rave on with no restrictions. I'm sure I left things out, and by the way, I tried not to go too, too crazy with too many from one band, but hope you dig it.

1. Judas Priest: *Killing Machine* (CBS/Columbia, October 1978)
2. Blue Öyster Cult: *Spectres* (Columbia, October 1977)
3. Black Sabbath: *Sabbath Bloody Sabbath* (Vertigo/Warner Bros., December 1973)
4. Angel: *On Earth As It Is in Heaven* (Casablanca, 1977)
5. Aerosmith: *Rocks* (Columbia, May 1976)
6. Blue Öyster Cult: *Some Enchanted Evening* (Columbia, September 1978)
7. Black Sabbath: *Technical Ecstasy* (Vertigo/Warner Bros., September 1976)
8. Kiss: *Destroyer* (Casablanca, March 1976)
9. Rush: *Caress of Steel* (Mercury, September 1975)
10. Blue Öyster Cult: *On Your Feet or on Your Knees* (Columbia, February 1975)
11. Sweet: *Off the Record* (RCA/Capitol, April 1977)
12. Ted Nugent: *Free-for-All* (Epic, October 1976)
13. Motörhead: *Overkill* (Bronze, March 1979)
14. Blue Öyster Cult: *Cultösaurus Erectus* (Columbia, June 1980)
15. Thin Lizzy: *Johnny the Fox* (Vertigo/Mercury, October 1976)
16. Blue Öyster Cult: *Extraterrestrial Live* (Columbia, April 1982)
17. Thin Lizzy: *Renegade* (Vertigo/Warner Bros., November 1981)
18. Tygers of Pan Tang: *Crazy Nights* (MCA, November 1981)
19. Scorpions: *Blackout* (EMI/Mercury, March 1982)
20. Motörhead: *Bomber* (Bronze, October 1979)
21. Black Sabbath: *Heaven and Hell* (Vertigo/Warner Bros., April 1980)
22. Kiss: *Alive!* (Casablanca, September 1975)
23. Blue Öyster Cult: *Fire of Unknown Origin* (Columbia, June 1981)
24. Gamma: *2* (Elektra, 1980)
25. Black Sabbath: *Never Say Die!* (Vertigo/Warner Bros., September 1978)
26. Deep Purple: *Burn* (Purple/Warner Bros., February 1974)
27. Nazareth: *Hair of the Dog* (Mooncrest/A&M, April 1975)
28. Blue Öyster Cult: *The Revolution by Night* (Columbia, October 1983)
29. Voivod: *Nothingface* (Mechanic/MCA, October 1989)
30. Uriah Heep: *Return to Fantasy* (Bronze/Warner Bros., May 1975)
31. Ted Nugent: *Weekend Warriors* (Epic, September 1978)
32. Rainbow: *Long Live Rock 'n' Roll* (Polydor, April 1978)
33. Whitesnake: *Lovehunter* (United Artists, October 1979)
34. Queen: *News of the World* (EMI/Elektra, October 1977)
35. Slayer: *Reign in Blood* (Def Jam, October 1986)
36. Demon: *Night of the Demon* (Carrere, 1981)
37. Legs Diamond: *Fire Power* (Cream, 1979)
38. UFO: *Obsession* (Chrysalis, June 1978)
39. Blue Öyster Cult: *Agents of Fortune* (Columbia, May 1976)
40. Nightwing: *My Kingdom Come* (Gull, 1984)
41. Judas Priest: *Sin after Sin* (CBS/Columbia, April 1977)
42. The Tubes: *Young and Rich* (A&M, April 1976)
43. Angel Witch: *Angel Witch* (Bronze, 1980)
44. Iron Maiden: *Iron Maiden* (EMI, April 1980)

45. Diamond Head: *Borrowed Time* (MCA, 1982)
46. Thin Lizzy: *Nightlife* (Vertigo/Mercury, November 1974)
47. Black Sabbath: *Black Sabbath* (Vertigo/Warner Bros., February 1970)
48. Coney Hatch: *Coney Hatch* (Anthem/Mercury, 1982)
49. The Tubes: *The Tubes* (A&M, June 1975)
50. Destruction: *Sentence of Death* (Steamhammer/Metal Blade, September 1984)
51. Blue Öyster Cult: *Tyranny and Mutation* (Columbia, February 1973)
52. Praying Mantis: *Time Tells No Lies* (Arista, 1981)
53. Rush: *A Farewell to Kings* (Mercury, September 1977)
54. Rainbow: *Rising* (Oyster/Polydor, May 1976)
55. Rush: *2112* (Anthem/Mercury, April 1976)
56. Ian Gillan Band: *Scarabus* (Island, October 1977)
57. Judas Priest: *Sad Wings of Destiny* (Gull/Janus, March 1976)
58. UFO: *Force It* (Chrysalis, July 1975)
59. Quartz: *Stand Up and Fight* (MCA, 1980)
60. The Dictators: *Bloodbrothers* (Asylum/Elektra, 1978)
61. Witchfynde: *Cloak and Dagger* (Expulsion, 1983)
62. Shakin' Street: *Shakin' Street* (CBS, 1980)
63. Iggy and the Stooges: *Raw Power* (Columbia, May 1973)
64. Paice Ashton Lord: *Malice in Wonderland* (Oyster/Warner Bros., March 1977)
65. Lucifer's Friend: *Mind Exploding* (Vertigo/Janus, 1976)
66. Nightwing: *Something in the Air* (Ovation, 1981)
67. Savage: *Loose 'n Lethal* (Ebony, 1983)
68. Judas Priest: *British Steel* (CBS/Columbia, April 1980)
69. Judas Priest: *Unleashed in the East* (CBS/Columbia, September 1979)
70. Holocaust: *The Nightcomers* (Phoenix/Filmworks, April 1981)
71. Robin Trower: *Victims of the Fury* (Chrysalis, 1979)
72. Metallica: *Master of Puppets* (Elektra, March 1986)
73. Ozzy Osbourne: *Blizzard of Oz* (Jet, September 1980)
74. Scorpions: *Tokyo Tapes* (RCA, January 1978)
75. Ethel the Frog: *Ethel the Frog* (EMI, 1980)
76. Ted Nugent: *Double Live Gonzo* (Epic, January 1978)
77. Grim Reaper: *See You in Hell* (Ebony/RCA, July 1984)
78. Vandenberg: *Heading for a Storm* (Atco, 1983)
79. Budgie: *Bandolier* (MCA/A&M, September 1975)
80. Hawkwind: *Sonic Attack* (RCA/Active, October 1981)
81. Anvil: *Metal on Metal* (Attic, April 1982)
82. Budgie: *Never Turn Your Back on a Friend* (MCA, 1973)
83. Moxy: *Ridin' High* (Polydor/Mercury, 1977)
84. Nazareth: *Loud 'n' Proud* (Mooncrest/A&M, November 1973)
85. Judas Priest: *Screaming for Vengeance* (Columbia, July 1982)
86. Legs Diamond: *A Diamond Is a Hard Rock* (Mercury, 1977)
87. Goddo: *Goddo* (Polydor, 1977)
88. Mercyful Fate: *Melissa* (Roadrunner/Megaforce, October 1983)
89. Agony Column: *God, Guns & Guts* (Big Chief, 1989)
90. Oz: *Fire in the Brain* (Tyfon, 1983)
91. Picture: *Eternal Dark* (Backdoor, 1983)
92. Starz: *Coliseum Rock* (Capitol, 1978)
93. Trouble: *The Skull* (Metal Blade, 1985)
94. Atomic Rooster: *Death Walks Behind You* (B&C/Elektra, September 1970)
95. The Rods: *Wild Dogs* (Arista, 1982)
96. Vandenberg: *Alibi* (Atco, 1985)
97. Van Halen: *Van Halen* (Warner Bros., February 1978)
98. Armageddon: *Armageddon* (A&M, 1975)
99. Motörhead: *Ace of Spades* (Bronze/Mercury, November 1980)
100. The Dictators: *Manifest Destiny* (Asylum, 1977)

APPENDIX 2
Ioannis's Top 100 Hard Rock Album Covers of the Vinyl Age

Let me start by saying that I love Martin's selections, both his choices for the book and his Top 100 list. It was not easy to do, I assure you. He is, as I am, a very accomplished artist, and thus our criteria of originality, color, and composition impacted our choices, and provided the impetus for much thought and discussion. So yes, our selections were based on art rather than on how hugely successful any particular album was. Furthermore, it was frustrating not to be able to choose Pink Floyd, Yes, Genesis, Supertramp, Weather Report, and so on, as these bands obviously do not fall within the hard rock genre. In addition, since I am primarily an illustrator, and have been since my humble beginnings, my choices lean heavily in that direction. I know that hard rock fans may be dismayed, for example, that I picked ELP over Judas Priest or Black Sabbath or another proper metal band for my top record cover choice, However, two points here. First, Giger's art is truly breathtaking, and aside from, say, the work of Iron Maiden artist Derek Riggs, his creations have been more widely imitated and copied in metal circles than any other—not to mention the fact that many clas- sically metal albums have also featured his work. Second, I saw ELP live during their heyday and it was the loudest, most grinding concert I have ever witnessed—very Gothic, sort of the granddaddy to bands like Nine Inch Nails, Gary Numan, and so on. I mean, feedback from synthesizers; explosions; distorted, thundering bass chords—all of it visually enhanced by Giger's cybernetic and chilling artwork. It could not get any more metal than that. Anyway, here is my list!

1. Emerson, Lake & Palmer: *Brain Salad Surgery* (Manticore, November 1973)
2. Judas Priest: *Killing Machine* (CBS/Columbia, October 1978)
3. Black Sabbath: *Black Sabbath* (Vertigo/Warner Bros., February 1970)
4. Deep Purple: *Machine Head* (Purple/Warner Bros., March 1972)
5. Led Zeppelin: *Houses of the Holy* (Atlantic, March 1973)
6. Uriah Heep: *The Magician's Birthday* (Bronze/Mercury, November 1972)
7. Black Sabbath: *Sabbath Bloody Sabbath* (Vertigo/Warner Bros., December 1973)
8. Judas Priest: *British Steel* (CBS/Columbia, April 1980)
9. Led Zeppelin: *Led Zeppelin* (Atlantic, 1969)
10. Iron Maiden: *Killers* (EMI, February 1981)
11. T. Rex: *The Slider* (EMI/Reprise, July 1972)
12. Queen: *Queen II* (EMI/Elektra, March 1974)
13. Rush: *Power Windows* (Anthem/Mercury, October 1985)
14. Deep Purple: *Fireball* (Harvest/Warner Bros., July 1971)
15. Motörhead: *Orgasmatron* (GWR, August 1986)
16. Kiss: *Destroyer* (Casablanca, March 1976)
17. Rolling Stones: *Sticky Fingers* (Rolling Stones/Atlantic, April, 1971)
18. Uriah Heep: *Demons and Wizards* (Bronze/Mercury, May 1972)
19. Scorpions: *Blackout* (EMI/Mercury, March 1982)
20. Judas Priest: *Sad Wings of Destiny* (Gull/Janus, March 1976)
21. Nazareth: *Hair of the Dog* (Mooncrest/A&M, April 1975)
22. David Bowie: *Diamond Dogs* (RCA, April 1974)
23. Blue Öyster Cult: *Fire of Unknown Origin* (Columbia, June 1981)
24. Celtic Frost: *To Mega Therion* (Noise, October 1985)
25. Black Sabbath: *Never Say Die!* (Vertigo/Warner Bros., September 1978)
26. Thin Lizzy: *Jailbreak* (Vertigo/Mercury, March 1976)
27. Nazareth: *No Mean City* (A&M, January 1979)
28. Aerosmith: *Toys in the Attic* (Columbia, April 1975)
29. Budgie: *Never Turn Your Back on a Friend* (MCA, 1973)
30. Rolling Stones: *Exile on Main Street* (Rolling Stones/Atlantic, May 1972)
31. Blue Öyster Cult: *Tyranny and Mutation* (Columbia, February 1973)
32. Nightwing: *My Kingdom Come* (Gull, 1984)
33. Metallica: *Master of Puppets* (Elektra, March 1986)
34. Be Bop Deluxe: *Sunburst Finish* (Harvest, February 1976)
35. Be Bop Deluxe: *Live in the Air Age* (Harvest, 1977)
36. Deep Purple: *Stormbringer* (Purple/Warner Bros., December 1974)
37. Black Sabbath: *Technical Ecstasy* (Vertigo/Warner Bros., September 1976)
38. Rainbow: *Rising* (Oyster/Polydor, May 1976)
39. Blue Öyster Cult: *Agents of Fortune* (Columbia, May 1976)
40. AC/DC: *Let There Be Rock* (Albert/Atlantic, June 1977)

41. Uriah Heep: *Fallen Angel* (Bronze/Chrysalis, September 1978)
42. Boston: *Boston* (Epic, July 1976)
43. Judas Priest: *Screaming for Vengeance* (Columbia, July 1982)
44. Rush: *Permanent Waves* (Mercury, January 1980)
45. Diamond Head: *Borrowed Time* (MCA, 1982)
46. Thin Lizzy: *Nightlife* (Vertigo/Mercury, November 1974)
47. Be Bop Deluxe: *Axe Victim* (Harvest, June 1974)
48. Kiss: *Hotter Than Hell* (Casablanca, October 1974)
49. The Tubes: *Remote Control* (A&M, March 1979)
50. Kansas: *Point of Know Return* (Kirshner, October 1977)
51. Hawkwind: *Warrior on the Edge of Time* (United Artists, May 1975)
52. Magma: *Attahk* (Tomato, 1978)
53. Queen: *Sheer Heart Attack* (EMI/Elektra, November 1974)
54. Budgie: *Bandolier* (MCA/A&M, September 1975)
55. Rush: *2112* (Anthem/Mercury, April 1976)
56. Ian Gillan Band: *Clear Air Turbulence* (Island, April 1977)
57. Montrose: *Jump on It* (Warner Bros., September 1976)
58. Cream: *Disraeli Gears* (Reaction/Atco/Polydor, November 1967)
59. Scorpions: *Love at First Sting* (EMI/Mercury, March 1984)
60. Angel: *Angel* (Casablanca, October 1975)
61. Judas Priest: *Sin after Sin* (CBS/Columbia, April 1977)
62. Molly Hatchet: *Molly Hatchet* (Epic, September 1978)
63. Black Sabbath: *Heaven and Hell* (Vertigo/Warner Bros., April 1980)
64. King Crimson: *In the Court of the Crimson King* (Island/Atlantic, October 1969)
65. T. Rex: *Electric Warrior* (Fly/Reprise, September 1971)
66. UFO: *Force It* (Chrysalis, July 1975)
67. Led Zeppelin: *In Through the Out Door* (Swan Song, August 1979)
68. Molly Hatchet: *Flirtin' with Disaster* (Epic, October 1979)
69. Iron Butterfly: *Scorching Beauty* (MCA, January 1975)
70. The Cult: *Electric* (Beggars Banquet/Sire, April 1987)
71. Thin Lizzy: *Black Rose: A Rock Legend* (Vertigo/Warner Bros., April 1979)
72. Wishbone Ash: *Argus* (Decca/MCA, April 1972)
73. Dio: *The Last in Line* (Warner Bros., July 1984)
74. Slayer: *Reign in Blood* (Def Jam, October 1986)
75. Bachman-Turner Overdrive: *Not Fragile* (Mercury, August 1974)
76. Nazareth: *Close Enough for Rock 'n' Roll* (A&M/Vertigo, March 1976)
77. The Who: *Quadrophenia* (Track/Polydor/MCA, October 1973)
78. Black Sabbath: *Mob Rules* (Vertigo/Warner Bros., November 1981)
79. Rainbow: *Difficult to Cure* (Polydor, February 1981)
80. Boston: *Don't Look Back* (Epic, August 1978)
81. Accept: *Balls to the Wall* (Lark/Portrait, January 1984)
82. Motörhead: *Bomber* (Bronze, October 1979)
83. Judas Priest: *The Best of Judas Priest* (Gull/RCA, 1978)
84. Golden Earring: *To the Hilt* (Polydor, January 1976)
85. Megadeth: *Peace Sells . . . but Who's Buying?* (Combat/Capitol, November 1986)
86. Voivod: *Nothingface* (Mechanic/MCA, October 1989)
87. UFO: *Space Metal* (Nova, 1976)
88. Jane's Addiction: *Nothing's Shocking* (Warner Bros., August 1988)
89. Guns N' Roses: *Appetite for Destruction* (Geffen, July 1987)
90. Saga: *Images at Twilight* (Polydor, 1979)
91. Saga: *Silent Knight* (Maze, 1980)
92. Black Sabbath: *Tyr* (I.R.S., August 1990)
93. Magnum: *Chase the Dragon* (Jet, March 1982)
94. Mötley Crüe: *Too Fast for Love* (Elektra, December 1981)
95. Whitesnake: *Slide It In* (EMI/Geffen, April 1984)
96. Alice Cooper: *Welcome to My Nightmare* (Atlantic, February 1975)
97. Quiet Riot: *Metal Health* (Pasha/CBS, March 1983)
98. Mercyful Fate: *Don't Break the Oath* (Roadrunner/Combat, September 1984)
99. Cirith Ungol: *Frost and Fire* (Liquid Flames/Metal Blade, 1980)
100. Scorpions: *Lovedrive* (Mercury, February 1979)

INDEX 1
Alphabetical by Artist

INDEX 2
Alphabetical by Album Title

Index 3

Illustrators, Designers, and Photographers

PICTURE CREDITS

Every effort has been made to secure permission and provide appropriate credit for photographic material. We deeply regret any omission and pledge to correct errors called to our attention in subsequent editions. Please contact us online through our websites at www.dangerousage.com or www.martinpopoff.com to alert us to any corrections.

A&M: Humble Pie, *Street Rats*, Feb. 1975: 74; Nazareth, *Malice in Wonderland*, 1980: 176; Nazareth, *No Mean City*, Jan. 1979: 150–51; Soundgarden, *Louder Than Love*, Sept. 1989: 256; The Tubes, *Now*, May 1977: 120; The Tubes, *The Tubes*, June 1975: 83; Y&T, *Black Tiger*, 1982: 205.
Active/RCA: Hawkwind, *Sonic Attack*, Oct. 1981: 189.
Albert/Atlantic: AC/DC, *Highway to Hell*, Aug. 1979: 154.
Ariola: Krokus, *Hardware*, March 1981: 186.
Arista: Krokus, *Headhunter*, Nov. 1983: 214; The Rods, *Wild Dogs*, April 1982: 198–99.
Atco: Axe, *Nemesis*, 1983: 216; Iron Butterfly, *Heavy*, Jan. 1968: 9; Iron Butterfly, *In-A-Gadda-Da-Vida*, June 1968: 10; Vandenberg, *Alibi*, 1985: 234.
Atlantic: Alice Cooper, *Welcome to My Nightmare*, Feb. 1975: 72–73; Badlands, *Badlands*, May 1989: 253; Foreigner, *Head Games*, Sept. 1979: 156; Led Zeppelin, *Houses of the Holy*, March 1973: 44; Led Zeppelin, *Led Zeppelin*, Jan. 1969: 11; Led Zeppelin, *Led Zeppelin III*, Oct. 1970: 25; MC5, *Back in the USA*, Jan. 1970: 20–21; Savatage, *Hall of the Mountain King*, Sept. 1987: 247; Vandenberg, *Heading for a Storm*, 1983: 215.
Aquarius/Capitol/EMI: April Wine, *The Nature of the Beast*, Jan. 1981: 182–83.
Beggars Banquet/Vertigo: The Cult, *Electric*, April 1987: 246.
Bronze: The Damned, *Strawberries*, Oct. 1982: 203; Motörhead, *Bomber*, Oct. 1979: 160–61; Motörhead, *Overkill*, March 1979: 153.
Bronze/Chrysalis: Uriah Heep, *Fallen Angel*, Sept. 1978: 139.
Bronze/Mercury: Uriah Heep, *Demons and Wizards*, May 1972: 36.
Bronze/Warner Bros.: Uriah Heep, *Return to Fantasy*, May 1975: 82.
Brunswick: The Who, *The Who Sings My Generation*, Dec. 1965: 3.
Capitol: Grand Funk, *Grand Funk*, Dec. 1969: 17; Grand Funk, *Live Album*, Nov. 1970: 26; Megadeth, *Rust in Peace*, Sept. 1990: 263; Starz, *Coliseum Rock*, 1978: 148; Starz, *Violation*, 1977: 129; W.A.S.P., *The Headless Children*, April 1989: 252.
Capitol/21/Mercury: Golden Earring, *Cut*, Aug. 1982: 201.
Casablanca: Angel, *Angel*, Oct. 1975: 92; Angel, *On Earth As It Is in Heaven*, 1977: 132; Kiss, *Alive!*, Sept. 1975: 89; Kiss, *Destroyer*, March 1976: 99; Kiss, *Dressed to Kill*, March 1975: 76–77; Kiss, *Rock and Roll Over*, Nov. 1976: 112–13.
Casablanca/Mercury: Kiss, *Lick It Up*, Sept. 1983: 209.
Charisma/Sire: Hawkwind, *Quark Strangeness and Charm*, June 1977: 121.
Chrysalis: Armored Saint, *Raising Fear*, Sept. 1987: 248; The Michael Schenker Group, *Built to Destroy*, Sept. 1983: 211; The Michael Schenker Group, *The Michael Schenker Group*, Aug. 1980: 173; Robin Trower, *Bridge of Sighs*, 1974: 69; UFO, *Force It*, July 1975: 84; UFO, *Lights Out*, May 1977: 119; UFO, *Phenomenon*, May 1974: 60.
Combat/Capitol: Megadeth, *Peace Sells . . . but Who's Buying?*, Nov. 1986: 243.
CBS/Columbia: Fastway, *All Fired Up*, 1984: 226; Hanoi Rocks, *Two*

Steps from the Move, Aug. 1984: 224; Judas Priest, *British Steel*, April 1980: 166–67; Judas Priest, *Hell Bent for Leather*, Oct. 1978: 146; Judas Priest, *Sin after Sin*, April 1977: 116; Judas Priest, *Unleashed in the East*, Sept. 1979: 158.
Columbia: Aerosmith, *Rock in a Hard Place*, Aug. 1982: 202; Aerosmith, *Rocks*, May 1976: 102; Aerosmith, *Toys in the Attic*, April 1975: 79; Blue Öyster Cult, *Cultösaurus Erectus*, June 1980: 171; Blue Öyster Cult, *Extraterrestrial Live*, April 1982: 200; Blue Öyster Cult, *Fire of Unknown Origin*, June 1981: 188; Blue Öyster Cult, *On Your Feet or on Your Knees*, Feb. 1975: 75; Blue Öyster Cult, *Some Enchanted Evening*, Sept. 1978: 142–43; Blue Öyster Cult, *Spectres*, Oct. 1977: 123; Blue Öyster Cult, *The Revolution by Night*, Oct. 1983: 213; Blue Öyster Cult, *Tyranny and Mutation*, Feb. 1973: 42–43; Iggy and the Stooges, *Raw Power*, May 1973: 46–47; Mott the Hoople, *Live*, Nov. 1974: 68; Mott the Hoople, *Mott*, July 1973: 51.
Cream: Legs Diamond, *Fire Power*, 1979: 163.
Decca/London: The Rolling Stones, *Let It Bleed*, Dec. 1969: 16.
Decca/MCA: Wishbone Ash, *Argus*, April 1972: 35.
Def Jam: Slayer, *Reign in Blood*, Oct. 1986: 242.
Ebony/RCA: Grim Reaper, *See You in Hell*, 1983: 217.
Elektra: Dokken, *Back for the Attack*, Nov. 1987: 249; Gamma, *2*, 1980: 179; MC5, *Kick Out the Jams*, Feb. 1969: 12; Metallica, *Master of Puppets*, March 1986: 238–39; Mötley Crüe, *Shout at the Devil*, Sept. 1983: 210.
EMI: Iron Maiden, *Iron Maiden*, April 1980: 170; Iron Maiden, *Killers*, Feb. 1981: 184–85; Iron Maiden, *Live after Death*, Oct. 1985: 228–29.
EMI/Elektra: Queen, *Jazz*, Nov. 1978: 147; Queen, *News of the World*, Oct. 1977: 124–25; Queen, *Queen II*, March 1974: 59; Queen, *Sheer Heart Attack*, Nov. 1974: 65.
EMI/Mercury: Scorpions, *Blackout*, March 1982: 196–97.
EMI/Reprise: T. Rex, *The Slider*, July 1972: 38.
Epic: Boston, *Boston*, July 1976: 104–5; Boston, *Don't Look Back*, Aug. 1978: 138; The Boyzz, *Too Wild to Tame*, 1978: 149; Cheap Trick, *Dream Police*, Sept. 1979: 157; Molly Hatchet, *Molly Hatchet*, Sept. 1978: 144–45; Ozzy Osbourne, *No Rest for the Wicked*, Oct. 1988: 250; Russ Ballard, *Barnet Dogs*, 1980: 177; Ted Nugent, *Cat Scratch Fever*, May 1977: 118; Ted Nugent, *Free-for-All*, Oct. 1976: 107; Ted Nugent, *Weekend Warriors*, Sept. 1978: 141.
Geffen: Guns N' Roses, *GN'R Lies*, Nov. 1988: 251.
Gull/Janus: Judas Priest, *Sad Wings of Destiny*, March 1976: 100.
Harvest/Sire: The Saints, *Eternally Yours*, May 1978: 137.
Harvest/Warner Bros.: Deep Purple, *Fireball*, July 1971: 31.
I.R.S.: Black Sabbath, *Tyr*, Aug. 1990: 262.
Island: Free, *Free*, Oct. 1969: 15; Free, *Tons of Sobs*, March 1969: 13.
Island/Atlantic: King Crimson, *In the Court of the Crimson King*, Oct. 1969: 14.

Island/Reprise: Jethro Tull, *Aqualung*, March 1971: 30.
Jet: Magnum, *Chase the Dragon*, March 1982: 195; Ozzy Osbourne, *Diary of a Madman*, Nov. 1981: 191.
Kama Sutra: Dust, *Dust*, 1971: 33; Dust, *Hard Attack*, 1972: 37.
Kirshner: Kansas, *Leftoverture*, Oct. 1976: 109.
Lark/Portrait: Accept, *Balls to the Wall*, Jan. 1984: 218.
London: The Rolling Stones, *The Rolling Stones, Now!*, Feb. 1965: 2; ZZ Top, *Fandango!*, April 1975: 80; ZZ Top, *Tejas*, Nov. 1976: 114.
Manticore: Emerson, Lake & Palmer, *Brain Salad Surgery*, Nov. 1973: 52.
MCA: Boston, *Third Stage*, Sept. 1986: 241; Budgie, *Never Turn Your Back on a Friend*, 1973: 56; Diamond Head, *Borrowed Time*, 1982: 207; Iron Butterfly, *Sun and Steel*, Oct. 1975: 93; Quartz, *Stand Up and Fight*, 1980: 178; Tygers of Pan Tang, *Spellbound*, April 1981: 187; Tygers of Pan Tang, *Crazy Nights*, Nov. 1981: 193; Tygers of Pan Tang, *Wild Cat*, Aug. 1980: 172.
MCA/A&M: Budgie, *Bandolier*, Sept. 1975: 90–91.
Mechanic/MCA: Voivod, *Nothingface*, Oct. 1989: 257.
Megaforce/Elektra: Metallica, *Ride the Lightning*, July 1984: 223.
Mercury: Bachman-Turner Overdrive, *Bachman-Turner Overdrive*, May 1973: 45; Bachman-Turner Overdrive, *Not Fragile*, Aug. 1974: 62; Legs Diamond, *A Diamond Is a Hard Rock*, 1977: 133; New York Dolls, *New York Dolls*, July 1973: 50; New York Dolls, *Too Much Too Soon*, May 1974: 61; The Runaways, *Live in Japan*, 1977: 130; The Runaways, *Queens of Noise*, 1977: 131; Rush, *A Farewell to Kings*, Sept. 1977: 122; Rush, *Caress of Steel*, Sept. 1975: 88; Rush, *Exit . . . Stage Left*, Oct. 1981: 190; Rush, *Permanent Waves*, Jan. 1980: 165; Uriah Heep, *Uriah Heep*, June 1970: 24.
Metal Blade: Fates Warning, *Awaken the Guardian*, Dec. 1986: 244–45; Fates Warning, *Perfect Symmetry*, Aug. 1989: 255; Fates Warning, *The Spectre Within*, Oct. 1985: 230; Trouble, *The Skull*, 1985: 235.
Millennium/Casablanca: The Godz, *Nothing Is Sacred*, 1979: 164.
Mooncrest/A&M: Nazareth, *Expect No Mercy*, Nov. 1977: 127; Nazareth, *Hair of the Dog*, April 1975: 78; Nazareth, *Loud 'n' Proud*, Nov. 1973: 53; Nazareth, *Razamanaz*, May 1973: 48.
Music for Nations: Manowar, *Hail to England*, July 1984: 220–21.
Neat/Combat: Venom, *Black Metal*, Nov. 1982: 204.
Noise/Warner: Helloween, *Walls of Jericho*, Dec. 1985: 232–33.
Oyster/Polydor: Rainbow, *Rising*, May 1976: 103; Ritchie Blackmore's Rainbow, *Ritchie Blackmore's Rainbow*, Aug. 1975: 85.
Oyster/Warner Bros.: Paice Ashton Lord, *Malice in Wonderland*, March 1977: 115.
Pasha/CBS: Kick Axe, *Welcome to the Club*, Aug. 1985: 227; Quiet Riot, *Metal Health*, March 1983: 208.
Philips: Blue Cheer, *Vincebus Eruptum*, Jan. 1968: 8.
Polydor: Billion Dollar Babies, *Battle Axe*, 1977: 134; Golden Earring, *To the Hilt*, Jan. 1976: 96; Pat Travers Band, *Crash and Burn*, 1980: 175; Rainbow, *Long Live Rock 'n' Roll*, April 1978: 136.

Purple/Warner Bros.: Deep Purple, *Burn*, Feb. 1974: 58; Deep Purple, *Machine Head*, March 1972: 34; Deep Purple, *Made in Europe*, Oct. 1976: 108; Deep Purple, *Stormbringer*, Dec. 1974: 70–71.
RCA: Budgie, *Deliver Us from Evil*, 1982: 206; Budgie, *Nightflight*, 1981: 194; Scorpions, *In Trance*, Sept. 1975: 87.
RCA/Capitol: Sweet, *"Give Us a Wink!"*, March 1976: 98; Sweet, *Off the Record*, April 1977: 117.
RCA/Portrait: Accept, *Russian Roulette*, April 1986: 240.
Reaction/Atco/Polydor: Cream, *Disraeli Gears*, Nov. 1967: 6–7.
Reprise: The Jimi Hendrix Experience, *Are You Experienced*, Aug. 1967: 4–5.
Roadrunner/Combat: Mercyful Fate, *Don't Break the Oath*, Sept. 1984: 225.
Roadrunner/Megaforce: Mercyful Fate, *Melissa*, Oct. 1983: 212.
Sire: Ramones, *Ramones*, April 1976: 101.
Stiff: The Damned, *Music for Pleasure*, Nov. 1977: 126.
Straight/Warner Bros.: Alice Cooper, *Love It to Death*, Jan. 1971: 28–29.
Sub Pop: Nirvana, *"Bleach,"* June 1989: 254.
Swan Song: Bad Company, *Desolation Angels*, March 1979: 152; Led Zeppelin, *In Through the Out Door*, Aug. 1979: 155; Led Zeppelin, *Presence*, March 1976: 97.
United Artists: Hawkwind, *Hall of the Mountain Grill*, Sept. 1974: 64; Hawkwind, *Space Ritual*, May 1973: 49; Hawkwind, *Warrior on the Edge of Time*, May 1975: 81; Whitesnake, *Live . . . in the Heart of the City*, Nov. 1980: 174; Whitesnake, *Lovehunter*, Oct. 1979: 159.
Vertigo/A&M: Status Quo, *Piledriver*, Dec. 1972: 39.
Vertigo/Mercury: Thin Lizzy, *Johnny the Fox*, Oct. 1976: 110–11; Thin Lizzy, *Nightlife*, Nov. 1974: 66–67.
Vertigo/Warner Bros.: Black Sabbath, *Black Sabbath*, Feb. 1970: 22–23; Black Sabbath, *Heaven and Hell*, April 1980: 168–69; Black Sabbath, *Never Say Die!*, Sept. 1978: 140; Black Sabbath, *Sabbath Bloody Sabbath*, Dec. 1973: 54–55; Black Sabbath, *Technical Ecstasy*, Sept. 1976: 106; Thin Lizzy, *Renegade*, Nov. 1981: 192.
Virgin: Iggy Pop, *Brick by Brick*, June 1990: 259.
Warner Bros.: Alice Cooper, *The Alice Cooper Show*, Dec. 1977: 128; Alice Cooper, *Billion Dollar Babies*, Feb. 1973: 40–41; Alice Cooper, *Greatest Hits*, Aug. 1974: 63; Alice Cooper, *Killer*, Nov. 1971: 32; Dio, *The Last in Line*, July 1984: 222; Jane's Addiction, *Ritual de lo Habitual*, Aug. 1990: 260–61; Montrose, *Warner Bros. Presents Montrose!*, Sept. 1975: 86; Van Halen, *1984*, Jan. 1984: 219; Van Halen, *Van Halen*, Feb. 1978: 135; ZZ Top, *Afterburner*, Oct. 1985: 231; ZZ Top, *Degüello*, Nov. 1979: 162; ZZ Top, *Recycler*, March 1990: 258.
Windfall: Mountain, *Nantucket Sleighride*, Jan. 1971: 27.
Windfall/Columbia: Mountain, *Twin Peaks*, Feb. 1974: 57.